The Revolutionary Urbanism of Street Farm:

Eco-Anarchism, Architecture and Alternative Technology in the 1970s

Stephen E. Hunt

Tangent Books

This edition published 2014 by Tangent Books

Tangent Books
Unit 5.16 Paintworks
Bristol
BS4 3EH
0117 972 0645
www.tangentbooks.co.uk

ISBN 978-1-906477-44-8

Publisher: Richard Jones (richard@tangentbooks.co.uk)
Design: Joe Burt (joe@wildsparkdesign.co.uk)

Front cover image adapted by Joe Burt from poster kindly made available by Paul Downton from his original Rotring ink pen drawing for Street Farm's visit to Cardiff in 1973 and inspired by their collage work.

A CIP catalogue record for this book is available from the British Library.

Acknowledgements

Boundless thanks are first due to Graham Caine and Peter Crump for their unfailing support and four decades' worth of fantastic stories. I am equally grateful to my partner Fiona Scott for all the love and enthusiastic reading of work in progress. Thanks for correspondence and encouragement are also due to Brenda Vale, Tom Woolley, Sandy Halliday, Godfrey Boyle, Paul Downton, Heathcote Williams, Louis Hellman, Bill Brown, Christopher Tyndale, Andrew McKillop, Brandy Ernzen, Christopher Squire, Terry 'Jakartass' and James Townhill. Without generous help from Stephen James in making Street Farm films available, and Claire Poyner of *Peace News* for rooting out archival material, some sections would not have been possible. David, Yvonne and Norman Gover at The Little Tipple, Long Ashton and Martin Muller of Boiling Wells Lane all warmly welcomed me into the natural habitat of the Bristol Gnome. Finally love and respect are due to all my comrades in the Bristol Radical History Group who provided the stream of inspiration and ideas that kept this project afloat. Cheersmedears!

Contents

Preface

Street Farm (Graham Caine, Peter Crump and Bruce Haggart) were a London-based collective of anarchist architects working in the early 1970s. The three friends put together *Street Farmer*, an underground paper that, alongside mutating tower blocks, cosmic tractors and sprouting one-way signs, propagated ideas for the radical transformation of urban living which they called 'revolutionary urbanism'. Taking inspiration from Situationism and social ecology, Street Farm offered a powerful vision of green cities in the control of ordinary people. As well as writing and drawing, the group took part in street activism and squatting, were exponents of autonomous housing and radical technology and became rock 'n' roll architects, going on the road with multimedia presentations to a recorded soundtrack of music by the likes of John Lennon and Jefferson Airplane. In 1972 Caine built and designed 'Street Farmhouse' with Haggart and other friends. It hit national and international headlines as the first structure intentionally constructed as an ecological house, appearing on an early BBC documentary introduced by a youthful Melvin Bragg. While their fame was brief, their ongoing influence on prominent green architects including Howard Liddell, Brenda Vale and Robert Vale and Paul Downton has been more enduring.

I should come clean at the outset and confess that I approach this territory, not as someone with an insider's knowledge of architecture and planning but from a Humanities background. I first came across Street Farm through Derek Wall's book *Earth First! and the Anti-Roads Movement*. So far as I know Wall made no contact with Street Farm but took the trouble to research some of the 1970s roots of the direct-actionist green movement for his study. So, how to get hold of members of a tiny, ephemeral group that had left a limited paper trail and in any case had split up forty years previously? In this respect time, geography and a little serendipity were on my side. Organising some speakers for the Radical History Zone at the Bristol Anarchist Bookfair, I managed to track down Graham Caine who had Bristol connections and had been interviewed by *Bristle* magazine a few years previously. Graham had since moved to Spain but still comes back to visit family and friends and was happy to meet up for a pint in my local when he was next passing through. After he'd told the story of his design of the first ecological house and shared forty years of anecdotes, he said: 'You'd better have a chat with Peter Crump who was a Street Farmer too. Pete's a born anarchist and has a cellar full of archives. He still lives in Bristol'. So I picked up the phone to speak to Pete. I'm pleased to say Graham was absolutely right on all counts and that Pete shared his memories and delivered a talk for the Bristol Radical History Group.

I realised a more thorough investigation of Street Farm's work was an unparalleled opportunity to look at the ideas of a unique grassroots activist group and to help understand the intersection between alternative architecture, the counterculture and the ecology movement in the 1970s. Political ecology emerged as a new social movement, differing from older concern for nature conservation in its critical foregrounding of a global threat caused by environmental degradation and the attribution of this to deficiencies in underlying political and economic structures. For this reason Street Farm and the wider ecology movement raised issues and adopted a spirit of resistance that have become even more relevant in the intervening decades. In the present day climate change is but the most prominent environmental issue as economic growth with the concomitant expansion of industry and infrastructure, together with rising populations of humans and domesticated animals, on a finite planet present ever more urgent challenges.

For Street Farm concern for ecology was the logical extension of their political grounding in anarchism. With ideas in keeping with those of the influential architectural writer the late Colin Ward, I shall suggest that Street Farm were proponents of community architecture before that term was coined. As such they understood that a house is far more than a physical construction with a function to shelter people. To design, construct and dwell in a house is a process. It is always built at a moment of transition and is a part of that transition, affecting in some modest way the character and viability of all that surrounds it. If it is built by its prospective tenants or with their participation it will more likely be a homely dwelling, contributing towards their autonomy in life choices; if imposed upon them by force of circumstance it will tend to their alienation. The conditions of a building's construction and maintenance in terms of its economic arrangements, interior organisation, aesthetic character and ecological impact will reflect and determine processes of change far beyond the immediate confines of its walls. It can tend towards the concentration of capital and political power or enhance social inclusion; it can exacerbate the loss of diverse habitats or land for food production or be designed in a low-impact, sustainable way to provide a prototype for others.

Graham said that for him Street Farm never really ended. While group labels may change, after walking through a door to understand the world in a particular way it is not possible to' unknow' and walk backwards through that door of perception. In the present time of crisis the current hegemony of state and capital offers solutions that increasingly fail to inspire confidence and lack credibility in the eyes of millions of world citizens. The principles of organising society for human well-being and justice and for ecological viability are enduring. Radical history learns from the past to inform the present and inspire the struggle for the future. The utopian current suddenly seems not so utopian; eco-anarchism offers a set of thinking tools to imagine alternative possibilities for that future. If we can demand the impossible, we can also refuse the inevitable.

Street-farming men

Such stuff dreams are made of. Imagine. A traffic jam of sheep flocked between the shop fronts and tenements, just a single bollard to suggest that this is a late twentieth-century street. Clun forest sheep by the look of them. Voting with their hooves perhaps in a triumphant ovine takeover. *Street Farmer* images playfully presented glimpses of a utopian transformation of urban life and ecology. They offered a creative visualisation of cities as liberated, even re-enchanted habitats, a 'revolutionary urbanism' in which a profusion of organic growth would replace predominantly concrete environments. The city / country dichotomy that characterises capitalist enclosure would be dissolved in order to bring about a reconnection of humanity with the non-human and natural environment. This directly anticipated the guerrilla gardening and Transition initiatives of the Nineties and Noughties. Such a transformation would constitute a thoroughgoing social revolution, not just top-down regime change. Or were these just stoned reveries, woolgathering in the afterglow of the summer of love and the *evenements* of 1968?

Street Farm, the editors of *Street Farmer* magazine, were an eco-anarchist collective of three friends, active in London and beyond in the 1970s, who collaborated on a number of original projects that fused architectural ideas with political media. Peter Crump (born 1942), Bruce Haggart (born 1948) and Graham Caine (born 1945), first met as students during the late 1960s at the Architectural Association (AA) in Bedford Square, London. They recognised each other as kindred spirits. Haggart had switched from a course at Aberdeen, while Crump had begun his studies seven years previously at London's Northern Polytechnic on a part-time basis on day from work. Caine, brought up on a council estate in Essex, had started as a 'teaboy' in an architecture firm where he developed the skills and experience to design and run projects. Since none of them had started their degrees at the AA, in order to be accepted they were each required to face an admissions jury, made up of a panel of existing staff and students. The future of the AA was in question at this time so there was a particular incentive to boost its academic credentials and practical output. All three future members of Street Farm had previously worked while they studied so they were able to walk in with a solid body of work, fresh off the drawing board, as well as some experience of the front-line of social housing provision in the public sector. Their substantial portfolios of design sketches proved to be impressive and not to be passed up lightly as many AA students could not boast equivalent tangible output. Haggart, Crump and Caine were therefore among 1969's successful applicants to the AA. Haggart and Crump quickly became comrades. As Crump wryly noted, this was partly because although there were many amazing lectures delivered, they were often among the few students that turned up to hear them. The chairs in the lecture halls were chillily vacant of the bottoms of attentive students, who were either partaking of the freewheeling pleasures of the time or, Crump surmises, likely to be still in bed. Caine, hit by a long-term and debilitating respiratory illness battled the condition in hospital for six months before starting at the AA where he also hooked up with Haggart and Crump.[1] The result, in due course, was Street Farm.

This was a momentous period for the Architectural Association. A battle raged to retain the independent character of the institution as students and staff, representing themselves as the 'School Community' fought off proposals to amalgamate with the

1 Graham Caine, e-mail message to the author, 12 March 2013. Graham Caine prefers to be on first names terms with those who take an interest in his work; consequently I have often used his given name in the text where appropriate and without ambiguity.

Imperial College of Science and Technology.[2] This opened up a space for student power, direct democracy and experimentation. Initially Haggart and Crump's work took the form of a challenging multimedia performance. An AA assessment became the occasion for an early Street Farm intervention, being a radical departure from the customary offerings and a rebellion against the expected style and discourse. Crump recalled:

> The earliest roots of Street Farm have their origins in our joint final-year presentation. At that time work was assessed by a jury. You invited an audience of your friends along – not of course, if you had any, your enemies – and delivered the presentation to them. However, one of the tutors also present was so enraged that he tried to pull one of the exhibits, a manifesto on a toilet roll, off the wall, perhaps because it wasn't like conventional architectural work but rather took the form of something more like a political manifesto.[3]

Street Farm's political edge was not incidental to their architectural work but predated it, informing and grounding all of their projects. Crump had worked in organic agriculture, in which his mother had been something of a pioneer when she started an organic market garden and farm near Eastbourne. This brought him into contact with Alan Albon, a contributor to *Freedom* and *Anarchy*, later involved in squatting and the City Farm movement.[4] Crump recalled, 'Albon was a rare thing, an anarchist farmworker', and they shared many discussions about anarchist ideas and literature.[5] Like Albon,

2 Grahame Shane, 'Obituary: Alvin Boyarsky (1928-1990)', *Journal of Architectural Education*, 45.3 (May 1992), 189 [online] http://www.jstor.org/stable/1425256 [accessed 22 March 2011].
3 Personal conversation with Peter Crump, Café Kino, Stokes Croft, Bristol 23 February 2011.
4 Nicholas Walters, 'Obituary of Alan Albon: Radical and Lovable', [online] *The Guardian* (25 May 1989).
5 Personal conversation with Peter Crump, Montpelier, Bristol, 24 August 2012.

Crump had been involved in the Committee of 100, the direct-action group that confronted the nuclear war machine during the 1960s. He also joined the huge anti-Vietnam War demonstrations and actions. The heat generated in the Situationist-inspired events of May 1968 and 'the Prague Spring' in Czechoslovakia in that year helped to kindle their activism as well. Caine cited the experience of these uprisings, just months before he started at the Architectural Association, as a political inspiration, recalling the pervading sense that anything was possible at that time.[6] The motivation behind Street Farm's particular form of political engagement was to earth more abstract theories by linking them to the reality of everyday life. As Crump put it, 'I was always interested in a range of political and cultural ideas and architecture became a hook to hang these politics on.'[7]

When Street Farm began, Peter Crump was living with his wife Glenys, and their daughters Bronwen and Bridget, at 63 Patshull Road, Kentish Town. This semi-detached 1860's Victorian house became the HQ for subsequent issues of *Street Farmer* magazine. The three-storey building had two spare rooms which were spacious enough to accommodate Bruce Haggart and his wife Kate when they moved in during Spring 1970. This arrangement nurtured the creative collaboration from which much of Street Farm's work sprang. The communal household reflected the anarchistic ethos of the two issues of *Street Farmer* with their collectively produced articles and images. Graham Caine self-built what has a strong claim to have been the first house intentionally constructed with ecological principles in mind, at Eltham, where he lived with his family until their eventual eviction (Chapter 6).

Street Farm is not easy to define as it defied neat categories. It

6 Personal conversation with Graham Caine, The Stillage, Redfield, Bristol 25 October 2010.
7 Personal conversation with Peter Crump, Montpelier, Bristol, 24 August 2012.

was a mash-up of practical projects, notably Street Farmhouse (as Caine's Ecological House became known), with alternative media, direct action and performance interventions, producing a heady, if short lived, synthesis. *Street Farmer* 1 proclaims itself 'an intermittant [*sic*] continuing manual of alterative urbanism', the ongoing nature of the project proving to be a statement of aspiration as much as description. It was at turns agit-prop sewage management, metropolitan pastoralism, a desire to liberate space from capitalist enclosure and an overlooked sprouting of the emergent ecology movement. The refusal of definition enabled Street Farm to take a flexible approach to their creative work. Godfrey Boyle acknowledged the inappropriateness of applying the 'straightjacket of definition' to Street Farm when he introduced an interview that he and Peter Harper conducted with Bruce Haggart and Graham Caine in 1974, contenting himself with a loose description:

> [...] If I describe them as a London-based group of anarchists practising, and and preaching, a unique brand of guerrilla architecture, I don't think they would disagree too much.[8]

Peter Harper's pithy description is in a similar vein: 'Green anarchists, [who] do urban guerrilla architecture that almost works, and are very funny'.[9]

This absence of a fixed programme enabled Street Farm to pursue particular interests and to engage with the community as they saw fit. Consensus decision-making is easier with a small number of like-minded folk. In addition to the core group of Crump, Haggart and Caine, two others regularly helped out with *Street Farmer*.

8 Godfrey Boyle and Peter Harper, 'Interview: Street Farmers', in *Radical Technology*, ed. by Godfrey Boyle, Peter Harper and the editors of *Undercurrents* (London: Wildwood House, 1976), 170.
9 Peter Harper, 'Directory of Alternative Technology', *Architectural Design* 44.11 (1974), 695.

Stuart Lever, who contributed to both issues of *Street Farmer* and provided technical assistance for their multimedia ventures, died on 24th October 2004. Roger Stowell, who contributed to *Street Farmer* 2 and helped to build the Ecological House, is also no longer alive. Other contributors to *Street Farmer* 1 were Mike Hickie on 'Street Gardening' and Martin Lipson and Barrie Hurrell on 'Agency Housing Co-op'.

The larger number of additional contributors to *Street Farmer* 2 also included Peter and Bruce's partners – Glenys Crump and Kate Haggart – and other like-minded comrades from the contemporary London alternative scene, namely Heather Burridge, Alan Mitchell, Fred Scott (Crump and Haggart's tutor at the AA), and Harriet and Dave (family names not listed).

Street Farm made a characteristically theatrical debut appearance on the streets of London wearing scarecrow masks in a blockade of Oxford Street in 1971. They supported the Oxford Street Action Committee and cooperated with other groups in taking direct action to confront traffic blight and to encourage a wider transformation of urban life. The immediate objective was to block every junction into Oxford Street, with the intention that bands would play in the reclaimed space while passers-by would be leafleted and treated to 'hot chestnuts and paper hats'.[10] The Oxford Street Action Committee's attempted street blockades against cars and lorries during the early 1970s anticipated the environmental activism of later groups such as Reclaim the Streets, Critical Mass and World Naked Bike Ride. Members of Commitment, an off-shoot of the Young Liberals (a more radically oriented group than in the present day!) coordinated the first event, demanding free public transport to liberate the streets from traffic congestion. A Police Commissioner's report recorded that:

10 Peace News, 'Blocking Oxford Street', *Peace News* (17 December 1971), 5.

> On Saturday 18th December, about 50 sympathizers of the "Young Liberals' *Oxford Street Action Committee*" met at Speakers' Corner and made their way into Oxford Street, where they attempted to close the street to vehicular traffic in effort to draw attention to pollution caused by the motor car. The demonstrators made various attempts to stop the flow of traffic but they were quickly thwarted by prompt police action and inconvenience to members of the public was kept to an absolute minimum. A total of 44 demonstrators were arrested.[11]

Demonstrators disrupted car traffic with their physical presence aided by a gigantic bunch of balloons. Alongside a broader network, Street Farm turned up to the first of two attempted blockades with the striking scarecrow masks designed to act as scare-cars (these appear in *Street Farmer* 2).[12] Victor Anderson, also a participant in the events, remembers that Street Farm joined forces with members of the green counterculture, such as the Dwarfs and the Planet Earth Survival Team. Acknowledging the peace movement's tactical influence, Anderson recalled: 'We said that there should be a Committee of One Hundred for the environment.'[13]

As we shall see, creative artistic propaganda provided Street Farm with rich mulch for the strategic propagation of alternatives in such multimedia as film sketches, road shows and *Street Farmer* magazine. There was never a third edition of *Street Farmer*, largely because the creative energies of the core collective were expended elsewhere

11 House of Commons Parliamentary Papers [online database], *Report of the Commissioner of Police of the Metropolis for the Year 1971* (Cmnd. 4986, 1971-72), 45 [accessed 22 November 2012].
12 Crump later recalled: 'We printed lots of them on brown paper bags but were worried that no one but us would want to wear them. In the event they did want to wear them'. Personal conversation with Peter Crump, Montpelier, Bristol, 7 May 2013.
13 Quoted by Derek Wall in *Earth First! and the Anti-Roads Movement: Radical Environmentalism and Comparative Social Movements* (London: Routledge, 1999), 29.

after 1972. Crump divided his time between paid employment in London and a rural commune in Wales called the EarthWorkshop (Chapter 6) before he eventually moved to Bristol for family reasons and actively supported the anti-nuclear movement. Caine worked tirelessly on the Ecological House (Chapter 6) until its eventual demolition after which he became involved in an urban farm project at Thamesmead before also moving to Bristol. Here, as we shall see, he became a 'Bristol gnome', devoting his talents to some unique and outstanding alternative architecture. Haggart too assisted Caine in the construction of the Ecological House and continued to propagate Street Farm ideas and work in liberatory technology. Bruce, Kate and Sholto Haggart and Caine moved to Camberwell in south London where they began a squatted community associated with Street Farm in the mid-1970s. By 1975 the postal address for Street Farm was 21 Flodden Road, SE5, described in *Alternative England and Wales* as 'Now a larger group squatting in a church and vicarage working things out in a less dramatic way'.[14] Bruce Haggart also lived in a squat in Crystal Palace Road and helped to tour manage the Pink Fairies[15].

Street Farm ran from 1971 to around 1976, after which time the group had run its course, their work as a collective diminishing following the dismantlement of the ecological Street Farmhouse, and the increasing involvement of the core members in new projects. From another perspective, Caine suggests, the Street Farm ethos continued independently throughout his later life: 'Well I've never seen it finished. I see it like I'm living the dream man, we've all got contradictions [...] I don't think I've ever been a capitalist', adding 'I feel like I've been a part of a few tribes, which is how I expect it's supposed to be'.[16] Haggart set up a website to bring

14 Nicholas Saunders, *Alternative England and Wales* (London: Nicholas Saunders, 1975), 266.
15 Graham Caine, e-mail message to the author, 10 February 2014.
16 Personal conversation with Graham Caine, Montpelier, Bristol 29 November 2012.

back some of Street Farm's work into the public domain in 2011.[17] Regrettably, given his major contribution to the Street Farm project, he was unwilling to take part in correspondence about the group or magazine stating that 'Streetfarm was of its time for its time. It is not ongoing' [18]. Nearly three decades after the collective disbanded, Peter Crump accepted an invitation from the Bristol Radical History Group to deliver a fascinating retrospective of Street Farm's work and ideas at the Bristol Anarchist Bookfair in May 2011.

17 http://www.streetfarm.org.uk/streetfarmer_one.html [accessed 14 June 2011]; republished as http://www.streetfarm.org.uk/Streetfarmer_One.html#0 [accessed 27 August 2013]. Further images from Street Farmer 2 are in the public domain at: http://www.flickr.com/photos/stefan-szczelkun/sets/72157623404365197/
18 Bruce Haggart, e-mail message to the author, 18 February 2013.

Digging up the Archives... and the WWWebb's Wonderful: Review of Literature from the Salad Days to now

It was in the context of enthusiasm for radical alternatives, a spirit of experimentation and increasing ecological awareness that Street Farm emerged during the early 1970s. They epitomise a particular historical moment, being the product of a time and place. Yet such grassroots activities not only reflect the circumstances of their time but also affect them. Street Farm provide a fascinating example of the issues and attitudes of optimistic, proactive radicalism and, although their story is largely untold, they helped to popularise approaches that have been noticed in several contexts.

Given their eclectic approach, it is unsurprising that Street Farm have been referenced for a variety of reasons, while they were still active under that name during the early 1970s and since. Although these were by no means mutually exclusive, four broad categories of interest can be identified:

1. Architectural writers and practitioners in radical and sustainable planning have recognised Street Farm as pioneering exponents of alternative technology and community architecture. Such recognition has mostly been based upon attention to Street Farmhouse.

2. Commentators upon, and historians of, the environmental movement have included Street Farm in their accounts as a grassroots group that exemplified the growing ecological awareness of the early 1970s. They have been seen as precursors of radical environmentalism in the following decades.

> 3. The publication of two issues of *Street Farmer* has secured the group a place in the history of the alternative press, especially relating to radical architecture.
>
> 4. Street Farm's particular blend of revolutionary urbanism as an expression of political resistance to state control and capitalism.

In 1972 Street Farmhouse made headlines in the architectural press and the national media. The notion of a purpose-built 'eco-house' was still a term that was novel enough to warrant quotation marks. Made of humble materials, the Ecological House was a radical and historic experiment in liberatory technology and design. It attracted international attention in the press and on television. In particular in a front-page story in *The Observer* Gerald Leach, the paper's Science Correspondent, gave an enthusiastic, account of Caine's project to construct 'Britain's first Ecological House'.[19] Leach was impressed and intrigued by the spirit of innovation and experimentation, coupled with attention to detail, that went into the design. He also noted the provisional support and endorsement this example of 'people's technology' in action had received from officialdom and commercial bodies. Aware of the political premises that were helping to structure the physical premises, Leach concluded:

> Ironically, the only cold shoulder has come from the Royal Institute of British Architects. But then, as a member of the anarchist architect group called 'Street Farmer,' [Caine] hopes that his eco-house will be a tiny step towards smashing the 'wasteland urban culture' that he feels official architecture has been largely responsible for creating.[20]

19 Leach, 'Living off the Sun', 1.
20 Leach, 'Living off the Sun', 2.

While Leach's feature was sympathetic, more often however, the acclaim was mixed with perplexity. Caine later recalled, 'the media didn't know quite what to do with us, and didn't always like us, because we linked what we were doing to anarchism'.[21]

Leach's news story generated a huge amount of publicity which soon gained in momentum. This increased exponentially when a team of BBC reporters arrived at the construction site and the world's first ecological house appeared on the BBC news the next night. Caine found himself the subject of an 'enormous story' which was quickly 'picked up in virtually every English-speaking country'. Inevitably such attention perpetuated even more interest, bringing in further correspondence and requests for information. This was particularly difficult at the project's start, before there was an ecological house to see! Caine recalls, 'I just couldn't keep up with it at all. I mean it was overwhelming and it just didn't let up, and it carried on for three years'.[22] To satisfy the demand for information, Caine and Haggart produced three different A3 information sheets over the course of the construction period (see Chapter 5).

Martin Pawley, a tutor at the AA during the 1970s, admired the inventiveness of groups such as Archigram and Street Farm, but felt that Street Farm's 'agrarian fantasies' were failing to engage with the 'real world' at a time of crisis and economic downturn. He feared that the potential and need for such flexible revolutionary solutions was great, but that opportunities to implement them were being shut down. Pawley, who interviewed Caine at the time, noted Street Farm's intriguing proposal for 'expanding and contracting inflatables which will respond to seasonal and crop variations'.[23]

F. P. Hughes's article for *Mother Earth News*, 'Ecologic House'

21 Personal conversation with Graham Caine, The Stillage, Redfield, Bristol 25 October 2010.
22 Personal conversation with Graham Caine, Montpelier, Bristol 29 November 2012.
23 Martin Pawley, 'The Need for a Revolutionary Myth', *Architectural Design*, 42.2 (1972), 79. See hedge plan in *Street Farmer* 1, [14].

(1973) examined the technical specifications of Caine's construction in detail and sought to identify ways that it might be adapted for the North American environment. David Dickson's book *Alternative Technology and the Politics of Technical Change* (1974) also describes Street Farm's Ecological House in a chapter on 'Utopian Technology'. Dickson noted Street Farm's advocacy of a 'people's technology', that involved decentralised political control. He recorded that at the time of writing they intended to adapt their ideas about 'self-servicing' to existing urban terrace houses and to expand food production as further means towards the achievement of this goal.[24] Brenda Vale and Robert Vale, partners who have taken a pioneering interest in alternative technology and environmental issues since the early 1970s continuing to write on such themes in the present day, drew attention to Caine's experiments in *The Autonomous House*, and took a particular interest in his attempts to deal with pathogens when attempting to recycle with human sewage.[25] The Vales met Graham Caine and went to see Street Farmhouse 'from a distance' shortly before it was dismantled.[26] In *Radical Technology* (1976), Godfrey Boyle and Peter Harper situate Street Farm's approach to alternative technology in the context of their political outlook in their extended interview with Haggart and Caine. Other publications that featured sketches of the Ecological House as a promising feat of innovative alterative technology and autonomous housing during the 1970s included Stefan Szczelkun's *Survival Scrapbook* 5 on *Energy* (1973) and E. J. DaSilva's 'Biogas Generation' (1979). Colin Ward regretted the obstacles provided by the planning regime that led to the dismantling of the experimental Street Farmhouse in his essay 'Do-It-Yourself

24 David Dickson, *Alternative Technology and the Politics of Technical Change* ([London]: Fontana/Collins, 1974), 132 and 144.
25 Brenda Vale and Robert Vale. *The Autonomous House: Design and Planning for Self-Sufficiency* (London: Thames and Hudson, 1975), 119-21.
26 Brenda Vale, e-mail message to the author, 17 April 2013.

New Town' (1976) published in *Undercurrents*.[27]

Since the collective had disbanded, Street Farm projects attracted less attention during the 1980s and early 1990s, perhaps because were many more available examples of the kind of alternative technology and sustainable housing had attracted mainstream interest. William Chaitkin, however, discussed Street Farm's approach in the 'Alternatives' section of Charles Jencks' comprehensive *Current Architecture*, paying attention to both the group's manifestos and their practical work in the form of the Ecological House. For Chaitkin, Street Farm exemplified a revolutionary approach to the autonomous house that was rarely present in American experiments in alternative technology. He observed that in Street Farm's art:

> [...] an ad-hoc post-industrial revolutionary dialectic is informed by horticultural similes – the decaying city as a compost heap for sprouting liberating tactics, a seed as a weapon, "weeding" existing technologies and graphic images: anarchist cows invade the metropolis, eating the office buildings.[28]

There has been a resurgence of interest during the new millennium and the pioneering status of Street Farmhouse has been recognised. Publications lost in archives have become digitised and newly accessible and the Internet facilitates the dissemination of research, making it possible to trundle the wheelbarrow of Street Farm's work and ideas along the information superhighway. Adrian Smith cited Street Farmhouse as an 'iconic example' of early alternative technology.[29] Simon Sadler also reproduced the Ecological House

27 Colin Ward, 'Do-It-Yourself New Town', *Undercurrents* 16 (June-July 1976), 33. Also published as a lecture text in Colin Ward, *Talking Houses: Ten Lectures* (London: Freedom Press, 1990), 32.
28 Charles Jencks, with a contribution by William Chaitkin, *Current Architecture* (London: Academy Editions, 1982), 275.
29 Adrian Smith, 'Governance Lessons from Green Niches: The Case of Eco-Housing', 89-109 in *Governing Technology for Sustainability*, ed. by Joseph Murphy (London: Earthscan, 2007), 94.

plan in his essay 'An Architecture of the Whole'.[30] In *Ecopolis* Paul Downton, a prominent practitioner in sustainable architecture, cited an occasion on which he invited Street Farm to the Welsh School of Architecture in Cardiff to explain their ideas and experiments in 1973 as an important stage in the evolution of his understanding of architecture's political dimension.[31] He commented:

> They were important to me then and have remained important to my thinking about cities, architecture and ecology. So I guess they did a good job![32]
>
> The reason I mentioned them in *Ecopolis* was because they became part of my philosophical and political DNA.[33]

A quarter of a century after they had originally written about them, Brenda Vale and Robert Vale recalled Street Farm's suggestion (in their interview in *Radical Technology*) that roads could be dug up to grow trees for providing fuel in an urban context.[34] Sandy Halliday included a description and colour picture of the Ecological House among the case studies in *Sustainable Construction*.[35] Halliday's husband, Howard Liddell, who took this photograph in 1974, also included Street Farmhouse in *Eco-Minimalism* (2008). Liddell was to attribute his long career as a leading practitioner and exponent of green architecture to seeing a 'knockabout act' by Graham Caine

30 Simon Sadler, 'An Architecture of the Whole', *Journal of Architectural Education*, 61.4 (May 2008), 108-29. [online] http://onlinelibrary.wiley.com/doi/10.1111/j.1531-314X.2008.00194.x/pdf [accessed 24 January 2012], 112.
31 Paul F. Downton, *Ecopolis: Architecture and Cities for a Changing Climate* (Dordrecht: Springer, 2009), 2 and 155.
32 Paul Downton, e-mail message to the author, 30 October 2012.
33 Paul Downton, e-mail message to the author, 5 November 2013.
34 Brenda Vale and Robert Vale, 'Is the High-Density City the Only Option?', 19-26 in *Designing High-Density Cities: For Social and Environmental Sustainability*, ed. by Edward Ng (London: Earthscan, 2010), 20.
35 Sandy Halliday, *Sustainable Construction* (Amsterdam: Elsevier, 2008), 13.

and Bruce Haggart in 1973.[36] Alison Shaw's obituary to Liddell again noted his acknowledgement that it was the Street Farmers that had first sparked his interest in ecology at this time.[37]

Other commentators on Street Farm have referenced Street Farm for their role in the early 1970's burgeoning ecological movement. In particular Richard Kimber and J. J. Richardson named them among other 'hippy' groups concerned with the environment in their 1974 book *Campaigning for the Environment*:

> It is not easy to accept that the London Oxford Street Action Committee, the Dwarves, the Street Farmers, and groups firmly embedded in the hippy world are part and parcel of a movement which includes bodies like the Civic Trust, the CPRE, and the National Trust. It is unlikely that such a wide variety of groups will find much common ground, particularly since many of the more radical groups see a fundamental change in the nature of British society as a prerequisite of any real improvement in the environment.[38]

In *Environmental Groups in Politics* (1983) Philip Lowe and Jane Goyder included them among a list of what they called the more 'doomful' environmental groups from the era:

> In the early 1970s, there was a gathering sense of impending environmental crisis with a number of pundits predicting imminent ecological collapse. Many of the groups springing up

36 Howard Liddell, *Eco-Minimalism: The Antidote to Eco-Bling* (London: RIBA Publishing, 2008), viii and 6.
37 Alison Shaw, 'Howard Liddell (1945-2013): Architect, ecology activist and charity worker', *The Herald* (Glasgow), [Features], 20. Sandy Halliday kindly drew my attention to her late husband's tribute to the Street Farmers, e-mail message to the author, 7 May 2013.
38 Richard Kimber and J.J. Richardson, 'Conclusion: Tactics and Strategies', *Campaigning for the Environment*, ed. by Richard Kimber and J. J. Richardson (London: Routledge and Kegan Paul, 1974), 224.

> questioned the direction of society and tended to view individual environmental problems as having a common cause in economic and population growth. Since then the whole climate of opinion has changed with the onset of recession – economic pessimism has displaced environmental pessimism as the downturn in the business cycle has set its own limits to growth. Groups that campaigned against 'growth mania' have been one of the casualties of the recession, and the more doomful groups of this period – such as the Movement for Survival, Population Stabilisation, the Street Farmers, Planners Against Growth and Green Survival – have proved ephemeral.[39]

It is misleading to bracket Street Farm with groups with titles that suggest that they take an apocalyptic, neo-Malthusian approach. In fact this is an opportunity to illustrate what Street Farm were *not*. The first two named groups for example reveal motives and attitudes behind some population concerns that they did not share, such as anti-immigration sentiments. The Movement for Survival was launched in the wake of the publication of the *Blueprint for Survival* and as such had close links to Edward Goldsmith and other editors of *The Ecologist* magazine. It was not so much 'ephemeral' but rather merged with the PEOPLE Party, eventually to be renamed the Ecology Party and, later still, today's Green Party.

The Population Stabilisation Group was launched by Labour and Conservative politicians advocating the availability of free birth control and better sex education alongside calls for welfare cuts in child support and maternity benefits.[40] While there are survivalist aspects to some of the images and ideas presented in the *Street Farmer*, a core claim is that impending 'biocide' is an inevitable

39 Philip Lowe and Jane Goyder, *Environmental Groups in Politics*, Resource Management series no. 6 (London: George Allen and Unwin, 1983), 181.
40 Ariadne, commentary in the *New Scientist* 55.807 (3 August 1972), 264.

outcome of capitalist expansionism, the impacts of which cannot be accounted for by population growth in isolation. For example, Graham Caine, detected underlying class assumptions implicit in the *Limits to Growth*, put together by representatives of big business in the form of the Club of Rome, noting that '"Limits to growth" only seemed to apply to the working class';[41] a justified concern in the light of sentiments expressed by the Population Stabilisation Group. They may have shared more common ground with the concerns of Planners Against Growth.

This group was set up to challenge and transform the current practices of establishment bodies such as the Royal Town Planning Institute, in the context of the impact of their commitment to the infinite expansion of the built environment upon the finite carrying capacity of the planet.[42] However, there are no links between Planners Against Growth and Street Farm. Finally the apocalyptically named Green Survival Campaign also appears not so much to have been 'ephemeral' but rather sprouted into the more august sounding Tree Council, a mainstay of respectable conservationism.[43] Nevertheless, Lowe and Goyder were right to observe that groups concerned with environmental issues fare less well during periods of economic recession.

Citing two aforementioned books by Kimber and Richardson and by Dickson, Derek Wall included Street Farm in his overview of the roots of radical environmental activism in his study of Earth First!.[44] More recently George McKay included them as part of 'the historic presence of [...] uncompromising greenness' in *Radical*

41 Personal conversation with Graham Caine, The Stillage public house, Redfield, Bristol 25 October 2010.
42 T. O'Riordan, *Environmentalism*, 2nd rev. ed. (London: Pion, 1981), 132.
43 Suggested by titles of documents in the Association of County Council archives held within the London Metropolitican Archives. See The National Archives: http://www.nationalarchives.gov.uk/a2a/records.aspx?cat=074-lma4243&cid=1-9#1-9 [accessed 15 October 2012].
44 Wall, *Earth First! and the Anti-Roads Movement*, 26.

Gardening, an account of the green counterculture.[45]

In recent years Lydia Kallipoliti, a researcher at Syracuse University, has done most to foreground Street Farm's work and explore their contribution in the context of alternative media in the field of architecture and planning. Kallipoliti has taken great interest in publications such as *Street Farmer*, travelling to England to interview Peter Crump and other editors in 2007 as a contribution to a broader collaborative project to produce an exhibition and published collection on European avant garde and radical media relating to architecture called *Clip, Stamp, Fold*, published in 2010. She interviewed Graham Caine in Spain the following year. *In 2010,* Kallipoliti included Street Farm's Ecological House in 'No More Schisms', a discussion of ecological tropes of sustainability and recycling in architectural representation, published as an article in *Architectural Design*.

This was followed up in 2011 with an article on Street Farm's television documentary *Clearings in a Concrete Jungle*, published in the *Journal of the Society of Architectural Historians*. Kallipoliti returns to the topic of the eco-house in her article 'From Shit to Food' (2012), a detailed analysis of the representational approach and scientific underpinning of Caine's work.

For Street Farm, liberatory technology, eco-activism and radical media were logical expressions of their collective and individual participation in the early 1970's political scene and their commitment to anarchism. Anarchist illustrator Clifford Harper, for example, had been a friend of Street Farm since they first met him as a part of the Kentish Town squatter community.

He later drew up a detailed plan for the EarthWorkshop in Wales[46] (see Chapter 7), and included both Caine and Haggart in

45 George McKay, *Radical Gardening: Politics, Idealism and Rebellion in the Garden* (London: Frances Lincoln, 2012), 195.
46 In Peter Crump's personal archive.

his acknowledgements for help in producing his *New Times Class War Comix* of 1974. This sets out to depict a hypothetical utopian society of about 2000 people living in a rural situation.

Revolution in the Air: Street Farm in Context

1968 and all that

In the late 1960s it was oddly normal that an after-effect of sticks and cobblestones hurled in fury in the Sorbonne, was somehow to cause structures to be built up from salvaged timbers, bricks and plastic on the other side of the Channel. Such distant emanating ripples were not seen as chaos theory at the time but many were alert to synchronicities. For Street Farm, in common with others of their generation, the 1968 events had been an inspiration; they were aware that it had opened up a space to imagine and dream. Graham Caine recalled that the upheavals had nearly routed Charles De Gaulle in France and, even in Britain, revolution was discussed as something that was possible, perhaps imminent. With a nod to France, Street Farm declared: 'The revolution is impotent without a vision as the dreamer is impotent without a revolution' (*SF* 2, 21). Furthermore, while the revolution would generate new forms and modes of social organisation, we would still need to produce food, provide shelter and deal with our shit. Such necessities would be part of the social revolution, central to the transformation of urban spaces. As we shall see, practical fantasies would demand fantastic practices.

Industrial capitalism had long had its discontents. In the early Nineteenth Century, William Cobbett raged against what he scornfully named 'The Thing'. The Thing was a nexus of the wealthy and powerful, a corrupt elite who ruled in their own political and economic interests. The Thing was a state of affairs in which the contrast between conspicuous consumption and grinding poverty marked a sharply divided society. Affairs of the state perpetuated cruel inequities through self-serving policies on the pretence that they were in keeping with Nature or the will of God. In the name of political economy, and under the majestic cloak of The Thing, deprivation, social dislocation and indignities were suffered. Then as now, The Thing was maintained by the old totalitarian threat – THERE IS NO ALTERNATIVE and the argument that any attempts to find one will lead, inevitably and inexorably, to catastrophe and chaos. Of course times and terms change. In the greatest challenge to the French state since the Paris Commune of 1871, the 1960's discontents called the problem 'The Spectacle'.

Countless historians have recalled Harold Macmillan's words 'You've never had it so good'. As the austerity of the 1940s eased, social mobility increased. In the industrialised West, many middle and working class people enjoyed greater disposable income and a higher material standard of living. So why was that generation discontented anyway? Weren't they destined to have angel delight, Cortinas, refrigerators to cool their prawn cocktails, lava lamps, Biba frocks, curvy chairs and spanglely ear-rings?

Situationists such as Guy Debord and Raoul Vaneigem updated and developed revolutionary theory for a time of plenty and universal adult suffrage. They spikily objected that, despite the greater abundance of material goods, people continued to be onlookers on their own lives, measured by their patterns of consumption and caught in an inauthentic world of fabrication and charade forever mediated by others. In *The Society of the Spectacle*, Debord wrote:

> The first phase of the domination of the economy over social life brought into the definition of all human realization the obvious degradation of *being* into *having*.[47]

47 Guy Debord, *The Society of the Spectacle* [1967] ([s.l.]: Rebel Press, 1987), para. 17.

These ingrates moaned that in the brave new world of modernity individuals were still powerless, alienated, constrained in the workplace and unfulfilled. The situation was worsening in fact, as communities were torn asunder while security specialists, technocrats and media barons instigated more sophisticated methods of control over populations. Vaneigem feared 'Ideological hypnosis is replacing the bayonet'.[48] There were still plenty of bayonets in the arsenal, however, should the occasion demand them. Beneath the neon lights of the consumer society dominance, competition and repression remained ever present realities. As such it was inseparable from the industrial-military complex complicit in two world wars, Hiroshima and Nagasaki and the escalating war in Vietnam. The background of the Cold War was a constant reminder that no progress towards greater harmony in human relations had been achieved. For critics coming together as the New Left, lethal underlying social tensions remained, whether a particular state leaned towards free-market capitalism, a mixed economy or a system of 'socialist' planning. In Vaneigem's words:

> Today, a planned economy allows us to foresee the final solution of many of the problems of survival. Now that the needs of survival are well on the way to being satisfied, at least in the hyper-industrialized countries, it is becoming painfully obvious that there are also human passions which must be satisfied, that the satisfaction of these passions is of vital importance to everyone and, furthermore, that failure to satisfy them will undermine, if not destroy, all our acquisitions in the realm of material survival. As the problems of survival are slowly but surely resolved, they clash more and more brutally with the problems

48 Raoul Vaneigem, *The Revolution of Everyday Life* [1967] ([s.l.]: Left Bank Books / Rebel Press, 1983), 73.

> of life, which, just as slowly and just as surely, are sacrificed to the needs of survival. In a way, this simplifies matters: it is now obvious that socialist-type planning is incompatible with the true harmonization of life in common.[49]

If such material gains were uncertain and a revolution of everyday life was as necessary as ever for the attainment of authentic liberation, the question remained as to from which quarter resistance might come in an advanced industrial society. Herbert Marcuse realised that, for the foreseeable future, economic conditions of material plenty militated against the traditional Marxist-Leninist model whereby the industrial proletariat would fulfil its historic mission to bring about such a revolution. However, not everyone was included in the warm embrace of the affluent society. In the United States there could be no more conspicuous instance of this than the enforcement of social and economic exclusion through racial segregation. The fictional notion of social peace was particularly laid bare after a week-long riot kicked off in 1965, when residents and police fought in the predominantly African-American Watts district of Los Angeles.

Elsewhere the shiny surface of the consumer society for the most part continued to be personified by smiling faces promising comfort, choice and freedom. Nevertheless flashpoints of resistance were soon to multiply across the heartlands of Western affluence. Over the next decade hippies and eco-freaks, black power and native American activists, draft-dodgers and women's liberationists, gays and New-Left revolutionaries began to expose a reality that was oppressive, alienating, stereotyping, exploitative, unjust, ruthless, frivolous, unhealthy and unsustainable.

The spirit of revolt famously exploded across Europe in 1968.

49 Vaneigem, *Revolution of Everyday Life*, 191.

Rather than await the correct material conditions, the here and now was the time to seize the moment, to liberate the beach beneath the street. Quoting demonstrators outside the French Embassy in London, Robin Fior's famous design for the front page of *Black Dwarf* roared in a huge font '**WE SHALL FIGHT, WE WILL WIN, PARIS, LONDON, ROME, BERLIN**', as the May 1968 festivals of the oppressed rocked the affluent society to its foundations.

The 1968 events erupted between Marcuse's completion of 'An Essay on Liberation' and its publication. Almost before the smoke from the Molotov cocktails had cleared, he added a preface, hoping that the audacious assault upon war, neo-colonialism and capitalism was an expression of the 'Great Refusal' and a harbinger of authentic social revolution to bring about the liberation of humanity. He was ecstatic that 'the radical utopian character of [the militants'] demands' once more conjured up the spirit of the *Communist Manifesto:*

> They have again raised a specter (and this time a specter which haunts not only the bourgeoisie but all exploitative bureaucracies): the specter of a revolution which subordinates the development of productive forces and higher standards of living to the requirements of creating solidarity for the human species, for abolishing poverty and misery beyond all national frontiers and spheres of interest, for the attainment of peace. In one word: they have taken the idea of revolution out of the continuum of repression and placed it into its authentic dimension: that of liberation.[50]

If ecological concerns were for the most part marginal to the

50 Herbert Marcuse, preface to 'An Essay on Liberation', [online] http://www.lifeaftercapitalism.info/downloads/read/Philosophy/Herbert%20Marcuse/Herbert%20Marcuse%20-%20An%20Essay%20on%20Liberation%20(Beacon,%201969).pdf [accessed 9 September 2012].

struggle that erupted on European streets in 1968, they increasingly became a part of countercultural and anti-capitalist agendas during the following years. One of the most prescient critics was Theodore Roszak, who called into question the reach of the street uprisings and strikes in terms of awareness of wider social consequences and from an environmental perspective. Later in 1968 he expressed concerns about the potential shortcomings of 'workers' control' following in the May General Strike in France:

> Surely the touchstone of the matter would be: how ready are the workers to disband whole sections of the industrial apparatus where this proves necessary to achieve ends other than efficient productivity and high consumption? How willing are they to set aside technocratic priorities in favor of a new simplicity of life, a decelerating social pace, a vital leisure? These are questions which enthusiasts for workers' control might do well to ponder. Suppose the French workers *had* taken over the economy, an objective which seems to have lost its general appeal in the wake of the new wage agreements the de Gaulle government has granted. Would the Renault workers have been willing to consider closing the industry down on the grounds that cars and traffic are now more the blight than the convenience of our lives? [51]

Roszak instantly recognised a potential divide between the dissidents. Many rebelled against the status quo because they felt excluded and marginalised and wanted to be emancipated from deprivation into order to enjoy the full fruits of the society of affluence. They rightly fought for justice, a part of which was to be included in the

51 Theodore Roszak, *The Making of a Counter Culture: Reflections on the Technocratic Society and Its Youthful Opposition* [1968] (Berkeley. CA.: University of California Press, 1995), 68-69.

economic bonanza. However there were already others who shared a desire to fundamentally transform the social and economic basis of society in a different vision of liberation. Andre Görz was one of the greenest members of the French *soixante-huitard* generation. He attacked the impact of cars upon urban communities and set out eco-socialist manifestos during the early 1970s. Later that decade Marcuse's 'Ecology and the Critique of Modern Society' (1979) also confirmed the arrival of political ecology. While the Situationist International had been early critics of the motor car's role in exacerbating alienation, Debord's concern about the ecological consequences of industrial capitalism, is more conspicuous in his 1988 book *Comments on the Society of the Spectacle* than in his original work of 1968. By 1988 he forcefully linked his critique of the spectacle to environmental degradation:

> The spectacle makes no secret of the fact that certain dangers surround the wonderful order it has established. Ocean pollution and the destruction of equatorial forests threaten oxygen renewal; the earth's ozone layer is menaced by industrial growth; nuclear radiation accumulates irreversibly. It merely concludes that none of these things matter. It will only talk about dates and measures.[52]

Graham Caine particularly cites reading Theodore Roszak's writings as an influence on his political and ecological development. Roszak coined the term 'counter culture'. His book *The Making of a Counter Culture* (1968) not only described, theorised and celebrated the burgeoning counter culture at this time, but helped to forge and develop the phenomenon. Reflecting on the 1960s in 1995, Roszak

52 Guy Debord, *Comments on the Society of the Spectacle* [1988], trans. by Malcolm Imrie (London: Verso, 1990), 34.

wrote that 'By 1960 the military-industrial complex quite simply *was* the American political system.'[53] Roszak was an astute social analyst, whose lively and compelling prose looked beyond the deficiencies of the capitalist military-industrial complex to the perils of an underlying technocratic mangerialism – a danger common to state socialism and capitalism alike. When I wrote a blurb that described the Street Farm as anti-capitalist Crump trenchantly extended this to socialist planners too.

After May 1968, as The Thing, The Spectacle, The Establishment, reasserted itself in the ensuing months, it also became apparent that there were limitations to the idea that the state could be overthrown at the barricades alone. The state knew all about violence, it was its lifeblood, so it would be difficult to out-brick or out-gun it. For a revolution to be successful and sustainable it was also necessary to create and develop alternatives. For a substantial section of the underground and the New Left, the revolutionary project was not to install the correct *Commissariat* of party leaders at the top but the total transformation of the means of production and conditions of life. Liberatory technology, ecology and communal living were to flourish as a part of this radical transformation, alongside a bewildering array of issues sometimes complementary, at others in competition or outright contradiction to each other. A cursory flick through contemporary countercultural publications, such as the *Whole Earth Catalog* or *Alternative London*, reveals countless preoccupations with the mind, body and spirit. There were new attitudes to child rearing and sexual liberation, attempts to change consciousness by meditation, psychedelic drugs or consciousness-raising groups, a revolution in the garden and kitchen through macrobiotic, wholefood and vegetarian diet, adventures in the occult, mysticism and non-western traditions, encounter groups and

53 Roszak, *Making of a Counter Culture*, xv.

psychodrama, alternative media and experiments in all areas of the arts. There were tensions between hedonism and simple living, self-indulgence and altruism, non-violent activism and the resistance of the street fighter or urban guerrilla. Indeed some entrepreneurial and individualistic ventures turned out to be less alternative in their outcomes, being readily recuperated into the disastrous Thatcherite 'Revolution' that followed. Out of this experimental dialectic sprang a counterculture at turns beautiful, tragic, self-destructive, innovative, nostalgic, utopian, liberating.

Green Earth Blues

> *The pride of having reached the moon is cancelled out by the humiliation of having gone so far towards making a slum of our own native planet.*
> (Max Nicholson)[54]

Concern for other species, the environment and the Earth itself became a significant part of the emerging cultural resistance. After all, behind the advertising hoarding was the decimated forest, beneath the gleaming new tower block was the bulldozed street market. The ecological costs of the consumer society were becoming clear. During the 1960s, Murray Bookchin was already beginning to elaborate the philosophy of social ecology with which he is closely associated. He identified the impact of pesticides on flora and fauna in 1962, shortly predating Rachel Carson's more famous critique of the pesticide industry, *Silent Spring*, later that year.[55] Ruth Harrison

54 Max Nicholson, *The Environmental Revolution: A Guide for the New Masters of the Earth* (London: Hodder and Stoughton, 1970), [5].
55 Lewis Herber [pseud. of Murray Bookchin], *Our Synthetic Environment* (New York: Knopf, 1962); Rachel Carson, *Silent Spring* [1962], (rpt. London: Penguin, 1999).

exposed the horrors of factory farming in *Animal Machines* (1964). The economist Barbara Ward made some prescient links between earth stewardship and social justice in her book *Spaceship Earth* (1966), a theme which she continued to develop in the decade to come. In the anarchist press, *Anarchy* magazine demonstrated an early awareness of green issues when it devoted a special issue to ecology in November 1966.[56] Friends of the Earth began in 1969 and Greenpeace was founded in 1971, quickly capturing the public imagination by taking direct action against nuclear testing and with daring 'David and Goliath' confrontations with whaling ships. (Sea Shepherd now fights this battle, its founder Paul Watson being another veteran 1970's activist). Also during the 1970s, women of the Chipko movement in India started a proud tradition of 'tree-hugging' in direct actions to protect forests from decimation due to cash cropping, while the Green Belt women of Kenya similarly began to plant thousands of trees to promote environmental responsibility, sustainability and economic independence.[57] On the party political front, in the UK emerging ecological ideas found a voice in the formation of the PEOPLE party in 1973 (later the Ecology Party; today the Green Party).[58]

There is no single explanation for the growth in ecological concern at this time, as several material factors contributed towards the increase in awareness. Many people in Western Europe had more discretionary time to think about the natural world, taking time to enjoy the countryside at home or to travel abroad and to take holidays where the impact might be obvious. Environmental

56 Michael Allaby, *The Eco-Activists: Youth Fights for a Human Environment* (London, Charles Knight, 1971), 6. It was Issue 69 – see *Autonomy: The Cover Designs of Anarchy 1961-1970*, ed. by Daniel Poyner (London: Hyphen Press, 2012), 157.
57 See Carolyn Merchant, *Radical Ecology: The Search for a Livable World* (New York: Routledge, 1992), 202-203.
58 Dick Richardson, 'The Green Challenge: Philosophical, Programmatic and Electoral Considerations', 4-21 in *The Green Challenge: The Development of Green Parties in Europe*, ed. by Dick Richardson and Chris Rootes (London: Routledge, 1995), 6.

impacts on everyday life became glaringly apparent whether through traffic congestion in the cities or the loss of hedgerows in the countryside. The development of sophisticated instruments and techniques to quantify and document environmental degradation is also significant. For example, James Lovelock invented an 'electron capture detector' that revealed pesticide residues in both the fatty tissues of penguins in the Antarctic and the milk of human nursing mothers, thus providing evidence to underpin Carson's *Silent Spring*.[59] At the other end of the spectrum, the Apollo astronaut William Anders' image of the Earth from the Moon, photographed in 1968, revealed our exquisitely illuminated, yet vulnerable looking, planet as never before. The resulting 'Earthrise' is one of the most well-known environmental photographs ever taken. The shifts in ideas about the planet that emerged in the scientific press and alternative publications soon also found their expression in mainstream political concern and the media. The substantial popular participation in the first Earth Day held in the United States in 1970 is often seen as the consolidation of a mass movement for environmental protection. Fears of nuclear and environmental catastrophe became increasingly prominent public concerns. By the mid-1970s looming ecological crises had become staples of popular culture, featuring for example in science fiction and television drama such as the environmental parables in *Doctor Who*, *Doomwatch* and, most apocalyptically, in *Survivors*.[60]

Concern for the impact of anthropogenic activity upon the natural environment, and the consequent effect upon human well-being and threat to other species and their habitats, moved to the top of national and international political agendas. The Council of

59 J. E. Lovelock, *Gaia: A New Look at Life on Earth* [1979], (Oxford: Oxford University Press, 1989), x.
60 See Dominic Sandbrook, *State of Emergency; The Way We Were: Britain, 1970-1974* (London: Allen Lane, 2010), 203-208.

Europe declared 1970 to be the European Conservation Year, an initiative to encourage all Europeans to both celebrate the beauty of the natural world and to be alert to pressing environmental threats.[61] In 1972 the United Nations Conference on the Human Environment held in Stockholm proved to be a landmark event as the world's first environmental summit. In the wake of the conference, still fresh in the minds of government ministers, the Heath Administration introduced the Protection of the Environment Bill (eventually be placed on the statute by Harold Wilson's government as the more limited Control of Pollution Act 1974). During the reading of the Bill in the House of Lords in November 1973, conservation-minded Lords debated the issues at hand, on one occasion alluding to the experiments of none other than Graham Caine. Lord Holford was particularly impressed by Caine's efforts to recycle wastes so far as possible in a closed system to reduce, even eliminate, pollution:

> I want to mention an experimental house built by a young architect, at a cost of less than £1,000, in which he disposes of all his waste, except of course bottles and plastic containers. He heats his dwelling and his domestic water system by solar panels; he derives supplementary energy from the wind by means of a small home windmill, and he provides his own gas for cooking and the auxiliary heating of his house and greenhouse—in which I was delighted to observe only last week that he is growing such things as pineapples and bananas and green vegetables of all kinds. I am not going to give your Lordships the address of this house because the young man, Mr. Graham Caine, is making a serious scientific model. Everything that happens is being properly and scientifically recorded by the Thames Polytechnic or by King's College biology departments, and obviously he

61 Allaby, *Eco-Activists*, 78.

> should not be plagued by too many unscientific visitors. But, meanwhile, similar and perhaps less primitive experiments in houses that absorb their waste and recycle their waste, and so on, are going on in Cambridge and elsewhere, on what might be termed generically "ecological lines". A feature of these experiments is that waste is reduced to an absolute minimum; costs are lowered, and where the systems are complete there is no pollution whatsoever.[62]

By the early 1970s the forecasted post-scarcity turned out to be not as imminent as observers such as Vaneigem and Murray Bookchin supposed. As is well known, the prevailing notion of continued abundance changed abruptly in during the Oil Crisis of 1973-74. Confidence about the inevitability of affluence diminished from the early 1970s onward, predating the Club of Rome's 1972 *Limits to Growth* report. Barry Commoner's *Closing Circle* (1971) had already attributed problems of environmental sustainability to the expansive nature of capitalism. Influential works such as E.F. Schumacher's *Small is Beautiful* (1973) aimed to adapt in a positive way to more straitened times ahead. Concerns relating to resource depletion, habitat loss, pollution and climate change began to loom large in influential publications such as 'The Blueprint for Survival' (1972) and the 'World Conservation Strategy of the International Union for the Conservation of Nature' (1980) which added the term 'sustainable development' to the environmental lexicon.

Doubts about the sustainability of prevailing economic trends encouraged and seemed to give credence to those who sought to live in a radically different way through tactical prefiguration, presenting a fundamental challenge by escaping or challenging existing social norms and priorities. Disillusionment with what

62 Hansard HL Deb 27 November 1973, vol 347, cols 51-52.

was described as technocratic urban society led to a substantial back-to-the-earth trend among a section of the counterculture who set up smallholdings and rural communes. This was not so much a primitivist urge but a quest to seek and dwell within a less complicated society; one more conducive to human happiness and efficient in meeting basic needs directly, rather than through the circumlocution of conspicuous consumption and drudgery towards endlessly deferred gratification. At its best this was more in a spirit of celebration and experiment than in rejectionism, an approach captured in books such as Schumacher's *Good Work* (1979) and Ivan Illich's *Tools for Conviviality* (1973), advocating among other ideas the use of appropriate technology. Not everyone was able or willing to leave the cities. Other countercultural groups, such as the Diggers in San Francisco, and the Kabouters and Provos in Amsterdam, preferred fight to flight by working for change in urban areas rather than rural communes. Peter Crump later included Street Farm within this approach because 'unlike other hippies' they 'didn't believe that the solution was to escape to the country'. He argued that to undertake countercultural resistance within the cities was, potentially, a more effective and powerful challenge to the state, though therefore likely to provoke a strong state response:

> You won't be able to achieve anything by going off into the country and escaping, the state can very well deal with that. The city itself is a manifestation of the state in a very clear way, but there *are* ways that you can take bits of the city back.[63]

Among groups that preferred to fight their corner in London, Street Farm shared common ground with The Dwarfs in Notting Hill and a group called PEST (Planet Earth Survival Team) who also

63 Peter Crump, 'Street Farm', talk at Bristol Anarchist Bookfair, 7 May 2011.

advocated a creative, ecologically sound and unalienated society in place of consumer society. According to Alan Dearling:

> [The Dwarfs] first appeared at the Portobello Carnival in 1971, where Hawkwind and the Pink Fairies played beneath the flyover. They modeled themselves on the Kabouters of Amsterdam and were quoted in *Time Out*: Dwarfs *"operate strictly as freak ambassadors...Dwarf power does not wish to be corrupted."* A bemused *West London Observer* reported that, *"Working out what the Dwarfs stand for is like trying to grab a fist full of air and bottling it in a jam jar."* Strange days indeed, and it didn't end there – Phil Russell, aka Wally Hope, [the ill-fated founder of the Stonehenge People's Festival] was one of them![64]

So Street Farm appeared at a time of fluid ideas, their autonomy as a group freely borrowing and weaving together strands of influence deftly seized from politics, ecology, architecture and popular culture. At the radical anti-capitalist edge of the late 1960's, early 1970's zeitgeist, they were both determined by, and a unique expression of, this cultural phenomenon as they drew upon, exemplified and offered a distinctive synthesis of contemporary ideas. In order to understand Street Farm we should consider their practice within the context from which they appeared in the Architectural Association and to compare, and as importantly contrast, them with other groups proposing radical change in architecture and planning.

64 Alan Dearling, 'Not Only But Also: Some Historical Ramblings about the English Festivals Scene', [online] http://www.enablerpublications.co.uk/pdfs/notonly1.pdf [accessed 25 September 2012], 4-5.

The Class of '71 at the Architectural Association

Founded as an informal association in 1847, the Architectural Association (AA) was slipping into a deepening crisis at the beginning of the 1970s. The idea of a merger with Imperial College of Science and Technology had been first mooted in 1964. Keen to defend the School's autonomous status, AA students and staff in London's Bedford Square fought off the proposal which was abandoned in 1970. The unpopularity of this perceived assault upon the AA's independence and integrity discredited the governing council and presented an opportunity for a real experiment in student power. Threatened with the institution's closure, students and staff staged a dramatic takeover of the AA's decision-making structures. For an interim period staff, students, councillors and members inclusively ran the AA under the provisionally convened School Community. Charles Jencks (an AA member at the time) gave a sympathetic account of this experiment in participatory democracy:

> The energy and creativity of the School Community was staggering; committees were formed to do every possible money-saving function, from cleaning the building at 6:30 in the morning to turning off the lights. There were committees on the school budget which showed methods for saving £70, 000, committees on a new appeal, long-term finance, academic structure, staff appointments, the graduate departments and so on. Over this three-month period about 200 people, mostly students, actively took part in creating and running their school. An interesting political fact emerged. With the participatory system, knowledge, skill and desire about politics decentralises so there is no longer any simple leader or fixed structure of government. As soon as one student would become exhausted

> with political activity, another one would fill relatively the same role. This showed the replicating nature of participatory democracy predicted by such theorists as Rousseau – its efficiency and energy compared to other systems. Imagine the difference between a leadership of five and one of two hundred and you see the potential.[65]

After three months, a more formally convened single governing body called the Forum succeeded the School Community. The title of Principal was abolished, to be replaced by a post with the designation of Chair which at least sounded more egalitarian, though in practice marked the passing of the most radical phase of the School Community's decision making by direct democracy.[66] The first Chair, Alvin Boyarsky, held this position for nearly two decades from June 1971 to his death in 1990.[67] This was an era that continued and accentuated the AA's critical tradition, with its ethos of eclecticism and experimentalism.[68] The appointment of Boyarsky, however, did not end the threat to the AA's future. The following year the crisis continued when the then Minister of Education, acceded to requests from local educational authorities to cease payments to the School. This Minister was a woman by the name of Margaret Thatcher. A defender of the School observed: 'She and her Department are unlikely to be overfond of the aims and priorities of the AA whose deinstitutionalised nature jars with the monolithic

65 Charles Jencks, '125 Years of Quasi Democracy', in *A Continuing Experiment: Learning and Teaching at the Architectural Association*, ed. by James Gowan (London: Architectural Press, 1975), 156-57.
66 Architectural Association, *Architectural Association: 125th Anniversary* (London: Architectural Association, [c.1973]), 115.
67 Architectural Association website, Edward Bottoms, 'AA History' http://www.aaschool.ac.uk/AALIFE/LIBRARY/aahistory.php [accessed 30 December 2011].
68 For an analysis of the AA's pedagogic practice and philosophical direction at this time, see Irene Sunwoo, 'From the "Well-Laid Table to the "Market Place": The Architectural Association Unit System', [online] *Journal of Architectural Education*, 65.2 (April 2012), 24-41.

organisations that she finds it easier to control'.[69] In the event the AA did lose its government grant, and survived only by marketing to international students which composed over 90% of its constituency by 1990.[70]

Several commentators have recalled the AA's extra-curricular and informal role as a nexus for the cross-fertilisation of ideas. In this respect the rooftop and bar, open to everyone, was its epicentre.[71] The jury system mentioned by Crump was one of a number of democratic and challenging features of the AA's educational approach. Students shared, debated and defended their final work with their peers in a process open to all other students, staff and interested parties within the AA.[72]

Members of Street Farm were therefore present at what was undoubtedly the most turbulent and experimental period in the AA's long history. As in other intellectual fields, fundamental questions about the control and direction of education were aired in energetic debates, prominently fought out in celebrated students' occupations in the London School of Economics, Hornsea and elsewhere. Graffiti that appeared at the Architectural Association satirised the libertarian spirit of the time: 'Do I have to do what I want again today?'[73] Nevertheless the outcomes could be impressive. Crump, reflecting on his experience as an AA student, shared Charles Jencks' assessment of the glorious months of the School Community. He largely corroborated the positive results of the extraordinary experiment in direct democracy:

69 [Anon], 'Save the AA'. *Architectural Design*, 42.9 (September 1972), 588.
70 Nishat Awan, Tatjana Schneider and Jeremy Till, *Spatial Agency: Other Ways of Doing Architecture* (London: Routledge, 2011), 98.
71 See Lydia Kallipoliti, discussion with Graham Shane, New York, 28 November 2006 and interview with Robin Middleton, 1 August 2007, in Beatriz Colomina and Craig Buckley (eds.), *Clip, Stamp, Fold: The Radical Architecture of Little Magazines 196X to 197X* (Barcelona and New York: Actar and Media and Modernity Programme Princeton University, 2010), 22 and 443.
72 *Architectural Association*, ed. by Nikki Hay (London: Architectural Association, 1975), 12.
73 Simon Sadler, *Archigram: Architecture Without Architecture* (Cambridge, MA.: MIT Press, 2005), 158.

> There was a student body that for a whole term ran the school by weekly meetings, where everybody was invited, everybody spoke, all decisions were taken collectively [...] The academics complained that we were not doing any work, but actually the student body produced more work, of more originality, in that term than at any other time in the history of the school. Even though they were entirely preoccupied with governing themselves [...] It's the first time I'd ever experienced it myself. I'd read about it, but never experienced it before. It was a very clear indication that it was a model that worked. But, people get fed up with it. It's hard work, it's bloody hard work, and you do have to be careful that you don't get bogged down into deciding how many rows of spinach you're going to have to plant, and who's going to peel the courgettes this week. Because you lose impetus like that and so the other thing it tells you – or at least it told us – was that all of these organisations are fit for purpose for a very short time and then they should go, just disappear and you get another one, because it's the people that make up the organisation that are significant, not the organisations themselves.[74]

AA tutor and member of Archigram, Peter Cook described 'The Street Farmers (Peter Crump and Bruce Haggart) [as] arrogant and neurotic but in the tradition of architectural rhetoric (and aesthetic too).' Of the fifth year of 1970-71 (of which the Street Farmers were a part) he recalled: 'Quite Simply – they were great'.[75]

74 Peter Crump, 'Street Farm', talk at Bristol Anarchist Bookfair, 7 May 2011.
75 Peter Cook, 'The Electric Decade: An Atmosphere at the AA School 1963-73', in *A Continuing Experiment: Learning and Teaching at the Architectural Association*, ed. by James Gowan (London: Architectural Press, 1975), 146.

Archigram: The White Heat of Cool

Of the groups that came out of the Architectural Association during the 1960s, Archigram made by far the greatest cultural impact. A core of six practicing architects – Warren Chalk, Peter Cook, Dennis Crompton, David Greene, Ron Herron and Michael Webb – sustained Archigram as a team and magazine from 1961 to 1974. In Simon Sadler's words:

> What Marshall McLuhan anticipated with media, and Timothy Leary engineered through hallucinogens, Archigram hoped to do with architecture: adjust environmental perception.[76]

Now high-profile in the annals of avant-garde design, Archigram formed part of the Britpop of their day. While they presented hundreds of images of their modernist visions, in practice few projects ever left the drawing board to be translated into physical structures under the Archigram name. Nevertheless the group had a flair and pizzazz that justly attracted attention. Their cutting edge, stylishly provocative approach generated a distinctive fusion of contemporary design with science fiction. Such enticing output, however, ultimately pushed 'techno-utopian' solutions that had a fading appeal by 1974. While Archigram set the standard for experimental audacity during the 1960s, by the mid-1970s a different spirit was abroad. Archigram had become a part of the architectural establishment against which to rebel. A consideration of Archigram here may help us to comprehend and to throw into relief what was revolutionary about the urbanism of Street Farm and other libertarian architectural groups whose attitudes of resistance were in marked contrast to both the old guard of the

76 Sadler, *Archigram*, 124.

Royal Institute of British Architects (RIBA), and also Archigram's radical formalism and the kind of modernist trends it represented, as well as a fundamentally different practice and approach based upon a political understanding of the urban environment and the living world.

There was much that was refreshing about Archigram with its modishly eclectic, pastiche approach. The Archigram team celebrated creativity, proposing innovative and imaginative approaches to urban design and planning. They were existential radicals, confident that environmental change affected by transforming architecture and planning could both have a fundamental impact on, and be an expression of, social well-being.

At least in intention, Archigram embraced a libertarian spirit. They sought to rescue and reinvent modernist architecture, widely disgraced by its association with the totalitarian regimes of the inter-war period. They did not put forward prescriptive blueprints. In Sadler's words, Archigram 'adopted a paradigm of indeterminacy', avoiding rigid principles of practice.[77] Peter Cook's belief that Archigram should initiate and inspire an ongoing cultural conversation about the nature and future of urban planning, presenting communities with a range of scenarios, and therefore choices, exemplified this non-prescriptive approach.[78]

Archigram aspired to the creative visualisation of a new aesthetic that married together what they considered to be visual elegance of form with the practical comforts demanded by a rapidly modernising society. The popularisation of adaptability and flexibility in design was surely one of their most valuable contributions. In the wonderful world of Archigram a building was not a rigid and fixed entity but a space that could be customised to accommodate its tenants' changing

77 Sadler, *Archigram*, 6.
78 Sadler, *Archigram*, 48.

needs and desires. The approach owed much to Buckminster Fuller's notion of a 'kit-of-parts'; dwellings and interiors that non-experts could quickly assemble and adapt using ready-made components. While, as we shall see, Archigram had penchant for 'throwaway' architecture, this feature of their work could be incorporated into sustainable construction as it enabled the kind of future-proofing that could keep buildings both current and durable.

A number of aspects of Archigram's work, however, help to explain why groups such as Street Farm and ARse (Architects for a Really Socialist Environment) began to question, challenge and propose different directions. For critics, Archigram's vision did not inspire confidence that renovated Futurist and Modernist grand plans would facilitate empowered or autonomous communities, any more than predecessors taking their lead from the Bauhaus or Le Corbusier. For all the talk of 'indeterminacy' and conversations, it seemed that outside experts would continue to determine the form and experience of urban communities. Furthermore there appeared to be limited analysis of the obstacles that state and corporate control presented to egalitarian models of direct democracy.

Sadler points out the irony that Archigram's utopianism was 'founded upon large-scale command/control systems'.[79] Archigram's theoretical approach seemed to cling to a questionable optimism regarding technological developments. In reality technocratic strategies and infrastructure are not 'neutral' in their social and political impact. If such systems are produced in context of the prevailing hierarchical and authoritarian military-industrial complex, it is indeed optimistic to anticipate that can they can be funded, researched, developed and implemented in such a way as to produce benign, emancipatory and democratic outcomes, rather than reproducing the values of their funders.

79 Sadler, *Archigram*, 117.

Free choice is central to Archigram's programme, based upon an assumption of the democratisation of abundance and affluence. In a capitalist market economy, however, 'free choice' always means offering choices and opportunities for wealthy consumers, with far more limited options for, and constraints upon, the liberty of producers. Archigram embraced free market forces that, during the intervening years, have significantly extended and exacerbated inequalities in wealth and their concomitant affect upon power relations. Those with the most capital determine projects and the production and distribution of goods and services. Noting the exclusive sub-text beneath Archigram's graphical representations, Sadler comments that they 'sought a constituency of young liberated, high-libido consumers – male or female'.[80] They failed to critically engage with the already apparent proliferation of social inequality, alienation and environmental deterioration.

Archigram's vision was in keeping with the contemporary expectancy of increasingly high inputs of resources and energy. Motorised urban transport, which Archigram celebrated as a healthy flow and circulation of energy, raises central dilemmas brought about by free choice and consumerism. The 'consumption of movement' – Sadler's suggestive term – was a conspicuous aspect of their schemes. This is particularly marked in their apparent enthusiasm for 'traffic interchanges' and 'motorised conurbations'.[81] It was hoped that through the availability of cheap consumer items a capitalist mixed economy could deliver socialism by producing and circulating at low cost the kind of exclusive luxury items previously reserved for the wealthy. There were analogies between automobile mobility and class mobility, as cheap cars met popular aspirations to move out of fixed hierarchical social relations. In practice the private

80 Sadler, *Archigram*, 183.
81 Sadler, *Archigram*, 80 and 77.

car brought about cities blighted by old enemies of urban conviviality such as pollution, oil dependency and reliance on big business, while undermining local resilience and resourcefulness. For critics the negative aspects of the car on urban life include death and injuries through accidents, divided communities, the blighting of street culture, often facilitating longer commuting journeys, disruption of public transport through traffic gridlock, poor air quality, inefficient fossil-fuel consumption and damage to buildings. David Pinder documents the Situationists' early attacks on cars as instruments of isolation and alienation, bisecting urban neighbourhoods and militating against authentic human encounters.[82] More recently, New Urbanist planners have sought to keep city centres car-free by introducing efficient advanced passenger transport schemes, retaining public spaces and reducing the distances between home, work and amenities.

Archigram's ideas about car design reflected their enthusiasm for planned obsolescence. They hoped that the rapid increasing trend for disposability in everyday plastic and paper items could be extended to private vehicles. Peter Cook went on to commend the appearance of 'limited-life-span houses', announcing provocatively:

> We must recognise this as a healthy and altogether positive sign. It is the product of a sophisticated consumer society, rather than a stagnant (and in the end, declining) society.[83]

One issue of Archigram's magazine featured a cover proclaiming: 'towards throwaway architecture'.[84] While temporary organic shelters are an age-old tribute to disposable design, Archigram's

82 David Pinder, *Visions of the City: Utopianism, Power and Politics in Twentieth-Century Urbanism* (New York: Routledge, 2005), 137.
83 Sadler, *Archigram*, 95, quoted from 'Discussion', *Archigram*, no. 3 (1963), np.
84 Peter Taylor's design, 'Expendibility', cover of *Archigram*, no. 3, (1963) reproduced in *Archigram*, ed. by Peter Cook *et al, Rev. ed.* (New York: Princeton Architectural Press, 1999), 14.

vision does not appear to be integrated with consideration of the recycling of parts, nor do they suggest what to do about the inevitable return of the repressed in the form of colossal quantities of waste. In retrospect, the celebration of disposability and expendability anticipated a trend that has continued. Nevertheless the concern for sustainability in succeeding years makes the Archigram model appear outmoded and unappealing. It is radical, but neither viable nor genuinely progressive. While all structures are of course ultimately temporary, the proposition that planned obsolescence is fulfilling is doubtful, even if material demand could be met in social and ecological terms. Archigram's approach is in contrast to Murray Bookchin 'economy of cherished things' in which high value is placed upon quality and durability as design virtues.[85] In this respect the cherishing of things in Edmund De Waal's novel *The Hare with the Amber Eyes* (2010) reverses the clinical functionalism of a throwaway society, celebrating the quiddity of objects. The pleasure embedded within meaningful and shared things and places can powerfully enrich and enhance life. Things gifted, told stories about, played with, transported and embellished can be important media through which joyful relationships are negotiated. This is surely also true of buildings. Disposable units are not designed to stand long enough to gather to themselves the community-nurturing patina of cultural memory.

Archigram's early enthusiasm for the supposed roles of expendability, disposability and planned obsolescence as somehow staving off a 'declining society' by representing dynamism and 'sophistication' over stagnation, was a departure from one of Buckminster Fuller's mantras, namely to always do more with less in the cause of hyper-efficiency.[86] Overarching such an approach

85 Murray Bookchin, *Post-Scarcity Anarchism* (London: Wildwood House, 1974), 135.
86 *Archigram*, editorial from *Archigram*, no. 3 (1963), 16.

is Archigram's 'Boy's Own' excitement for all things gleaming with novelty and searing with velocity. In keeping with the spirit of the 'white heat' of technology, objects of innovation and change became desirable fetishes in their own right. This is radicalism, however, only in the scope of its physical impact. Whatever Archigram's theoretical intentions, there was a danger that the kind of change they proposed was quantitative rather than something able to qualitatively and profoundly transform society for the better. During the 1960s Herbert Marcuse made a significant differentiation between quantitative change, being the development of physical and technical living conditions and qualitative change which he defines as 'authentic liberation.'[87] In the present-day, although somewhat slowed by the plateauing economy, city centres are permanently under reconstruction. This is no doubt pleasing to Archigram given, as David Greene wrote in a retrospect of 1998, that in Archigram's 'new terrain', 'the city becomes a continuous building site in a very literal sense'. Nevertheless, despite claims that this would engender 'the power to reshape social relationships', features such as the hierarchies of power, anti-social behaviour and patterns of deprivation remain obstinate fixtures in urban life.[88] In Marcuse's terms, for all the acceleration of technical innovation and physical construction, qualitative change has proved to be elusive. Just as clichéd terms of the Nineties and Noughties such as 'excellence' and 'vibrancy' have become diluted by overuse, the force of the term 'innovation' has been expended. And identifying with youthful innovation is of course to instigate one's own ephemeracy.

Archigram celebrated consumerism and individual choice in a

87 Herbert Marcuse, 'Liberation from the Affluent Society' (1967 lecture in London), 175-192 in *The Dialectics of Liberation* ed. by David Cooper (Harmondsworth: Penguin, 1968), 180, [online] http://www.marcuse.org/herbert/pubs/60spubs/67dialecticlib/67LibFromAfflSociety.htm [accessed 12 June 2012].

88 David Greene, Prologue to *Concerning Archigram*, ed. by Dennis Crompton (London: Archigram Archives, 1998), [ii].

way that was welcomed in the aftermath of post-War austerity. As we have seen, however, by the start of the 1970s the Situationists and other critics had increasingly shifted radical opinion towards the rejection of consumer society. To base an economy upon expendable consumerism is to become reliant upon vast and increasing inputs of raw materials and energy, to mass-produce its throwaway cars and glass, steel and concrete buildings. Archigram's output was drafted in the context of an affluent society with increased leisure time, a time of the space race and the Cold War, when conspicuous consumption was a weapon against Eastern Bloc austerity. To feed Cornucopian fantasies of approaching post-scarcity assumed immense, stupendous plenty. It was predicated on an assumption of continued abundance for all, an idea that has come increasingly anachronistic. For many in the West, real term wages have stagnated, job security diminished and discretionary time reduced during subsequent decades.

Like most futurists, Archigram anticipated the shape of things to come as an accelerating trajectory of the present. This was a reasonable assumption. But it is a wise axiom that we should be cautious about predicting anything, especially the future. As expectations of global abundance began to fade, Archigram's early hi-tech proposals correspondingly appeared less feasible. Even with lighter materials and a trend towards dematerialisation, citizens of Archigrametropolis would be dependent upon systems which wouldn't have their own needs at heart – for food, energy and their basic service infrastructure. In the context of Vietnam and the Cold War, sophisticated and expansive command and control systems had social consequences beyond a neutral logistical function in ordering chaos. Residents and communities living in an Archigram future would also be heavily dependent upon experts. Extravagantly original mega-projects that have been translated into reality in recent years may be technically innovative but they are, of course, not necessarily socially progressive, egalitarian or democratic. In recent years some of the most iconoclastic architecture has been the proliferation of ecologically invasive developments, for instance Palm Jumeirah Island, in Dubai.[89] This was created through a radical recontouring of the natural environment. Such spectacular complexes are real estate designed for the elite and super-rich in the socially conservative nations of the United Arab Emirates, far from the vision of democratic consumerism of which Archigram dreamed. In our post-Postmodernist present, innovation itself has become old hat.

While both Archigram and Street Farm were closely linked to the Architectural Association, a consideration of the former helps to illustrate and clarify what Street Farm were not. There are several similarities. The libertarianism, the faith in the environment for the amelioration of social ills, the kaleidescoping and telescoping of collage and splintered manifestos are common to both. Both groups were to be closely associated with the output of their magazines, although *Street Farmer* was a more ephemeral publication. Both disseminated playful, experimental graphics, making use of montage style over-written by radical slogans for a new era of urban living. Nevertheless, as we shall see, while both groups used montage, the content, effect and significance of Street Farm's assemblages is markedly different from those of Archigram. Despite the undoubted affinities and common ground that existed, their approaches diverged sharply. Crump registers a fundamental political difference between Street Farm, 'primarily a collective for social revolution', and Archigram, who by contrast 'had no time for social revolution', recalling that 'Archigram's current project at the time of our graduation was for an underground palace for

89 'Meet the first resident of Dubai's palm-shaped man-made island', *Daily Mail Online*, 22 June 2007: http://www.dailymail.co.uk/news/article-463694/Meet-resident-Dubais-palm-shaped-man-island.html [accessed 25 August 2013].

Prince Rainier!'[90] Archigram foregrounded themes of disposability consumer choice and cornucopian technology, while Street Farm emphasised autonomy, self-sufficiency and sustainability.

Peter Cook of Archigram was Haggart's tutor at the AA.[91] However while Archigram and Street Farm were near contemporaries in London's radical architecture scene during the early 1970s, there was little prospect of a working relationship between the Archigram tutors and their street farming students. In a 2007 interview with Lydia Kallipoliti, Peter Crump commented:

> [...] We did not have very much to do with Archigram. They did not like us. They thought of us as 'antitechnology'. And although this is not entirely true, in the bucolic sense, we were mostly involved in politics. Technology for us was incidental. On the contrary, they were interested in the kind of technology of building complex systems and equipped houses and cities.[92]

It is true that contrasting attitudes to technology reflected a clear divide between Street Farm and Archigram approaches. Warren Chalk of Archigram challenged the assumptions of the ecology movement, writing:

> This technological backlash we are experiencing must be fought with a more sophisticated technology, a more sophisticated science... If we are to prevent eco-catastrophe it can only be done by more sophisticated environmental systems, not by dropping out.[93]

90 Peter Crump, e-mail message to the author, 29 April 2013.
91 Zak Kyes and Wayne Daly, 'Street Farmer', *AArchitecture*, 4 (Summer 2007), 19-22: http://www.aaschool.ac.uk/Downloads/AArchitecture/AArchitecture04.pdf [accessed online 24 January 2012], 22.
92 Kallipoliti, interview with Peter Crump, Bristol, 11 July 2007, *Clip, Stamp, Fold*, 254.
93 Warren Chalk, 'Touch not...', *Architectural Design* 4 (April 1971), 238.

Rejecting 'hippy philosophy', Chalk provocatively looked forward to the emergence of the 'electronic tomato' and the 'personalised robot' in the belief that:

> Experiments such as these could achieve a people-oriented technology of human liberation, directed towards pleasure, enjoyment, experimentation: a try-it-and-see attitude.[94]

Chalk argues that an accommodation between the natural environment and the synthetic environment is to be attained. Writing at a time when the teargas of the Sorbonne and the marijuana of Woodstock had not long dissipated, he concludes that 'hopefully some environmental magic will then prevail and we will again think up the impossible in order to be realistic'. In this way Chalk seemingly echoes the sentiments of the counterculture. However, while Archigram ostensibly shared with Street Farm a desire for production for social needs, there is no critique of the dynamics of capital and the consequent remit of mainstream research to meet the needs of the military-industrial complex. Street Farm understood that obstacles to human liberation were fundamentally social and political rather than technological in nature. In retrospect Street Farm's gloomier prognosis of the trajectory of capitalism was more prescient. At the time of writing, forty years after the confident assumptions of a coming post-scarcity society, some pundits predict a decade of austerity in Europe, with both precarious employment prospects coupled with longer working hours and later, more frugal, pensions. The environmental catastrophe that Chalk hoped to avoid has become a fact of life rather than a prediction for countless refugees displaced due to climate change, while the critical loss of habitats and species continues apace. Despite exponential technological

94 Chalk, 'Touch not...', 238.

development, principal forms of energy remain unchanged as the economy is based upon the consumption of bunker fuel and other fossil fuels and uranium.[95] The economic drives for competition, centralisation, division of labour, commodification in turn impact upon the superstructure to reproduce social systems that do not for the most part facilitate liberation or enjoyment.

In the aftermath of the austere 1940s and early 1950s, Archigram celebrated the emerging consumer boom as a liberating and democratic trend. Street Farm's political attitudes and sympathy for the Situationists' critique of consumerism however signalled a marked distinction. Again in this they were to be prescient, anticipating the shortcomings of the individualistic neo-Liberal era that has followed, during which for those in employment the consumer bonanza was often purchased at the cost of life as a treadmill of debt and overwork.

There was little manifest antipathy between the two groups. However, despite the proximity of their activities, they inhabited different mental universes and had divergent motivations. While Street Farm certainly rejected a technocratic approach, the notion that its relationship to Archigram defined its theory and practice, therefore, is spurious. Crump rejects outright Stefan Szczelkun's comment that 'The Street Farmers had arisen from the Architectural Association as a kind of radical eco response to the technological supremicism of Archigram'.[96] He counters that this statement 'has no basis in fact because The Street Farm ideas arose without any reference to Archigram at all'.[97]

95 At the time of writing the significance of the first long-distance flight by a solar-powered plane remains to be seen: AP, 'Solar-powered plane lands near Washington', *The Independent*, 16 June 2013 [online] http://www.independent.co.uk/news/world/americas/solarpowered-plane-lands-near-washington-8660648.html [accessed 16 June 2013].
96 Stefan Szczelkun, 'Earth Workshop', http://www.stefan-szczelkun.org.uk/phd103.htm [accessed 26 August 2011].
97 Peter Crump, e-mail message to the author, 29 April 2013.

The response of Street Farm and Archigram to ecological matters is a significant distinction. In this respect Graham Caine was explicit that his projected ecological house was 'a deliberate attempt to opt out of the concept of developing yet more "super technology to save the world," and also reduces the dependence upon a centralised supply source.'[98] Quoting Szczelkun, Paul Downton, an architect who also met with Street Farm members while the group was still active, took an interest because of their practical application constructing 'an uncompromisingly ecological building on the basis of an anarchist philosophy and a radical vision of urbanism.'[99] It is worth emphasising here that the *basis* of Street Farm's theoretical approach was their anarchism, this being the ground from which their green practice sprouted. Street Farm made it clear in several places that their motivations were not initially ecological but rather that self-sufficiency, low-impact, autonomous projects and concern for the natural environment were a logical outcome of their beliefs.

ARse and the Derrière-Garde

If for many Archigram magazine was the face of avant-garde thinking in English architecture, snapping from its rear was ARse. Also linked to the Architectural Association through the involvement of David Wild, and near contemporary with Street Farm, *ARse* magazine was published from 1969 to 1972. This was the strapline of what was loosely termed Architects for a Really Socialist Environment or Architectural Radicals, Students and Educators – the editors were happy for readers to decide for themselves what the acronym stood for. The capitalisation was a cheeky allusion to the *Architectural*

98 Graham Caine, 'The Ecological House', *Architectural Design* 42.3 (1972), 140.
99 Downton, *Ecopolis*, 155.

Review. Unlike Street Farm or Archigram, *AR*se was primarily a publication and did not function as a group of practising architects, and so, surely mercifully, no constructions were designed under the name of ARse. In the words of writers for the Spatial Agency project, editors Tom Woolley and David Wild produced a magazine that 'was a resolutely left-wing publication that set out to critique the architectural profession's complicity in capitalist society'.[100]

There was much common ground with Street Farm both in *ARse*'s robust anti-capitalist politics and their sympathy for the squatting movement and workers' struggles. Both ARse and Street Farm were also willing to take direct action and make public statements beyond the printed page and in the wider struggle. ARse, for example, were behind the 'ARse-orchestrated protest' against Buckminster Fuller's lecture at the Institute of Contemporary Arts on the grounds that he was the '"Ambassador-Priest of United States Technological Imperialism"'.[101] They particularly objected to the role of Buckminster Fuller's designs and ideas in bolstering the American state at a time when it was engaged in an imperialist war in Vietnam, upholding a principle that the widely revered designer, by now a global celebrity, should not be beyond critique. Street Farm shared this ambivalence towards Buckminster Fuller, and also rejected his formalist approach. Peter Crump explained:

> We saw him as somebody who had brilliant structural ideas, and despite the fact that he fascinated me as an intellectual, his discourse was overwhelmingly formal. It was precisely this formal obsession that *Street Farmer* was trying to fight against.

100 Spatial Agency, 'Alternative Publishing / Zines', http://www.spatialagency.net/database/where/organisational%20structures/alternative.publishing.zines, [accessed 17 May 2011], para. 2.
101 Irene Sunwoo, text on *ARse* no. 3 for Clip/Stamp/Fold exhibition: The Radical Architecture of Little Magazines 196x–197x, NAiM / Bureau Europa, Maastricht, Netherlands, 27 June – 26 September 2010 [online]: http://www.clipstampfold.com/detail.html?id=58 [accessed 17 May 2011].

> *Street Farmer* never suggested archetypal structures and forms; we tried to avoid that at all costs.[102]

ARse also directly lampooned Archigram. Issue 3, for example, features Peter Cook on the front cover as Archigoon demonstrating his project for the Monte Carlo Entertainment Centre. In an interview conducted in 2006, David Wild outlined the specific objections that underlay the parody of Archigram:

> [We were] appalled that Archigram were so distanced from the radicalism that was going on everywhere in the student world. Everything that they were proposing was a rip-off of Russian Constructivism, but without the politics; instead of 'workers of the world unite,' it was 'come on down and get groovy,' and the collages were all of dolly birds and enviable people. It was all very optimistic – and there is nothing wrong with that – but it was just at the wrong point in time. It was when students worldwide were involved in radicalism. The first big demonstration against the Vietnam War was attended by almost all of us, while Archigram were just in their own little world, which was totally rooted in consumer culture and completely object-fixated, but with a very unpleasant sort of technologically fetishistic edge to it…[103]

Wild suggests that the polemical issue of *ARse* did not reflect any ongoing animosity between the individuals involved. However, he intimates that, while he regrets the mode of expression, he remains unrepentant about ARse's attitude to Archigram:

> This kind of distance from politics and this obsession with

102 Kallipoliti, interview with Peter Crump, Bristol, 11 July 2007, *Clip, Stamp, Fold*, 253.
103 Irene Sunwoo, interview with David Wild, London, 7 October 2006, *Clip, Stamp, Fold*, 515.

> technology have continued up to the present, and of course their success now shows that we were absolutely right.[104]

Although ARse's first production, the Vienna Manifesto, was first published in *Anarchy* magazine, edited by Colin Ward, ARse's activism leaned towards a more party political approach than Street Farm. Subsequent issues were printed by Socialist Review Publishing, a Trotskyite publisher. Nevertheless ARse didn't follow a party line and contributions reflected a diverse range of libertarian opinions within a New-Left current, aiming at political education and the demystification of the architectural profession. The final issue was published in 1972. Tom Woolley commented:

> We killed off *ARse* because it was too successful as we thought it had become a consumer product, such was the demand for it .This was very much David [Wild]'s influence. He produced thousands of paper bags with the Vietnam NLF flag on it which also sold like hot cakes!![105]

With ARse at the front of his career, Woolley took up employment at the AA in 1974. His work with the AA's Hugo Hinsley was instrumental in establishing an architects' co-operative called 'Support'. Woolley recalls that this initiative 'pioneered genuine participatory design in London' through the establishment of the Community Technical Aid movement and the creation of centres to help communities resisting the imposition of mass redevelopment projects and housing issues.[106] Writing in the *Architects' Journal* in 1977, Woolley offered a definition of 'socially responsible' architecture, usefully citing what he considered to be 'four elements

104 Irene Sunwoo, interview with David Wild, London, 7 October 2006, *Clip, Stamp, Fold*, 515.
105 Tom Woolley, e-mail message to the author, 26 September 2013.
106 Tom Woolley, e-mail message to the author, 26 September 2013.

of real alternative practice':

1. Changed relationships between architectural workers; breaking down employer/employee alienation.
2. New sectors of work in which services are available to wider sections of the population, the actual building users as opposed to remote corporate clients.
3. New participatory techniques to de-mystify the status of expertise and to help lay people understand architectural problems more fully.
4. A commitment to greater public accountability of the profession as a whole.[107]

Architects' Revolutionary Council

The Architects' Revolutionary Council (ARC) was another group that advocated community empowerment and rejected 'top down' planning. ARC was also closely connected to – though eventually separate from – the New Architecture Movement. ARC members George Mills and Peter Moloney (creator of many of the group's agit-prop posters) record that its origins stem from an eastern European initiative for 'socially inspired architects' to unite in national movements while working towards an eventual objective to form an ARC International.[108] A British section of the ARC, initially from within the Architectural Association, became part of the revolutionary milieu within architecture. Brian Anson, a lecturer at the AA, founded the British section of the ARC in 1974, in collaboration with several of his students at that time.

107 Tom Woolley, 'Alternative Practice', *Architects' Journal* 42.166 (19 October 1977), 735.
108 George Mills and Peter Moloney, 'Architects Revolutionary Council -- Its History and Its Present Aims', *Building Design*, (297) (7 May 1976), 9.

Anson was a passionate advocate of community empowerment and control in planning decisions (notably a prominent and formidable campaigner in the successful fight to save Covent Garden from development). The ARC's main target was RIBA, but its wider attacks included Archigram and, echoing the so-called Anti-Uglies of the 1950s, resisted the broader trend towards the imposition of brutalist architecture and gentrification:

> We wish to create a situation whereby every time a student passes a building such as Centre Point he vows that he will never work in a practice that is involved in such obscenities. Whenever a student walks through a gentrified area where massive improvement grants have enabled landlords to evict long standing tenants and raise the value of their property a hundredfold, he will vow never to work in firms that indulge in such activities.[109]

In keeping with this determination to fight with tenants against hostile development, Bill Brown, a former ARC activist, outlined the group's outlook and tactics as follows:

> The ARC took a libertarian Marxist approach, with ideas about urban community action particularly inspired by Henri Lefebvre. We believed very much in providing tenants with the tools so that they could take control of their own neighbourhoods. The emphasis on the control of living spaces and a better overall quality of life came to have an environmental aspect as it inevitably involved a desire to include and protect green spaces. It was this insistence on finding ways for people to take real

109 AA Events List, Week 21 (18–21 March), 1974, quoted by Edward Bottoms, 'If Crime Doesn't Pay: The Architects' Revolutionary Council', *AArchitecture*, 5 (Winter 2007-08) [online]: http://www.aaschool.ac.uk/aalife/library/arc.pdf [accessed 24 November 2012], 16.

> control of their communities that marked us and groups like the Street Farmers as revolutionaries rather than just radicals. ARC was a small number of activists often only a dozen, who had considerable success on several occasions. One of these was at Bridgetown [Staffordshire] where the ARC fought alongside tenants and local people and for the first time successfully stopped the demolition of an old neighbourhood of solid working class housing. The campaign included direct action such as lying down in front of, and even sabotaging, bulldozers. By contrast the Colne Valley project involved support and advice rather than a campaign of direct resistance.[110]

In Britain ARC continued to be closely associated with Anson and ended its six-year existence with his departure from the AA in 1980.[111] In keeping with Street Farm's approach, and Woolley's later outlines for 'socially responsible' architecture, he supported community self-management as an alternative to both capitalism and state socialist approaches to architecture.[112] However, while they may have shared an antipathy towards the establishment RIBA, and despite Anson's criticism of the 'Authoritarian left', the implicit vanguardism of Mills and Moloney's account of ARC as deliberately 'tight-knit' in order to 'remain a revolutionary, as opposed to a reformist organisation', distinguishes the group from Street Farm's more inclusive politics of revolutionary urbanism.[113]

The New Architecture Movement (NAM) was another thorn in the side of RIBA. NAM was a direct descendent of the ARC, being formed at an ARC conference in 1975. It put the case

110 Personal conversation with Bill Brown, Harbourside, Bristol, 30 September 2013.
111 Spatial Agency, 'Architects' Revolutionary Council', http://www.spatialagency.net/database/architects.revolutionary.council.arc [accessed 2 January 2012].
112 Louis Hellman, 'NAM Working to Redistribute Power in Architecture', *The Architects' Journal* 163 (2 June 1976), 1067.
113 Mills and Moloney, 'Architects Revolutionary Council,' 9.

for the unionisation of architectural workers and also brought concern for urban environmental issues into the profession by working closely with the Birmingham Green Ban Action Group and other conservation groups. NAM adopted the strategy – first implemented in Sydney, Australia – of using trade unionist industrial action such as strikes and boycotts as a means to uphold socially responsible principles and block the destruction of historic buildings, for instance the successful campaign to save the Central Post Office in Victoria Square, Birmingham in 1973.[114] After *ARse* was discontinued, Tom Woolley also channelled his energies into the New Architecture Movement (NAM). He cites *ARse* as an important inspiration for the NAM, whose '*SLATE*' magazine was to become the 'main focus of antiestablishment architects' during the later 1970s.[115] Woolley has since continued to advocate green remedies, such as low-impact building techniques and organic agriculture. He has promoted sustainable architecture and design, both educationally and professionally, through several institutions and organisations, including the Centre for Alternative Technology.

Design historian John A. Walker, links architectural activist groups such as Street Farm, ARse, and NAM as a part of a broader movement of Community Architecture. Such groups sought to resist the kind of social engineering imposed in the interests of the state and capital, in favour of a community-oriented and community-controlled approach to the local environment.[116]

Another group from the Architectural Association that seem to have much in common with the Street Farm approach was the Rational Technology Unit, which AA tutors Gerry Foley and George Kasabov founded in response to the high profile energy – and

114 Anne Karpf, 'The Pressure Groups', *Architects' Journal*, 166 (1977), 728-29.
115 Irene Sunwoo, interview with Tom Woolley, London, 27 June 2007, *Clip, Stamp, Fold*, 544.
116 John A. Walker, *Glossary of Art Architecture and Design Since 1945*, 3rd ed. (London: Library Association Publishing, 1992), entry 158.

environmental – crisis in 1973.[117] They were near contemporaries with Street Farm, being at the AA's premises in Bedford Square in 1973-1974. Members D. Taylor and Kevin McCartney participated at the same time as Caine and Haggart in Bath's Comtek 'exhibition of Technological Alternatives', largely organised by the Bath Arts Workshop, that took place in 1974. With links to BRAD (Biotechnic Research and Development), the Rational Technology Unit, similarly to Street Farm, combined demonstrations of practical experiments in alternative technology with a political underpinning. While they were influenced by Caine's experiments in people's technology and he believed 'they did great stuff' he declined to join them, not wishing to continue in the academic environment at Bedford Square at that time.[118] Taking an ascetic, survivalist approach, the Rational Technology Unit questioned the most fundamental purposes of architecture and planning in the context of a changing present and, in their view, deteriorating future:

> The current technocratic, highly wasteful, energy intensive society is reaching its end. Even if its own contradictions do not bring about this, the awakening consciousness of countries with primary resources, notably all the oil producers, has changed the world. The old conventional wisdom of architecture has to be re-considered. Not only are there new social and technical problems; there is the whole question of what the role of the architect is, in this rapidly changing society.[119]

Street Farm's relationship to the Architectural Association, therefore, placed them at the heart of a London scene that was undergoing a

117 Irene Sunwoo, 'From the "Well-Laid Table to the "Market Place": The Architectural Association Unit System', [online] *Journal of Architectural Education*, 65.2 (April 2012), 34.
118 Personal conversation with Graham Caine, Montpelier, Bristol, 29 November 2012.
119 Comtek, *Comtek '74* (Bath: Comtek, 1974), 14. See also Patrick Rivers, *The Survivalists* (London: Eyre Methuen, 1975), 106-108.

fundamental re-examination and contestation of the purposes and principles of architecture at that time. This critical tradition has since continued in several publications including the big-hitting *Architectural Design*, Martin Pawley's *Ghost Dance Times*, the experimental and eclectic journal *NATØ* (*Narrative Architecture Today*) of the 1980s, through to the more recent *Fulcrum, Civic City Cahier* and *P.E.A.R.* However Street Farm's relationship to the AA was an ambivalent one and it was to the unofficial world beyond academia that they were drawn; to the squats, communes and festivals of the counterculture. So it is to these, their more natural home, that we should now turn.

Plots and Squats

It may be no coincidence that the first City Farm in England was set up in Street Farm's neighbourhood of Kentish Town in 1972. The project had its origins in a squat comprising the disused stables and allotments on its present site on a railway siding.[120] One of the original squatters, Ed Berman, developed the initiative into a more organised project, under the auspices of a group called Inter-Action in 1968. Graham Towers describes Inter-Action as 'a co-operative of community workers, teachers and artists', which 'developed several initiatives to improve environmental awareness and help inner city London voluntary groups organize their own projects in the arts, media and education'.[121] First known as the Fun Art Farm, Kentish Town City Farm evolved from a community gardening project involving local families and pensioners. Formally designated a City

120 David Nicholson-Lord, *The Greening of the Cities* (London: Routledge and Kegan Paul, 1987), 150. See also McKay, *Radical Gardening*, 176.
121 Graham Towers, *Building Democracy: Community Architecture in the Inner Cities* (London: UCL Press, 1995), 110.

Farm from 1972, this project was based on a former timber yard and British Rail owned land off Cressfield Road, Kentish Town.[122] The Oral History Project that is collating memories and other research about the origins of city farms notes their development from grassroots community initiatives to provide access to land in urban areas during the 1960s.[123]

Kentish Town's radical character was also reflected in the presence of Britain's largest population of squatters, numbering a community of around 400 people during the early 1970s. This concentration of squatters enabled them to make a significant impact on the area. A report by John Pollard, written in conjunction with his fellow squatters in 1972, itemised their contributions which included the creation of 'Free Space Park', a free food restaurant, a store with free and nearly free goods, a crèche and the publication of two community newspapers, the *Crescent Community* and *Here and Now Times*.[124] 'Free Space Park' was to feature as a 'Street Farmyard', a 'groovy place' for a range of community activities in a Street-Farm related paper called *Community Gardening*.

When Pollard wrote a follow-up article for *Architectural Design* the next year this alternative infrastructure and barter and gift economy was still thriving. In 1973 the Camden and Kentish Town squatters' organised a spring neighbourhood festival and a 'Neighbourhood Community Action' candidate even stood in the local elections.[125] Street Farm members both took part in squatting

122 Details gleaned from City Farm Group, *Where to Find City Farms in Britain*, produced and ed. by the City Farm Advisory Service (London: Inter Action Group / City Farm Advisory Service, [1980?]), 8 and 37.

123 See Federation of City Farms and Community Gardens Oral History Project webpage: http://www.farmgarden.org.uk/farms-gardens/oral-history-project [accessed 22 May 2011] and Kentish Town City Farm webpage: http://www.ktcityfarm.org.uk/history.htm [accessed 22 May 2011] and Kentish Town Memories: 40 Years of Kentish Town City Farm webpage: http://40years.ktcityfarm.org.uk/ [accessed 28 September 2013].

124 John Pollard, *Squat: A Report Written in Conjunction with the Squatters in West Kentish Town, September 1972* (London: [self-published?] 1972), sections 3 and 4.

125 John Pollard, 'Squatting in the City', *Architectural Design* 43.8 (1973), 506.

and had close connections to the wider London squatting community at this time. Crump recalled that he used to regularly hang out at the health shop at Good Vibes Corner where he bought muesli which had to be mixed on the spot and was always an opportunity for a chat. He got to know Stefan Szczelkun and Clifford Harper during the time when they were involved with the Kentish Town and Camden squatting scene.[126]

Indeed the proactive experimental work that the squatters were carrying out locally in creating an alternative infrastructure and society was something of a tangible model for the kind of utopian social relations that Street Farm were trying to inspire. A letter from Camden Street Farmers to Maya of *The International Times* sets out the classic Street-Farm strategy to squat the land with food, outlining their experiments in turning 'waste land into productive agricultural land'.[127]

This creative approach is reflected in the squatters' enthusiasm for repurposing buildings, contrasting starkly with the council's urge to wipe them out to start again (an approach that might have met with Archigram's approval). A lot of ingenuity and energy was dedicated to retrieving and transforming buildings that the local authorities had attempted to put out of commission by extensive damage. Crump commented:

> The council used to break the toilets and plumbing, and sometimes the roofs, to stop people moving in. One house looked normal from outside in the street but the council had totally gutted the inside – it was so damaged that they set up floors using a scaffolding structure essentially inside the shell

126 Personal conversation with Peter Crump, Montpelier, Bristol, 24 August 2012.

127 Camden Street Farmers, [Dear Maya letter], *The International Times* 3.2 (July 1975), 6. Strategies for urban food production are discussed in more detail in a later article which looks to be the work of a Street Farmer or acquaintance: A London Farmer, 'Urban Farming', *The International Times* 3.4 (November 1975), 3.

of the house to fill the space so that it could be used as a home again.[128]

> […] all that big area was full of derelict Victorian houses and Camden Council owned most of it. The council's plan was to knock it all down and build housing, while at the same time all kinds of young people were moving into the area with no resources at all, constructing wonderful rooms, turning this area into a very exciting urban development; not at all like a city though.[129]

Acknowledgements on the inside cover of *Street Farmer* 2 record that it was printed by Gus and Sarah of I.R.A.T. Printers of 13 Prince of Wales Crescent (Good Vibes Corner). This indicates that it was printed at premises known as The Dairy, a building run by the squatting community. I.R.A.T. (Institute for Research in Art and Technology) was closely connected to the London Film-Maker's Coop, then based at these squatted premises and linked to another underground institution, The Arts Lab. The squatted Princes of Wales Crescent was also a temporary home to Boy George and Marilyn and hosted gigs such as that by the influential anarcho-punk collective Crass, supported by the Nipple Erectors whose vocalist Shane McGowan was soon to become frontman of The Pogues. Despite the entrepreneurial efforts of the squatters, the Crescent was demolished during the late 1970s.

128 Personal conversation with Peter Crump, Montpelier, Bristol, 24 August 2012. This is likely to be the structure in Castle Road, Kentish Town a photograph of which features in Graham Wells, 'London Squatters', 100-101 in Lloyd Kahn (ed.) *et al. Shelter* [1973] (2nd ed. Bolinas. CA.: Shelter Pub. [nd]), 100.
129 Kallipoliti, interview with Peter Crump, Bristol, 11 July 2007, *Clip, Stamp, Fold*, 256.

'Revolutionary Urbanism': Street Farm's Praxis

It concerns a form of co-operative liberation, the process of which is at least as important as the unperceivable end.

The revolution has to be fought not only in the official demonstration Square and at work but in the very fabric in which we live.
(Caine, 'A Revolutionary Structure', *Oz* (November 1972))

Beautiful Processes

It is necessary to set out some thoughts on what a radical and sustainable approach to architecture and planning would entail. Street Farm's approach is broadly in keeping with the principles of community architecture in so far as they advocated an inclusive, participatory approach to planning, wholly rejecting the top-down imposition of design by outside experts with its tendency to alienate residents. Indeed they can be considered as exponents of 'community architecture' before that term was coined (1975 according to Nick Wates and Charles Knevitt[130]). However, the collective asserted that 'Street Farm revolts against linear argument' (*SF* 2, iii). It will be in vain, therefore, to look for a bullet-pointed manifesto of precepts and action in their work. It is more appropriate to understand *Street*

130 Nick Wates and Charles Knevitt, *Community Architecture: How People are Creating their own Environment* (London: Penguin, 1987), 32n.

Farmer 1 and 2 as mind maps. In this sense it is fruitful to consider the ideas as related to each other as a net of loosely mapped themes rather than as progressing on a logical, straight-line continuum on a flat surface. Clusters of images and text on the printed pages make up nodes and curves incorporating a lacework of organically connected ideas. These at once critique capitalism and state socialism and sketch strategies towards their vision of 'revolutionary urbanism', meaning 'urbanism that is used in a revolutionary way' (*SF* 1, [17]). Together the themes and ideas constitute nothing less than an overarching revolution or 'transmogrification' in the organisation of urban and rural life. In keeping with this topical metaphor of a net, there is no hierarchy of ideas – they are inter-related, mutually dependent and equivalent. In this respect 'revolutionary urbanism' is about the contestation of socio-spatial aspects of the city life by confronting oppressive control and surveillance, as well as reforming technological modes of production and construction. Street Farm's alternative technology is as much about the political and psychological task of unwinding power as the generation of wind power. Indeed while the terms 'alternative technology' is used interchangeably with similar terms, Haggart and Caine argue for a crucial Bookchinite distinction:

> The alternative mentality is the mentality of the original thinker motivated by and responsive to their own alienation, as the isolation of the self-sufficient mentality, is a process and a produce of existing systems. A liberatory technology is a technology that will change the existing situation, alternative technology is one that will make that existing situation more tolerable.[131]

131 In their two-sided bulletin called 'Ramifications and Propagations of Street Farm'. The notion of 'liberatory technology' derives from Bookchin's essay 'Towards a Liberatory Technology' (1965).

Street Farm propose that only a social revolution can break down alienation and mystification. The collective are strongly committed to community empowerment and participation in the decisions that determine the built environment. They favour autonomous living and decentralised organisational structures, liberated from interference and coercion by the destruction of the state or capitalist enterprises. There is an ecological sensibility that aspires to human interaction with the natural environment and other species and looks to confront and abolish the urban / rural divide. Invoking Vaneigem, Crump insisted that, if it is to be measured as a success, 'the moment of revolution must bring an improvement in life for *everyone*, not just for the suppressed and the poor and the needy, but to *everyone*, because actually nobody's happy under the present capitalist system.'[132]

Alienation

Alienation is a slippery term, indicating a sense of splitting away or estrangement, and appearing in economic, cultural, political, social and ecological forms. However, these different forms, as Street Farm were all too keenly aware, were intimately linked, and stemmed from the same root causes. They held that 'The real problems are to do with the alienation of people from their environment, the isolation of individuals from the community and the disintegration of community' (*SF* 1, [25]).

The idea of economic alienation has its origins in Karl Marx's *Economic and Philosophical Manuscripts of 1844*. Here Marx argued that wage-earning workers inevitably experienced alienation, due to their lack of control over workplace processes and output in a capitalist system dominated by bourgeoisie ownership of the means

132 Peter Crump, 'Street Farm', talk at Bristol Anarchist Bookfair, 7 May 2011.

of production. Workers' experienced employment as fragmentary and disempowering. Such alienation crushed the potential for creative work to unleash human potential as an integrated and purposive part of self-realisation. During the 1960s Herbert Marcuse updated the theory of alienation for the consumer society, arguing that if people had little control over their working lives, superficial freedom to choose between branded gadgets and services merely accentuated and sustained their alienation.[133]

This analysis critiques an economic system in which working populations are compelled to compete on the labour market and to sell their personal skills. There are constraints upon where, and how, we spend our days and lives, and to what purpose. In such a discourse the owners of the means of production determine much of our waking activity; by means not of our own choosing, we make products or provide services not to meet our desires, for aims and outcomes divorced from our own aspirations. The surplus value produced is for others' profit. We participate in an amoral production process in which any pleasure in creativity, social usefulness, impact upon the environment or other ethical consequences are secondary, incidental considerations, and for the most part irrelevant.

Street Farm draw upon the Situationist critique of consumerism when they reveal the way that this economic system also brings about political and cultural alienation. In reference to Debord's notion of the 'society of the spectacle', they declare in 'A Threatening Letter to ALL architects': 'Modern urbanism organises the reaction of all social life to a spectacle, but the only spectacle it can stage is that of our own alienation.'[134] They argue that production of disposable consumer items not only wastes resources, but also underpins a

133 Herbert Marcuse, *One-Dimensional Man: Studies in the Ideology of Advanced Industrial Society* [1964], 2nd ed. (London: Routledge, 1991), 8-9.
134 Street Farm, 'A Threatening Letter to ALL Architects', *Architectural Association Quarterly* 4.4. (Autumn 1972), 17.

system of control:

> The most abhorent [*sic*] aspects of consumerism are the aspects that work to enforce the State most successfully. The products on display in [the] world supermarket are the products of a system in which those who actually produce have no control over the nature of the products. The State controls the people by controling [*sic*] the means of production (*SF* 2, 4).

Given Street Farm's assertion that 'Mass production is mass alienation' (*SF* 2, 4), it follows more positively that:

> The process of converting our energies from the useless to the useful will involve the conversion and reversion of all that is alien to the will of the people (*SF* 2, 4).[135]

A collage in *Street Farmer* 2, 'A mountain of uselessness in a desert of futility' (*SF*2, 8), makes the link explicit as it piles together symbols of the British state (Big Ben) and capital (a banknote depicting The Queen) with a heap of consumer items.

In order to reduce economic unit costs, human labour and raw materials are commodified and state and capital work together to impose and organise a system of domination based upon centralisation and specialisation. In the process humanity becomes not only divided against itself, through the barriers of hierarchy and competitive rivalry, but estranged from the natural world. By the 1970s therefore it was clear to critics of capitalism that this template of domination was also applicable to the impact of Industrialism upon the world's ecosystems. The emergence of

135 The subtitle 'Useful Work versus Useless Toil' is a reference to William Morris's 1884 essay of that name.

urbanisation since the Industrial Revolution had sharpened the divide between city and country, intensifying the separation and alienation of humanity from the natural world. Such a critique of existing patterns of urban life and organisation is fundamental to Street Farm's approach, distinguishing them from more productivist and urban minded socialists who would be content to seize the means of production, while largely maintaining the old capitalist infrastructure in its familiar form so long as it was under workers' control, or organised by a party vanguard under the guise of a 'dictatorship of the proletariat'. Street Farm assert that 'Modern urbanism, the physical manifestation of hierarchical systems, is but a further aspect of the ecological disorder that follows the very logic of capitalism' (*SF* 2, 1). For this reason revolutionaries should pay attention to the underlying source of the commonwealth in the real economy of natural resources and achieve sustainable production through organic agriculture. Street Farm reject a definition of economic well-being based upon increasing growth measured by G.N.P. while the '"soil-bank" is depleted year by year' due to chemically intensive farming (*SF* 2, 2). Street Farm's concern about the commercial application of vast amounts of pesticides was in keeping with a growing scepticism about the impact of agribusiness, particularly in the decade following the Rachel Carson's explosive bestseller *Silent Spring*. Glenys Crump, Heather Berridge and Harriet (no second name given) express this concern for industrial capitalism's complicity in human alienation in 'Wasteland Farming', a contribution to *Street Farmer* 2:

> Capitalism with its extreme division of labour leaves people with neither time nor energy to collect and use plants. People have become alienated from themselves – they have lost control over their own lives and their own internal balance (*SF* 2, 12).

> If we are to regain our at-oneness with ourselves, we must find again the time to know, use, love and sustain our natural environment and fight the industrial capitalism which has forced the people away from themselves, to reach a way of life in which we can use technology and nature for our mutual advantage rather than mutual destruction (*SF* 2, 13).

Richard Mabey also captured the enthusiasm for reconnecting with a form of subsistence outside of the monetary economy, in his enduringly popular *Food for Free*, first published in the same year, 1972, and still in print over four decades later.

Street Farm believed, however, that limited improvements were possible within capitalism and that we did not need await the day of the glorious revolution before achieving meaningful change. Self-activity and community organisation and action facilitated thoroughgoing change that was necessary to raise consciousness and confidence. Urban revolutionaries – aware that 'the omnipresence of the state is both its strength and weakness' (*SF* 2, 6) – should identify strategic means to subvert and attack the state by modifying the state environment. They therefore advocated the exploitation of 'loopholes in capitalism and state' (*SF* 2, 3).

Significantly alienation is a factor in two tests by which Street Farm assessed revolutionary urbanism. First, in order to facilitate revolutionary change, they suggest it is only actions and ideas which confront alienation and reverse alienation which constitute authentic alternatives:

> The nature of the alternative is irrelevant. Any real alternative is an act of rebellion and is subversive. The quasi-alternative will make the alienation of our situation more tolerable. The real alternative changes the situation (*SF* 2, 6).

Second, quoting Vaneigem, they argued that it is the experience of integration and 'totality' rather than the fragmentation and estrangement of alienated existence that brings about pleasure for all and is the measure of authentic revolutionary change:

> For everyone the beginning of the revolutionary moment must bring an immediate increase in the pleasure of living a consciously lived beginning of totality (*SF* 2, 21).

In the 1976 film documentary *Clearings in the Concrete Jungle*, Bruce Haggart's comments on the experience of constructing the Ecological House at Eltham capture in an immediate way the practical realisation of Street Farm's ideas. He contrasts the alienation inherent in the conventional construction and inhabitation of housing unit with the more joyous and empowering experience of dwelling in older homes, or those produced by authentic participatory architecture:

> You see we've only experienced modern house building as a function of capitalism. And it's money that's created them, it's not been people. You know, so money employs a plumber, money employs a bricklayer and no one's involved in loving the building that's put up, there's no parties involved in building a house, there's no good times. It's all work, alienated work, and you can see that in the houses that are around. Older houses kind of transcend that alienation just because people will have lived there for so long and people will manifest themselves in the house. And it's just that we had a chance to manifest ourselves in the house from the beginning so that it comes out looking like something weird, you know something that's landed on the Earth rather than grew up from it. That's a strange but rather beautiful process (*Clearings in the Concrete Jungle*).

Street Farm's predictions regarding capitalism's failings have in many cases been born out during the intervening years. Social scientists have continued to find gainful employment in mapping such intractable urban problems as the widening gap between rich and poor, alienating concrete environments, traffic gridlock, precarity in the labour market and insufficient affordable housing. Ecologists have found that, despite hopes for a weightless economy, it has so far not been possible to decouple economic growth from environmental degradation as species' extinctions, climate change and habitat destruction have continued apace. On the other hand, despite continuing anti-capitalist dissent, a new world has yet to emerge from the ruins.

(Renewable) Power to the people

If a transition to a society liberated from alienating capitalism was to be realised it would come about through the efforts and awareness of ordinary people and communities engaged in practical everyday struggle. Street Farm's activities therefore were a praxis forged from anarchist philosophy and practical ideas about changing the world. According to their revolutionary urbanism, workable alternatives and an envisioning, revolutionary spirit would have to come together if they were to inspire and effect profound qualitative change in the conditions of everyday life. For Street Farm, a replacement of personnel at the top would be futile; grassroots transformation was necessary to bring about an authentic social revolution.

Power should be dispersed and diffused among the population as a whole, through the empowerment of communities linked by wider networks of cooperation and solidarity. Street Farm didn't attempt to recruit members to form lobbying associations but advocated provisional grassroots structures to implement practical solutions to social problems:

> These committees, street communes, village councils are not representative Councils, they are not democratic, they are ad-hoc groups formed without coercion in response to the situation [...] The councils have no need of specialist management boards, committees, or 'professional' services. These serve only to alienate the problems from the people (*SF* 2, 23).

This was more than a theoretical proposition as Street Farm itself was a loose collective of close friends living in shared households, housing co-ops and communes. Boyle described communal life at 'The Vicarage', home of the Haggarts and friends in South London as 'vividly reminiscent of Alice's Restaurant' – the popular hippy film of 1969 based on Arlo Guthrie's album of that title.[136] Also, as mentioned earlier, *Street Farmer* 2 was printed by a squatter collective and Street Farm had close connections to Kentish Town and Camden's squatters. Proactive exponents of the kind of practical idealism that the group favoured created 'Squat City', the heart of the political squatters' movement.

The nature of architecture and planning determine a community's relationship with, and experience of, its own immediate environment. The Austrian architect, artist and dreamer, Friedensreich Hundertwasser, beautifully captured the fundamental importance of home and environment to human identity and well-being in his sketch of the five skins. In Hundertwasser's holistic model of humanity, the home exists as a third skin after a person's epidermis and clothes, 'nature and other people' help to define identity, while 'earth ecology nature' and finally the wider universe provide the

136 Boyle and Harper, *Radical Technology*, 170.

all-encompassing context for existence.[137] This also suggests an existential definition of who we are because the fluid determinants of self are in permanent flux. The degree of community control – or often lack of control – in matters of housing, the wider built environment and the relationship to the natural world is therefore of central concern for socially-responsible architecture. The amount of liberty and autonomy which individuals and communities share to take responsibility for such matters, and their consequent ability to use such liberty and autonomy wisely, is a fundamental measure of social well-being and progress. It is not a means for society but an end.

The desire to reclaim architecture from the mystification of the orthodox architectural profession is evident in the pages of *Street Farmer* which imagines moving to a situation in which 'people realise that architecture is intuitive [and] concepts of what architecture is and is not are forgotten... concepts of enclosure and lifestyle are infinitely transmogrified' (*SF* 1, [11]). Street Farm directly confronted hierarchy within the architectural profession and the alienation they believed it produced in communities. It was essential that processes should be demystified, and maximum participation through direct democracy should be cultivated, if the dictatorship of experts was to be overthrown. In 'A Threatening Letter to ALL Architects', published in the *Architectural Association Quarterly*, Street Farm mocked what they regarded as the imperialist aspirations of 'Architex – the pigs with drawing boards'. Two pigs clad in expensive looking suits sport badges declaring 'Today the High Street, Tomorrow the World'.[138]

In order to meet another key aspiration of radical architecture it

137 Wieland Schmied, *Hundertwasser 1928-2000. Personality, Life, Work* (Köln: Taschen, 2005), 394-395, with reference to Pierre Restany, *Hunderwasser, The Painter-King with the 5 Skins* (Köln: Taschen, 1998).
138 Street Farm, 'Threatening Letter', 17.

would be necessary to raise 'community consciousness' as a prelude to, and part of the process of, achieving a community's participation in the conditions of its own existence. Graffiti was seen as potentially part of this process, not an instance of anti-social behaviour. If 'buildings become the blackboards of community consciousness', such unofficial street expressions can become a medium for inhabitants to voice their own ideas. By wresting meaning and control from the developers and planners who have imposed their functional, utilitarian notions of architecture ordinary people can start to reclaim their own surroundings. For Street Farm graffiti is empowering as 'an agent which can be used by individuals to alter their environment, to communicate and to decorate' (*SF* 1, [8]). A blank wall is also a contested space – the corrugated iron fence in the photograph accompanying these words appears to be incongruously daubed not only with 'Thank you tree' but also with the initials 'NF', signifying the far-right National Front, over-written as NLF, the National Liberation Front, the anti-Imperialist group opposing the Vietnam War, still ongoing at that time. As a Situationist tactic, graffiti can 'détourn' visual spaces increasingly appropriated by advertisers and officialdom, so as to immediately and directly make radical claims and demands visible through sloganising counternarratives.

More organic means were preferred to toxic aerosol paints. The idea of a 'hydraulic grass seeding canon' is, improbably, an instance in which life has come to imitate Street Farm art. The idea of the canon was to fire seed at tower blocks, spelling out words so that it 'metamorphoses a tower block with growing graffitti [*sic*]' (*SF* 1, [9]). Peter Crump was later amused to note the irony that apparently similar equipment is now available to age and weather buildings and that tractors have been reclaiming such urban areas as the centre of Detroit where the residential population has collapsed due to unemployment and deprivation.[139] Street-Farm-like, groups including Evolve Detroit, Detroit Urban Agriculture and Detroit Summer have cultivated substantial swathes of the bankrupt Motor City. Ironically this successful harvest from dereliction has opened up new opportunities for profit making, leading punk permaculturalists to mock would-be urban farmer John Hantz, a Detroit financier, who fears that the city now suffers from a lack of scarcity and 'stultifying abundance'.[140] In Exarchia, the revolutionary district of riot-torn Athens, too, locals have created people's parks and guerrilla gardens to mark their resistance and reclamation of space.[141]

For Street Farm progress consisted not in merely lobbying to influence local administrative bodies but to participate far more substantially by taking over community structures for local governance through direct decision making. In one Street Farm vision, in images anticipating the recent Occupy movement, urban campers take over parks and other public spaces. Again life seemed to be imitating Street Farm art. Captioned 'Peoples parks are used for urban camping' (*SF* 1, [9]), the montage images of tents cut and pasted on to a park scene later became a reality in occupations such as Zuccotti Park (New York), St Paul's and Finsbury Square (London), College Green in my own city of Bristol and throughout the world. This was to be an exercise in temporary, low-impact self-housing and political demonstration all in one since camps became

139 Personal conversation with Peter Crump, Café Kino, Stokes Croft, Bristol 23 Feb 2011.
140 Anon., 'Can Permaculture Save Detroit?', *Punk Rock Permaculture E-Zine* [online blog] http://punkrockpermaculture.wordpress.com/2010/01/11/can-permaculture-save-detroit/ [accessed 16 August 2012]; David Whitford, 'Can Farming Save Detroit?', *Fortune*, [online] CNN Money website,http://money.cnn.com/2009/12/29/news/economy/farming_detroit.fortune/index.htm?cnn=yes [accessed 16 August 2012].
141 Andi Stasis Agria, 'An Image from the Future of Revolutionary Ecology: Greek Insurrection and the Eco-War to Come', excerpts from *We Are an Image from the Future* (AK Press, 2010) *Earth First! Journal* (2010) [online] http://www.earthfirstjournal.org/article.php?id=525 [accessed 17 September 2012]; Julian Bolger, 'Anarchists and Blackshirts take up their Spraycans in War of Words', *The Guardian* (12 May 2012), 23.

sites of protest and micro-communities, as previously in peace camps such as Greenham Common and camps for direct action against new roads and airport expansion.

Dismal, functionalist tower blocks, office blocks and other junk Modernist buildings exemplify the old world to be transmogrified. Street Farm unleash the imagination to repurpose and transform the entire metropolis. To enter the liberated space that remains is to wander through a refreshingly topsy-turvy world of subversive role reversal where 'Buildings seen to limit lifestyles are unbuilt' as 'Architects become office demolition men'. Not only are concrete structures unbuilt but monolithic political and economic edifices are removed too as 'Lawyers dismantle the law' and 'Buisness [*sic*] is replaced by small scale super efficient cooperatives mass producing variety' (*SF* 1, [10]). The technical implementation of such mass production is unclear – unless somehow division of labour could be bypassed – given that as quoted above, *Street Farmer* 2 perhaps inconsistently asserted that 'mass production means mass alienation' (*SF* 2, 4). The polemics take on a provocative tone of heartless nihilism and lack of empathy:

> Every traffic jam makes us laugh
> Every train delay makes us jump for joy
> Every empty office block brings smiles to our faces
> Every homeless family is a cause for celebration (*SF* 1, [27]).

Their optimism for the potential for change was thus ironically rooted in the manifest failings of the contemporary system and a rejection of incremental reforms within capitalism. *Street Farmer* 1 concludes with resounding (though unattributed) slogans from earlier revolutionaries – namely Spanish anarchist Buenaventura Durruti's lines: 'We are not in the least afraid of ruins [...] We carry a new world here in our hearts' and Russian anarchist Mikhail

Bakunin's 'The passion for destruction is a creative passion' (*SF 1*, [26]). In Street Farm's own words: 'A revolutionary urbanism will result from a process of creative vandalism, manifesting as a catalytic agent in the process of Urban Alchemy' (*SF* 2, 25) *Street Farmer* 2 is also strongly in the revolutionary tradition, supporting the street struggles of the late 1960s, early 1970s:

> At the moment of rebellion we must remove ourselves from the control of the state by destroying the state environment around us, separate our environment from the states machinery this is done by building barricades around the liberated areas – Paris Londonderry etc to immediately disconnect the state agencies of control. (*SF* 2, 21).

If there was to be true decentralisation so that communities were empowered to control their localities, it was also essential that they made steps towards autonomy so that they would not be dependent upon the state or private business for services and commodities. To this end they encouraged local food production and the development of autonomous architecture. As we shall see (chapter 6), projects such as Street Farmhouse were initiated to prove that dwellings could be liberated from dependence by the creation of off-grid energy and autonomous sewage supplies. Such features were not only ecologically sustainable but motivated by a political desire to be emancipated from outside control.

The eco-anarchist alternative is a life affirming vision, hopeful for renewal. Counter to the capitalist model of production and distribution for profit according to the dictates of market forces, is a decentralised system in which cooperatives deliver abundance while rejecting standardisation and promise diversity. Goods are produced for their use value and, together with services, delivered to meet social needs rather than for profitable exchange. In this socialist model the means of production are held in common rather than private or state ownership so producers are not wage slaves. In this way people's lifestyles are 'transmogrified' alongside the physical surroundings so that economic and environmental alienation are prevented.

Transmogrification

So far such ideas are axiomatic in anarchist circles. However, there is a particular idiom of expression, visual imagery and synthesis of ideas that sustains Street Farm's distinctive identity. The trope of 'Transmogrification' for example is a key idea and visual effect in *Street Farmer* 1, suggestive of a radical metamorphosis of existing conditions. Before such a metamorphosis existing buildings are joyless and monolithic edifices, constructed and organised along gridlines. The process of transmogrification implies a profound change, being an unexpected transmutation not only of an entity's form but its very nature. The *Oxford English Dictionary*, for example, defines such shape shifting thus: 'to alter or change in form or appearance; to transform, metamorphose (utterly, grotesquely or strangely)'. The classical idea of metamorphosis has long been familiar from Ovid's *Metamorphosis* in which Daphne changes into a tree. The cover of *Street Farmer* 1 gives this an ecological twist as a tower block sprouts branches among which hippy faces (Haggart and Crump) peer, while inside a gigantic crow pecks another high-rise building to the ground (*SF* 1, [1-7]). Ovid's gods and goddesses unleash their mischief in the inner-city.

When transmogrification is depicted in a cartoon series of visual puns in *Street Farmer*, organic nature usually wins out. Concluding this sequence an adept hedge trimmer uses a pair of shears as a magic tool to transform a single dwelling in a street of respectable, though monotonously identical, houses. When a gigantic hedge smothers the house, our heroic topiarist deftly clips a quaint and unique Gothick home from the box or privet, complete with club-shaped windows, pinnacles and ornamental birds. This fantastical liberated space is in stark contrast to both the brutalist aesthetics of uniform tower blocks and suburban conformity. To step into the interior of the (transitory) Gothick home is to reveal what looks to be an enchanted glade within, achieving, Crump explains, a reversal in which 'the identical house behind the hedge transmogrifies itself into a hedge while the original hedge becomes the dwelling place!'[142] The Gothick home is reminiscent of the nesty nooks and cosily enfolding organic spaces that the philosopher Gaston Bachelard celebrates in his phenomenological *Poetics of Space* (1958).

The idea of radical transmogrification is germane to Street Farm's strategy to encourage a root and branch transformation of urban spaces. This was in reaction to the bourgeois tradition of moving to suburbia to avoid the crowds and pollution of city squalor and the popular trend to return to the land to enjoy a supposedly simpler and more self-sufficient lifestyle in the countryside. Crump himself attempted a move to rural Wales during the mid-1970s, a relocation that was in keeping with the decentralist appeal daubed across another tower block in *Street Farmer* 1: 'Workers of the world disperse', at once celebrating, yet artfully subverting, Marx's rallying cry (*SF* 1, [8]). However, while this was liberating for many striving to create alternative spaces during this era, Street Farm recognised the limitations of this form of escapism within capitalism because they were aware of its class dimension. Even during the 1970s, when land was cheaper and more available than in the present day, many could not afford to support themselves in rural areas. For a more complete revolutionary change it would be necessary to undermine

142 Peter Crump, e-mail message to the author, 29 April 2013.

and confront the county / city dichotomy. The way forward was to achieve a metamorphosis of the city.

Gutkind and the 'Rise of Communities'

The now rarely read German thinker Erwin Anton Gutkind (1886-1968) influenced the ideas of Crump in particular.[143] Gutkind's books are no longer widely available but some short excerpts from his writing on community illustrate his relevance as an inspiration for revolutionary urbanism. Gutkind's *The Expanding Environment* (1953) was predicated upon the idea that what is now called globalisation would inevitably come about as atomic power, aviation and super-highways could at once enable populations to be widely dispersed yet interconnected, effectively ending the age old divide between country and city.[144] This 'New Mobility' would eventually bring about a social revolution as cities and national frontiers become increasingly redundant. While subsequent events have not, so far, proven Gutkind's proficiency as a futurist, he took a broader historical view and situated such changes within five generations. Despite the technocratic sounding tone of aspects of Gutkind's account, he strongly favoured 'humanization' over 'mechanization'.[145] Street Farm were able to take from Gutkind the notion of the erosion of the divide between city and countryside and the creation of cooperative communities in which human values took precedence over the priorities of capitalist economics.

143 Personal conversation with Peter Crump, Montpelier, Bristol, 7 May 2013. Gutkind features prominently in Crump's unpublished history dissertation, *Freedom and Decentralisation*, written at the AA and marked by Charles Jencks.
144 E.A. Gutkind, *The Expanding Environment: The End of Cities – The Rise of Communities* (London: Freedom Press, 1953), 18.
145 Gutkind, *Expanding Environment*, 61.

Gutkind was forthright in his rejection of conservative values, identifying nationalism, religious sectarianism and capitalism as the root causes of profound and extensive suffering and obstacles to human potential for spiritual progress. If humanity were able to transcend the barbarity and irrationality of war, brought about by state, ideological and religious rivalry, it would be possible to meet human needs and achieve social justice. As an architect of Jewish descent who had escaped from Nazi Germany, Gutkind was writing in a world traumatised by the Holocaust, the bombings of Hiroshima and Nagasaki and the loss of over 50 million lives in World War II. He regarded progress beyond factional competition, therefore, not as naïve idealism but a prerequisite if humanity is to be resilient to disaster and to progress towards a viable and civilised future.

Gutkind wrote in a tradition of decentralists such as Peter Kropotkin, Lewis Mumford and Frank Lloyd Wright (who associated centralisation with monarchy, and decentralisation with democracy[146]), but sought to extend the notion of decentralisation further. He envisioned a coming time in which regions without frontiers would supersede present States and structural concentrations in urban centres and conurbations. New patterns of settlement would emerge in the form of human-scale communities, resulting in something that 'looks like confetti strewn over the country by a rather orderly and methodical visionary', a 'new regionalism', being:

> [...] more than a mere decentralization which proceeds always in relation to a centre. Hence its name. It is a dispersal, a scattering apart, and its final result will be the End of Cities and the Rise of Communities.[147]

146 Frank Lloyd Wright, *The Living City* [1958] (New York: New American Library, 1963), 87.
147 Gutkind, *The Expanding Environment*, 61.

In the context of this imminent shift in human geography, Gutkind believed the challenge for the post-War generation was to try to cultivate the power of cooperation and mutual aid in order to attain the security and well-being of all humanity. For Gutkind, it is necessary to rise above limited managerial and quantitative priorities in order to unleash the realisation of a profound cultural renaissance:

> Our civilization has not understood to free the creative impulses and the imaginative spontaneity in the common run of men. It has cultivated more than anything else a superficial familiarity with things and the lop-sided knowledge of experts. Our most cherished ambition is to save time. But we have no clear idea what to do with it when we have saved it. The docile acceptance of the shuttle-service between home and work as the dominating factor of life is another form of escapism avoiding the responsibility to think for ourselves and to experience ever anew what life in the fullness of spiritual re-creation and in the unending stream of transformation and manifoldness can be.[148]

Gutkind's anarchistic rejection of the state and hierarchy (the anarchist publisher Freedom Press printed some of his writing), as ultimately incompatible with functional communities, provides a theoretical foundation for ideas that Street Farm promoted:

> Some timeless characteristics will always be inherent in the conception of a community: mutual aid, immediateness of personal relations, smallness of scale, and reciprocal adaptation of man and environment in a spirit of understanding and insight, not as a fight of man against Nature. But what we should

148 Gutkind, *The Expanding Environment*, 66.

> not repeat is to allow a community to fall under the influence of a leader. Even if this word had not a particularly ominous ring nowadays, the leader-principle as such is incompatible with the spirit of a community. It is incompatible because it upsets the dynamic equilibrium on which the harmonious working of a community depends. It creates and tends to maintain economic and social differences, while it impedes diversity and emulation, levelling them down to an obedient conformity. Around the institution of a leader, even if the term of office of the individual leaders is restricted to a short period, cliques develop which grow gradually into the role of institutionalized minorities. In this way a structure is shaped which can but lead into the lifeless organization of a State, and consequently to the negation of a true community spirit.[149]

Gutkind's holistic thinking led him to an ecological approach. His emphasis upon understanding human activity in terms of ecological relationships and our situation within the living world significantly informed Murray Bookchin, the Twentieth Century's most influential eco-anarchist. Indeed, Gutkind coined the term 'social ecology', shortly to be the bedrock of Bookchin's philosophical and political thought.[150] He defines 'Social Ecology' as follows:

> It stresses the indivisibility of man's interaction with his environment and the need for extending the hitherto rather narrow field of sociological studies to all those factors which are connected in one way or another with the habitat of man.[151]

149 E. A. Gutkind, *Community and Environment: A Discourse on Social Ecology* (London: Watts and Co., 1953), 17-18.
150 Janet Biehl, *Mumford Gutkind Bookchin: The Emergence of Eco-Decentralism* (Porsgrunn, Norway: New Compass Press, 2011), 33.
151 Gutkind, *Community and Environment*, 47.

He advocated the recalibration of the social sciences, favouring a paradigm shift towards what he termed social-ecological thinking, casting aside a preoccupation with what, anticipating Marcuse, he considered to be 'greatest absurdity' of 'economic man'.[152] A total reframing of priorities would be required for this divided and alienated creature to mature and evolve a more integrated understanding of its social and environmental context:

> The vital problem that, which our age has to face is: How can fractional man grow into full man, and how can a new approach towards the variety of life development which is commensurate with the transformation of man's personality and leads away from the over-estimation of analysis and the neglect of synthesis.[153]

'Up Against the Hedge Mother Earth Fuckers'[154]

Street Farm claimed that they did not primarily regard their priorities and concerns as ecological. In 1974 Bruce Haggart commented:

> [...] we had a load of polemic and theory about the State, capitalism, freedom, collectives and anti-capitalist society. Our main motivations were never ecological, really, though Graham was working on a house called the Ecological house... that was unconscious. A house organised the way the Street Farm House is seemed appropriate to the sort of anti-capitalist society we were talking about.[155]

152 Gutkind, *Community and Environment*, 17-18.
153 Gutkind, *Community and Environment*, 72-73.
154 From 'Ramifications and Propagations of Street Farm'.
155 Boyle and Harper, *Radical Technology*, 170.

However, the conceptual divide between town or city and country is one of the first dualisms in the evolution of society, the ensuing development of the natural environment becoming the primary process fuelling the engine of capital accumulation with the emergence of a market economy. It is inevitable therefore that Street Farm, familiar with Gutkind and Bookchin, would confront such an opposition and the domination of the natural environment. Their very name goes some way towards collapsing the distinction between city and country. In taking such an approach they reclaimed a space for the living world and non-human species, thus following a logic that, even if initially unconscious, tended towards an ecological practice. This was much in common with the wider cultural politics emerging from the hippy underground at that time. From the evidence of psychedelic publications such as *Oz*, Simon Rycroft identifies the recognition of nature as physical process and the desire to live in 'ecosystemic harmony' as one of the counterculture's most prominent themes and something that could be strived for as part of 'the renaissance of the human spirit' in urban environments as much in the countryside.[156]

Street Farmer presents no intention to prettify urban life with a picturesque adornment of illusory 'nature' through the introduction of a cosmetic *rus in urbe*. In any case 'nature' is one of the most complex and slippery words in the English language. Raymond Williams was to devote five pages to 'nature' in *Keywords* in 1976, identifying no less than fourteen uses for the term.[157] In keeping with their anti-capitalist 'polemic', however, Street Farm challenged the binary opposition that had arisen between the urban built environment and the countryside. The prevailing version of progress

156 Simon Rycroft, *Swinging City: A Cultural Geography of London 1950-1974* (Farnham: Ashgate, 2011), 141.
157 Raymond Williams, *Keywords, A Vocabulary of Culture and Society* (London: Croom Helm, 1976), 184-189.

too often involved, and involves, a process of drainage, clearance of vegetation and construction of an inert environment composed of dead matter in the form of concrete, glass and steel. Street Farm proposed the reversal of his process to bring about a more people-friendly living environment:

> Office blocks crumble within a matter of months. When the city has again been made habitable ie green & beautiful a few people drift back while the rest are content to play in the country' (*SF* 2, 7).

The assault upon the town /countryside divide is taken further in 'A Threatening Letter to ALL Architects' where Street Farm argue that the logical corollary of their approach entails the abolition of the present construct of the countryside:

> the reversal of inorganic evolution, necessary to resolve the contradictions between town and country is a process that means the end of the countryside just as much as the end of cities [...].[158]

In the green spaces that sprout up beneath the ruins, the city becomes an edible socialist commonwealth in which the 'land belongs to everyone equally' (*SF* 1, [12]). For the most part remnants of the 'old urbanism' are not obliterated but constructively reused or recycled. It is not clear how the useful functions of residual items from the era of Industrialism, including old electric fences and motorway flyovers, would be met when they are eventually used up or worn out. Nature is allowed to take its course as, in scenes reminiscent of Richard Jefferies's nineteenth-century novel *After London* (1885),

158 Street Farm, 'Threatening Letter', 19.

such familiar landmarks as St Paul's Cathedral and the Post Office Tower slip gently beneath the silt. So icons of the old theocratic order and the new technocratic establishment (the Post Office Tower was completed in 1964) go down together. What appears to be Nelson's Column is scythed (*SF* 2, 21). It is to be expected that horticulture would feature prominently in *Street Farmer*. As well as community gardening, the transmogrification and revitalisation of the urban landscape takes place in the most direct sense imaginable – in *Street Farmer* 1 a tractor literally ploughs up the tarmac of city streets, a task that shire horses undertake in *Street Farmer* 2 (*SF* 2, 22). In this striking image of revolutionary urbanism the plough literally turns over the existing conditions of the street. As in William Morris's *News from Nowhere*, where the citizens put the Houses of Parliament to good use as a dung market, Street Farm suggest that the 'accumulated plans government papers and secret files and currency' of the state can be composted (*SF* 1, [12]). Street Farm explicitly recycle this image later with their quotation from Morris's utopia (*SF* 2, 23). In keeping with Morris's approach, for Street Farm, hands-on farming denotes not a return to a feudal past but a revolutionary over-turning of the present social order:

> Street Farmers till their land… physical transmogrification of urban land with radicalisation of lifestyles. Urban land is revitalised using compost from all sources (*SF* 1, [13]).

In this way Street Farm anticipate the activities of groups such as Reclaim the Streets and The Land Is Ours who also sought to root and ground their direct-action politics in the soil. In *Street Farmer* 2 a plentiful harvest of stooks takes place next to tower blocks (*SF* 2, 23), accompanied with the declaration 'Spring is here and the time is ripe for planting in the street' (*SF* 2, 22) (the nod to the Rolling Stones 1968 hit 'Street Fighting Man' helped to create a sense that this cultivated corn was a product of 'hip and with-it' farming, fighting for a future rather than looking back to a bucolic past). After this germinal, new seasons of campaigners advocated revolutionary gardening in succeeding decades. Reclaim the Streets's high-profile guerrilla gardening action in Parliament Square on Mayday 2000 took place beneath banners proclaiming 'Resistance is Fertile' and 'Let London Sprout'. Again, partying helped as an incentive to the toiling. In *Street Farmer* 2 a hilarious Piccadilly Region Provisional Farm Plan is put forward, its somewhat Maoist overtones tempered by 'subject to the will of the people' (however this might be ascertained) (*SF* 2, 21).

The farming communities that Street Farm envision are based upon itinerant rather than settled practices. Liberated from 9-5 wage slavery, citizens of a post-capitalist London are often nomadic, dwelling in such provisional homes as a hedge community shelter' (apparently a geodesic dome, *SF* 1, [14], popularised but not invented by Buckminster Fuller) or an 'antibuilding shelter' (*SF* 1, [16]). Crump remembered some fascinating exchanges on such topics at the time. Stuart Lever, for example, came up with the idea of 'the countryside with a huge net into which people could plug (way before the Internet), and tap into energy to power the set-up of 'instant tree platforms'.[159]

Such ideas also echo Archigram's work, inspired by Buckminster Fuller's ideas and inventions. The plug-in kettle in a 'well serviced field' (*SF* 1, [16]), for example, resembles David Greene's notion of a plug-in grid that enables people to live comfortably in what he terms 'botteries' away from city life. Technical innovations such as this 'net', if such a magical mesh could be woven, would address the twin issues of urban overcrowding and rural depopulation that had exercised thinkers such as Ebenezer Howard at the beginning

159 Personal conversation with Peter Crump, Café Kino, Stokes Croft, Bristol 23 Feb 2011.

of the century. Howard proposed to set up garden cities such as Letchworth to combine the opportunities of the town with the healthy open spaces of the country in a synthesis he called town-country.[160] Street Farm's suggestion that homes themselves could combine the natural and the human-made takes this synthesis one stage further. Low-impact, ecologically benign dwellings are partly made up of living plants: 'houses of living tissue, the wall taking up carbon dioxide and returning oxygen growing and diminshing [*sic*] to accomodate [*sic*] needs' (*SF* 1, [16]). Hundertwasser put this into practice in some of his Viennese buildings in which 'tree tenants' help to regulate air quality. Among strategies to deconstruct the conventional divide between city and country through low-impact dwelling and nomadism, Street Farm even featured images of urban campers pitching tents in Piccadilly Circus, the brash epicentre of consumer capitalism, 'pirating' telegraph poles to affix their guy ropes (*SF* 1, [17]).

While such images border on a self-parody of the Street Farm project, the two issues of *Street Farmer* have an explicitly 'green' tone. In *Street Farmer* 1, for example, Stuart Lever contributes a graphic article on tree housing, encouraging readers of the benefits – 'Ecology appreciation – help restore your natural harmony by spending time up in a tree' (*SF* 1, [23]). *Street Farm* 2 continued the theme with the previously mentioned article 'Wasteland Farming' and Roger Stowell's contribution of an ecological protest poem illustrated by Glenys Crump (*SF* 2, 11).

Certainly Street Farm came to be inspired by, and contributed to, the early ecology movement in its widest sense, experimenting with alternative technology and self-sufficiency. It blends the fantastical and utopian with a practical and rooted approach, its hippy idealism rejecting the emergent new age movement on the grounds that:

160 Ebenezer Howard, *Garden Cities of To-morrow*, 2nd ed, (London: S. Sonnenschein, [1902]), 1.

> The new age vision is the product of a reaction to old age situations and is perverted by old age language and systems. The new age vision is not a plan but a fable… (*SF* 2, 21).

Practical, tangible measures were required. This led to ideas that resulted in pioneering projects, including the prototype ecological house (discussed in Chapter Five), incorporating sewage recycling, solar power and the use of reused building materials. Obviously such features have since become recuperated into the mainstream. Street Farm's approach was a more radical form of tactical prefiguration – an idea captured in the phrase 'be the change you want to see in the world' (often attributed to Gandhi), lighting a route to utopia by creating practical, achievable examples in the here and now. Stuart Lever contributed a sketch of a model five-acre homestead to support four adults to *Street Farmer* (*SF* 2, 3) which drew upon a contemporary enthusiasm, in part popularised by John Seymour and Sally Seymour's *Self-Sufficiency* (1970). In Lever's plan, activities such as growing Russian comfrey for green manure, coppicing for fuel and useable wood and installing a wind turbine for water pumping and electricity generation, help to minimise fossil-fuel inputs. Equipment and infrastructure that is shared on a cooperative basis, such as a community-owned tractor, ensures efficient use.

In *Street Farmer* a desirable city is alive rather than inert. A profusion of sprouting, breathing, photosynthesising, living things surround and entwine human dwellings. In one image of practical surrealism, the hydraulic seed cannon in *Street Farmer* 1 reclaims tower blocks by making them sprout green with 'growing graffitti [*sic*], thus making the static and inert edifices literally vegetate (*SF* 1, [9]). While grooviness and sci-fi lighten the iconography of Archigram's tower blocks, in the pages of *Street Farmer* they are hostile fortresses which inmates should transform or destroy for the sake of their own liberation.

While Street Farm's ecological approach grew out of an initial commitment to autonomous self-sufficient living, they moved beyond an anthropocentric outlook, declaring in Caine's words that 'The land belongs to the communities of the biosphere not individuals of the human race'.[161] Other animals besides humans populate the pages of *Street Farmer* – a crow predates upon a tower block, while gulls flock around the tree observatories in issue 1; in issue 2 working horses plough on through another tower block, cleaving it in two as flocks of sheep and herds of cows undertake to reclaim the streets. Two sheep are labelled as 'animal friends' in issue 1 (*SF* 1, [14]) while feisty cows and chickens are set free in 'A Threatening Letter'. So alongside the re-examination of the city / country divide, the human / non-human divide is also questioned. For cultural theorist, Jennifer Wolch, such an approach would both enrich human experience and enhance the environment for the benefit of other species. Setting out her vision of Zoöpolis, Wolch cites evidence that suggests:

> [...] concrete interactions and interdependence with animal others are indispensable to the development of human cognition, identity, and consciousness.
>
> To allow for the emergence of an ethic, practice, and politics of caring for animals and nature, we need to naturalize the cities and invite the animals back in, and in the process re-enchant the city. I call this renaturalized, re-enchanted city *zoöpolis*.[162]

Such interactions would be possible with the greater proximity of

161 Street Farm, 'Threatening Letter', 20.
162 Jennifer Wolch, 119-138 in 'Zoöpolis', in *Animal Geographies: Place, Politics, and Identity in Nature-Culture Borderlands*, ed. by Jennifer Wolch and Jody Emel (London: Verso, 1998), 122 and 124.

other animals. The solution for Wolch, seemingly in keeping with Street Farm's approach, is not to flee to the countryside to seek pastoral idylls, but a more inclusive project to transform the urban environment to one that is more environmentally benign and to permanently ameliorate the city / country dichotomy. To relocate to a rural area might provide a strategic space to experiment with alternatives and deliver some positive benefits such as increased intimacy with the natural world and lower concentrations of air pollution. Nevertheless, for an individual, family or collective to move to a country cottage did little to challenge the fundamental city / country dichotomy. Street Farm's strong primary objective to live autonomously in order to challenge the state and capital is inextricably linked to concern for, and a desire to connect with, the natural world. This might be easier in rural areas where land prices were cheaper but the main aim was to avoid dependence upon a large mortgage. Caine explained in a 1973 interview with F. P. Hughes for *Mother Earth News*:

> The provision of shelter as a provision of mortgage merely extends the potential for exploiting the individual and endorses the myth of the ever expanding GNP.[163]

Street Farm understood that the natural environment was a primary source of capital accumulation and, the planet being finite, that it constituted a barrier to the inexorable economic growth upon which capitalism relies. The effective exploitation of natural capital has for the most part held in abeyance the kind of apocalyptic predictions for human suffering on a global scale made by Paul R. Ehrlich and Garrett Hardin during the 1960s, notwithstanding devastating

163 F. P. Hughes, 'Ecologic House', *Mother Earth News* [20] (March / April 1973). Online: http://www.motherearthnews.com/nature-community/ecologic-house-zmaz73mazraw.aspx [accessed 22 April 2012], 8.

catastrophic regional famines (such as Biafra and Ethiopia, instances largely due to war and failures of distribution) and eco-disasters with human causes (such as Bhopal and Chernobyl, Deepwater Horizon and Fukushima). Constraints upon growth will indeed be severely tested if presently projected trends continue as current United Nations projections anticipate that the world's population will increase to 9-10 billion by 2050; especially if this is accompanied by aspirations for a lifestyle based on the high consumption of goods and energy, and a population boom of domesticated animals to support a meat and dairy diet (all to be achieved while stabilising climate change and other forms of environmental deterioration). From a capitalist perspective, to ensure the continued expansion and acceleration of economic growth, it is necessary to drive down production costs through technological innovation, constraining labour and distribution costs and the exploitation of raw materials, while avoiding the costs of externalities such as pollution and habitat destruction. Whether an environmentally sustainable capitalism is possible is a doubtful article of faith. Murray Bookchin rejected the idea:

> To speak of 'limits to growth' under a capitalistic market economy is as meaningless as to speak of limits of warfare under a warrior society. The moral pieties, that are voiced today by many well-meaning environmentalists, are as naive as the moral pieties of multinationals are manipulative. Capitalism can no more be 'persuaded' to limit growth than a human being can be 'persuaded' to stop breathing. Attempts to 'green' capitalism, to make it 'ecological', are doomed by the very nature of the system as a system of endless growth.[164]

164 Murray Bookchin, *Remaking Society* (Boston, MA.: South End Press, 1990), 93-94.

Street Farm were familiar and in sympathy with Bookchin's ideas. Caine and Haggart referenced an excerpt from Bookchin's *Post-Scarcity Anarchism* in 'From Here we Grow', a photocopied circular featuring images from the 'experiment in free living' at Street Farmhouse. They also put up a banner emblazoned with the exuberant legend 'From here we grow' on Street Farmhouse for the television documentary *Clearings in a Concrete Jungle*, thus proffering an alternative notion of growth.[165] After all self-sufficiency and autonomy on Caine's model could be a pathway to economic sustainability and therefore to grow well-being, but not for the kind of economic growth that capitalism demanded. For Bookchin and other social ecologists, domination of the natural world was a primary form of hierarchy that provided a model for subsequent forms of domination including, eventually, capitalism. Social progress required a total paradigm shift beyond hierarchy and capitalism. In keeping with this approach, anti-capitalist critics such as Street Farm rejected capitalism for its tendencies to replicate conditions of alienation and disempowerment, both within the field of the architectural profession and throughout society as a whole. To bring about socially responsible planning through projects within capitalism would therefore at best offer partial amelioration, failing to resolve underlying problems, protracting rather than tackling inequality, injustice and deprivation. For Street Farm, a 'revolutionary urbanism' was necessary – capitalism and statism alike were slum ideologies that required clearance.

In the long run ecological sustainability provided a surer measure of the value and viability of human endeavour. This particularly applied to architectural practice, but ironically set Street Farm well

165 Kallipoliti, 'Review: Clearings in a Concrete Jungle', 241. Caine recalled that the Street Farmhouse slogans were short-lived as he was threatened with prosecution under the Town and Country Planning Act for advertising! Personal conversation with Graham Caine, The Farmhouse, St Werburghs, Bristol 21 May 2013.

outside of conventional architecture as a commercial enterprise. In the 1998 documentary *Travels with my Chainsaw* Caine claimed 'Believe it or not in 1970 a lot of architects wouldn't have known what the word "ecology" meant. And as to its applicability to architecture, absolutely nothing.'[166] Caine still argues that consideration for the sum of ecological connections and impacts provides a more realistic principle to assess the worth of activities, again asserting a fundamentally difference in approach: 'Ecology is a great way of looking at the way things are done, whether it has integrity or not; fucking capitalism has no integrity – just get it, use it, dump it.'[167]

It follows that, while Street Farm rejected a small 'r' romantic attitude, in so doing, I would argue that they implicitly, though forcefully, situate themselves within the tradition of Romantic anti-capitalism. Discussing his experimental Ecological House in 1973, Graham said:

> I consider the project not to contain a romantic attitude but a revolutionary one in that it indicates both a possible means to revolution and the stimuli, in that it exhibits a realistic alternative to the exploitational vision of the environment.[168]

Cultural critics Michael Löwy and Robert Sayre argue that 'Romanticism is essentially a reaction against the way of life in capitalist societies.'[169] They use this over-arching definition to identify several distinct, indeed mutually antagonistic, categories of Romanticism, ranging from feudal, right-wing and Fascist forms

166 Graham Caine (guest presenter), *Travels with my Chainsaw*, Art Trails series (produced and directed by Steve Gear), broadcast HTV West, 1998.
167 Personal conversation with Graham Caine, Montpelier, Bristol 29 November 2012.
168 Quoted in Hughes, 'Ecologic House', 8.
169 Michael Löwy and Robert Sayre, *Romanticism Against the Tide of Modernity*, trans. by Catherine Porter (Durham, NC.: Duke University Press, 2001), 17.

through to 'Revolutionary and/or Utopian (which includes Jacobin-Democratic, Populist, Utopian-humanist, Libertarian or Anarchistic and Marxist)'.[170] Street Farm clearly fall within the latter strains of Romanticism. By this definition, Romanticism also includes worldviews held since the Nineteenth Century up to the present day and onwards. Max Blechman argues this is in keeping with Karl Marx's assertion that Romanticism is 'the historically inevitable counteroffensive to the "complete emptiness" of bourgeois life' and in some form will continue to accompany capitalism "as its legitimate antithesis up to its blessed end"'.[171] To this end revolutionary Neo-Romanticism uprears its head in surrealism, situationism, the late 1960s, early 1970s counterculture, campaigns for peace and ecology, anti-racism and feminism as well as less progressive, even fascist manifestations. It is unsurprising then that Street Farm should reference the works of earlier troublemakers such as William Morris (*News from Nowhere* and 'Useless Toil v Useful Work') and Robert Tressell (*The Ragged Trousered Philanthropists*), as kindred anti-capitalist spirits. Their own fight against 'the exploitational vision of the environment' is therefore in the same tradition of revolutionary Romantic anti-capitalism. Only if the kind of revolutionary urbanism which Street Farm advocated were to be successful in its transcendence of capitalist alienation would it be able to move beyond Romanticism, given that in Blechman's words, 'romanticism is coterminous with the division of consciousness caused by capitalism and inextricable from it'.[172] It follows that Romanticism is dependent upon capitalism; if Romanticism is an umbrella term

170 Robert Sayre and Michael Löwy. 'Figures of Romantic Anti-Capitalism', *New German Critique*, 32 (1984), 60-62.
171 Max Blechman, 'Reflections on Revolutionary Romanticism', 237-250 in Max Blechman, (ed), *Revolutionary Romanticism* (San Francisco, CA.: City Lights Books, 1999), 237; quoting from Karl Marx, *Grundrisse: Foundations of the Critique of Political Economy (Rough Draft)* [first pub.1939], trans. by Martin Nicholaus (Harmondsworth: Pelican / Penguin, 1973), 162.
172 Blechman, 'Reflections on Revolutionary Romanticism', 247.

for a miscellany of political and cultural ideas linked only by their antagonism to capitalism, a post-Capitalist society would also be a post-Romantic society.

Anti-Lectures: Street Farm's Multimedia Adventures

Architecture has never been a popular art. Its clients have always been the rich. Its legacy is one of palaces, fortifications, office blocks, commemorations to those with power and wealth. It is an old role that architects play. Paradoxically they try to rationalise this old role in a world of new circumstances and consciousness.

Better to become entertainers, jesters, clowns, trapeze artistes, alchemists singing songs of the new age. [...] *Not planning men but stirring their imagination.* (Haggart, 'Italian Trip', 202).

Street Farm's published output as a collective was not extensive; publication was not their only, or even their main, strategy for the dissemination of ideas. In addition to the two issues of *Street Farmer*, Caine and Haggart produced two illustrated A3 information sheets to explain the thinking behind Street Farmhouse, as a response to the substantial number of enquiries they were receiving by post and in person about the ecological house. Haggart also published a short pamphlet called *The Street Farmers Windworkers Manual* and a newsletter called *Community Gardening*. Additionally there were contributions to magazines such as *Oz*, *Architectural Design*, *Architectural Association Quarterly*, *Mother Earth News*, *Domeletter* and occasional interviews. On many occasions, Street Farm also put on green boiler suits and propagated their ideas through a number of slide-show and performance events. Street Farmhouse also attracted attention in the mainstream media including, as we have seen, the

BBC news and *The Observer* in 1972, and the group's work and ideas were discussed in architectural and alternative publications. Finally, in their most ambitious multimedia ventures, they were involved with two BBC television projects. They presented Street Farm ideas in one of the 'Open Door' series in 1973. In 1976 *Clearings in a Concrete Jungle* particularly featured Graham Caine and Bruce Haggart explaining the ethos behind the Ecological House in a longer television documentary introduced by up-and-coming presenter Melvyn Bragg.

The Street Farm project had its origins in presentations at the Architectural Association. Bruce Haggart and Peter Crump were given an assignment which involved drawing up plans for an area of Greater London which included Notting Hill and the vicinity of Wormwood Scrubs. The output from this was Crump and Haggart's joint submission for a diploma which they successfully achieved in 1969. Crump recalled that in some ways what they produced was 'very unarchitectural' in conventional terms but that, because some of the material was 'at least architectural in its form and about the environment' they 'got away with it'. They produced a black and white film based on their work which was combined with collages and cartoon strips to create a formal, if unconventional, presentation. The film had a second, more utopian, half which was made in colour that, unfortunately, no longer exists. However, Crump could remember three aspects of the content:

> We decided that commuting was often the most engaged and interesting part of working life. Therefore, in utopia, working life could be transformed into something far more enjoyable if people spent the first half of the day commuting into work and the second half commuting back again. To this end, we staged ourselves setting off to work in a rowing boat on the Regent's Canal wearing bowler hats for the film. This was accompanied

> by the sound track 'We are normal and we want our freedom, we are normal and we dig Burt Weedon' by the Bonzo Dog Doodah Band. Related to this was the thought that if this was the case then there was no real reason to commute to work at all. The trains could just be parked outside people's flats. However we didn't wish the train drivers and railway staff to suffer from unemployment. We had the idea that the carriages could be transformed into gardens by filling them with plants which the train drivers and other staff could maintain. This part of the film was created using a miniature model 00 train set. It would of course be possible to make a much better job of this with today's technology. A third element of the film's content featured a plan to turn Wormwood Scrubs prison into a hotel.[173]

Train carriages filled with plants could then form a series of linear parks that would interlace the city with greenery. The idea of verdant railway carriages sprouting with indoor gardens also uncannily anticipates a feature of the transport system in Ernest Callenbach's 1975 futuristic novel *Ecotopia*, in which the chief protagonist, journalist Will Weston, finds that the Ecotopians of 1999 travelled in train carriages with recycling facilities and that were 'full of hanging ferns and small plants I could not identify'.[174]

The Urban Pastures of *Street Farmer*

From such creative collaborations came *Street Farmer*. In the web of Wyrd that was 1970's ephemeral publishing, *Street Farmer* bridged the heyday of the alternative press, between the flowering of late

173 Personal conversation with Peter Crump, Montpelier, Bristol, 24 August 2012.
174 Ernest Callenbach. *Ecotopia: A Novel about Ecology, People and Politics in 1999* [1975] (London: Pluto, 1978), 7.

1960's underground classics including *The International Times*, *Oz*, *Gandalf's Garden*, *Frendz* and *Black Dwarf*, and the explosion of zine publishing such as the punk cut-and-pastes and homespun radical press circulating from the mid-1970s, and ongoing during the next quarter of a century. The emergence of Web-based agit-prop from the mid-1990s has brought about the steady demise but, certainly not the extinction, of the print format. *Street Farmer* shared thematic and visual affinities with the aforementioned *Archigram* and *ARse*, the bucolic and quixotic *Country Bizarre*, alternative technology and environmental magazines such as *Undercurrents* and *The Ecologist*, and papers with more political priorities, such as *The Leveller*, *Green Line*, *Green Anarchist* and *Schnews*. A comprehensive archival catalogue of such publications is essential if systematic research into them is to be carried out in the future, given that online and physical holdings are currently patchy.

The first issue of *Street Farmer*, 'incorporating *Amateur Architecture*', was published in September 1971. According to the cover there was a print run of 500 and the price was 30p. The pages were printed in a professional printshop in Soho, a convenient but relatively costly way to produce the magazine. The litho print was reproduced from text and artwork delivered on large pasteboards. Although the raw artwork was in colour, the price for colour reproduction was prohibitively expensive, so individual pages appeared in single colour inks on a white background. It was packaged as a bundle of thirty loose-leaf sheets in a cellophane bag so that the reader could browse them in any order he or she chose.[175] This disarrangement neatly affirmed Street Farm's rejection of linear argument, accentuating holistic, non-hierarchic relationships between the themes and ideas within. However there are identifiable

175 Peter Crump suspects that the idea was inspired by a B. S. Johnstone novel which he came across in draft form (e-mail message to the author, 29 April 2013).

sections, colour-coded in blue, green and red inks. Following the front cover, Haggart's opening sequence is a blue cartoon strip on the theme of transmogrification. Green-tinted collages putting forward the Street Farm's theories of revolutionary urbanism make up the largest proportion of the magazine, appearing in several blocks of pages that are of a piece. The contribution of fellow AA student Mike Hickie, a short surrealist cartoon strip in green on 'Street Gardening', features pruned and grafted cuttings of street furniture such as one-way signs and parking meters which need to be cut back in order to sprout back more vigorously. This comically reiterates the theme of transmogrification. In red, Graham Caine's prototype sketches for an 'ecological house' was to be an important practical aspect of the Street Farm project (manifest as Street Farmhouse a year later). Other discrete sections are Martin Lipson and Barrie Hurrell's short feature on the Agency Housing Co-op, a project to occupy vacant land and find cheap housing options in London[176] and tree house drawings credited to Stuart Lever.

Street Farm delivered the artwork for a second issue of *Street Farmer* to I.R.A.T. Printing, based in a squatted building at Good Vibes Corner, where their comrades turned their presentation boards into letter-size prints.[177] *Street Farmer* 1 must have attracted enough readers to warrant an increase in the print run of *Street Farmer* 2 to a slightly more ambitious 700 copies. The cover price had gone up to 50p, for a 36-page publication. It was collated and stapled so there was less opportunity to juggle the pages. This time green ink alone was used for the entire publication with light-green tinted stock used for the cover. It now boasted an international reach, as outlets in Swansea, Amsterdam, Florence and Paris were

176 See also Stefan A. Szczelkun, *Survival Scrapbook 1: Shelter* (Brighton: Unicorn Books, 1972),
[unpaginated Section 8 [p. 4]].
177 Kallipoliti, interview with Peter Crump, Bristol, 11 July 2007, *Clip, Stamp, Fold*, 255.

listed. For Kyes and Daly it references 'the visual excesses of the underground comix movement while anticipating the pragmatic DIY aesthetic of punk zines'.[178]

Street Farmer 2 was more of a collective effort with a larger number of contributors in addition to the core Street Farmers. The inimitable Street-Farm style is still evident, however, in the largest proportion of the magazine which consists of Peter Crump and Bruce Haggart's collages on pages 1, 4-6 and 22-27. By the time it was being produced Haggart and Crump had left the AA. Haggart was soon to start work with Caine, in the ongoing implementation of alternative technology at the Ecological House, which constituted a practical realisation of some of Street Farm's ideas. House meetings took place at Patshull Road to look at content, which was also provided by partners at that time, Glenys Crump and Kate Haggart, along with other friends and colleagues from the AA. On pages 2-3 Stuart Lever supplies a manifesto for organic agriculture with an accompanying plan for five-acre homestead to support four adults. Alan Mitchell imagines a similarly utopian space on page 7, with sketches of a 'renaturalised' city in which alternative technology is constructed from the detritus of industrial society such as motorway signage. Pages 8-15 are concerned with matters botanical and herbal. Pages 8-9 feature excerpts from herbalist Juliette de Bairacli Levy's writings with accompanying lunar chart. Kate Haggart's cartoon of emancipated flowers and trees on page 10, is followed by Roger Stowell's contribution 'No-one goes to ask the plants and animals why' illustrated with Glenys Crump's floral psychedelia. An article on 'Wasteland farming' on pages 12-15 by Glenys Crump, Heather Berridge (a friend from the AA) and Harriet (no second name given) advocates the culinary delights of wild plants. Peter Crump supplies a cartoon in which, happily, a gigantic foxglove devours a

178 Kyes and Daly, 'Street Farmer', 22.

bomber jet and tower block on pages 16-17. Graham Caine sets out his proposal for an alternative entry to a housing competition in Bracknell (see Chapter 6) on pages 18-21. The back cover features some fabulously eccentric correspondence received in response to *Street Farmer* 1 and other Street Farm activities.

Bruce Haggart's ingenious and fantastical Statue of Liberty cartoon strip fills the penultimate pages 27-31. There is much playful visual wit in this sequence of frames in which Liberty, tired of being frozen in time on her pedestal, liberates herself by hurling her flaming brand at the skyline, stripping off, and plunging into the Upper New York Bay. Modelled on Jefferson Airplane's Grace Slick (Crump recalls Haggart was 'quite keen' on her[179]), Liberty swims the ocean until reaching a faraway shore where she seizes a tractor and begins to cultivate the land. She crashes through a car, liberating the driver who walks free and naked. He goes forth to unloose some cattle from their paddock who then wander free and munch their way through nearby tower blocks. Meanwhile the emancipated Liberty, like a cosmonaut Lady Godiva for the Space Age, goes into orbit on her tractor, finally spelling out the legend 'Farmage' across the universe, and weaving constellations into gigantic intergalactic cobwebs.

The pages of *Street Farmer* 2 are even busier than *Street Farmer* 1, brimming over with ideas and images. There is no minimalist desire for the ample white-space deserts considered excellent design and good taste in the slick production of twenty-first century graphic design. In keeping with the content, this dense profusion creates a forest-garden of diverse text, drawings and graphics in defiance of monoculture. Unfortunately this representation can sometimes be to the detriment of visual accessibility.

True to Allen Ginsberg's maxim, 'first draft, best draft',

179 Peter Crump, 'Street Farm', talk at Bristol Anarchist Bookfair, 7 May 2011.

Street Farmer, with its occasional typos, also creates a refreshing visual impression of spontaneity. This homespun appearance is accentuated by the mix of handwritten and typed text, suggesting that the pages were improvised and put together with materials that were immediately to hand. They appeared current, ephemeral and almost still warm from their creators' imaginative processes. This effect, however, belies the extremely time consuming and labour-intensive process of producing the newsletters before the availability of personal computers.

The medium of collage lends itself readily to this approach. Peter Crump recalled that they met Terry Gilliam who was living in a nearby part of London at that time, making a name for himself as the animator for Monty Python. He offered some of the hints and tips of his craft:

> He advised that, as the work was ephemeral, not to spend too much time being precious about it. For the collages, don't bother with scissors. You get the same effect or better by tearing the components and putting them together. Again with the animation the viewer just looks at the main components and if they are interested will collaborate with the fact that it is all an optical illusion anyway.[180]

A favourite medium for the Dadaists and Surrealists, the art of collage also has a subversive political pedigree. The German anti-Nazi artist John Heartfield was surely the greatest exponent of the form which he developed as photomontage. During the 1930s photomontage became such a powerful propaganda weapon in Heartfield's hands that he could be described as taking on the Third Reich with a

180 Personal conversation with Peter Crump, Café Kino, Stokes Croft, Bristol 23 Feb 2011.

pair of scissors.[181] This political tradition has since continued, for example in the anti-consumerist paste-ups of Barbara Kruger and the anarcho-punk aesthetic of the materials produced by bands such as Crass (Gee Vaucher's work), The Buttocks and The Hit Parade and in zines such as Laura Oldfield Ford's *Savage Messiah* series. Quick and cheap to reproduce through cut 'n' paste and photocopying, collage made art accessible. Once collage styles had emerged they survived after cheap open source graphic design software made it no longer necessary to make mash-ups using scissors and glue.

Collage enabled the creative collision of city and country that characterises the inimitable pages of *Street Farmer*. Throwing together mundane images and altering context subverted expectations and created surreal effects. The sheep, horses, Friesian cows and tractors became established motifs, being as emblematic for Street Farm as chimpanzees and rats are to Banksy. Like Alice's discovered world, much of the topsy-turvy city wonderland in *Street Farmer* 1 is first encountered as one which reverses expected proportions, where people, trees and toadstools (the hallucinogenic fly agaric) rear up above tower blocks.

However, while this is a realm where an adult may step from an egg, an angel can take flight and a tractor can soar across the universe, it is also grounded in reality. Its utopianism was rooted by its affinity with such solid and practical contemporaries as the *Whole Earth Catalog* and Stefan Szczelkun's *Survival Scrapbooks*. A range of contributors, and quotations from earlier writers as diverse as William Morris, Robert Tressell, Kurt Vonnegut and Raoul Vaneigem, together with snippets from newspaper cuttings, comic strips and sales catalogues add to the mix.

There is a cheeky and surreal humour throughout Street Farm's

181 Richard Cork wrote an article on John Heartfield called 'Fighting Fascism with Scissors', *The Times* (21 August 1992).

writings which always leavens the prose. In 'A Threatening Letter', for example, they use the *Architectural Association Quarterly* own ink to cock a snook at the authority of their old institution's respected publication:

> Note to casual readers, earnest researchers and pornographers alike: the authors of article above take no responsibility for the contents of the rest of this God awful magazine neither do they concur with what has been written elsewhere even though they have not read it.[182]

In addition to two copies of *Street Farmer*, a detailed information sheet called 'Ramifications and Propagations of Street Farm', published in 1972, set out to explain the theoretical basis for Street Farmhouse. It was produced when Street Farmhouse was near completed and featured an annotated photo-essay of the construction process on the reverse. A second information sheet, captioned 'From Here we Grow' is also likely to date to late 1972. Printed on light green tinted paper, this featured technical specifications, sketches and further contacts interspersed with *Street Farmer* content and a quotation from Murray Bookchin on one side, and a reproduction of Graham's article 'A Revolutionary Structure', written for *Oz* magazine, on the other.

Community Gardening (c. 1972-1973) was an organic gardening paper written and drawn by Bruce Haggart of 'Farmage Press' at Patshull Road and 'Dr John' [Pollard] of the Prince of Wales Crescent squat and typed by Kate Haggart. It was packed with tips for green-fingered squatters, also featured feisty-looking brassicas, carrots and alliums accompanying the legend: ''Vegetables of the Rising Revolution: Allies in the Liberation of All Things'.

182 Street Farm, 'A Threatening Letter', 20.

All three core members of Street Farm collaborated on 'Some Proposals on the Reservicing of an Urban Terraced House', for *Domeletter*, a small-press magazine published in Philadelphia.[183] Again the plan to retrofit older existing houses so that they are more autonomous in their use of services has proven to be a forward-looking aspiration. This would enable people to achieve some of the key objectives of Street Farmhouse, such as using liberatory technology to decrease dependence upon external services and enjoying greater self-sufficiency at the neighbourhood level, while avoiding some of the planning obstacles that were to thwart the project at Eltham.

Bruce Haggart's also published *The Street Farmers Windworkers Manual* of 1973. This was a short pamphlet which, as the name suggests, gave practical advice on producing small wind turbines for the microgeneration of electricity.

Its publication in *Peace News* underpins the role of liberatory technology as a literal means to help to devolve physical production and therefore shift the control of power (in the senses of both energy and political leverage) to communities liberated from dependence upon the state or the commercial private sector. Haggart's aims are modest in their means but far-reaching in their implicit critique of capitalist alienation:

> No attempt has been made to give instructions about calculating the output you expect, nor has the usual measure of efficiency been evaluated. These considerations seem more fitting to marketing and alienated production systems, and as you can't sell the wind, consider anything you can build yourself from scrap materials and that gives you light and power to be

183 Graham Caine, Bruce Haggart and Peter Crump, 'Some Proposals on the Reservicing of an Urban Terraced House', *Domeletter*, 4, ed. John Prenis, 1–6 (Philadelphia, Penn: Self-Published, 1972).

alchemic rather than efficient. Do it and see, but don't expect to run factories off them.[184]

Haggart expresses a desire to unite a practical love of creating, tinkering and repurposing with more visionary aspirations. Again this is a Romantic anti-capitalist critique of a calculating quantification of value rather than qualitative appraisal of worth – any energy or enlightenment that comes about due to the creation of these windmills is an end in itself, not a step towards other unspecified, and infinitely deferred, objectives of economic growth. The *Collected Fables of Urban Alchemy* were also referenced in *Street Farmer* 2 (*SF* 2, 23). Allusions to alchemy not only gesture towards esoteric, experimental traditions but recall the Street Farmers' affinity with the New Alchemy Institute in Cape Cod, Massachusetts.[185] Street Farm sourced practical information from like-minded founders – John Todd, Nancy Jack Todd and William McLarney – fellow anarchists with similar underlying principles, sharing ideas in correspondence about the politics of radical technology, one nexus in a myriad of international countercultural exchanges at this time.

Taking the call for 'all power to the imagination' literally, they put across ideas about experimental architecture, planning and design in multimedia 'happenings' that incorporated manifestos and rock and roll. In his 2007 interview with Lydia Kallipoliti, Peter Crump described *Street Farmer* as 'a magazine and a slide show; it was a sound-and-light performance'.[186]

184 Bruce Haggart, *The Street Farmers' Windworkers Manual* (London: Peace News, [1973]), 1.
185 Awan, Schneider and Till, *Spatial Agency*, 176-177.
186 Kallipoliti, interview with Peter Crump, Bristol, 11 July 2007, *Clip, Stamp, Fold*, 252.

Film Shoots in Green Boiler Suits

Street Farm's forays into interventionist performance was therefore another facet of their approach. In a short article written for the Architectural Association's *AArchitecture*, Zak Kyes and Wayne Daly write 'In collaboration with friends, the duo [Bruce Haggart and Peter Crump] carried out urban interventions clothed in a uniform of green boiler suits'.[187] This is likely to have been sourced from an online posting by Stefan Szczelkun, a close acquaintance of Street Farm , who recalled that they 'would make public actions dressed in green boiler suits'.[188] Such activities were in keeping with the popularity of the Happening during the early 1970s.

Happenings were engaging multimedia performances with unpredictable and radically experimental form and structure. Breaking down and dissolving the distinction between performers and spectators, happenings transformed the relationship between them so all became participants in events intended to engage, explore and challenge and thereby raise consciousness around particular themes. Although drawing upon older artistic movements such as the Dadaists' games of shock and chance, the current phase of experimental theatre had only started to establish itself as a widespread cultural phenomenon during the 1950s through the pioneering work of the Fluxus network and the Gutai Group in Osaka.[189] Michael Kirby provided a theoretical basis for considering the proliferation of happenings in his influential essay

187 Kyes and Daly, 'Street Farmer', 19.

188 Stefan Szczelkun, 'EarthWorkshop' [n.d.], http://www.stefan-szczelkun.org.uk/phd103.htm#_ftnref2 [accessed 23 April, 2011], footnote.2.

189 See Udo Kultermann, *Art-Events and Happenings*, trans. by John William Gabriel (London: Mathews Miller Dunbar, 1971), 80; Michael Kirby, 'Happenings: An Introduction', in *Happenings and Other Acts*, ed. by Mariellen R. Sandford (London: Routledge, 1995), 16-17. Allan Kaprow's 'Eighteen Happenings in Six Parts' (1959) was the origin of the term 'happening' in the sense of referring to an artistic event.

'The New Theatre' (1965).[190] Kirby felt that a new critical theory and vocabulary was required to understand and frame such new forms and developments. He defined the new theatre as non-matrixed performance – by which he meant fluid shows that did not observe the constraints that stage conventions imposed, such as expected formats and characterisation. Caine captured the theatricality of Street Farm's approach in a reminiscence of a typical roadshow opening:

> It started off with our pre-recorded murmuring as the students started coming in and while we'd be getting the show together our murmur would be increasing, increasing so that you could hear them all getting up and up and up and until everybody was shouting at each other virtually and then our murmur would just go "STOP!" and immediately everybody stopped and it was like "it's a great time to be alive boys and girls and if you don't think it's so fucking great to be alive, you better leave now because this show will really bring you down." [blasting out Frank Zappa's 'Call any Vegetable'] – and "BANG!" into this music, and the projections of the animations, like tearing down New York and cows invading and Jefferson Airplane coming. I mean it was fantastic, it was absolutely fabulous.[191]

In the new drama and happenings linear or predetermined narratives and the niceties of stage sets were abandoned in such a way as to disrupt place-time continuums. The intention was to experience a range of feelings not simply to portray them – any emotions are those not of a characterisation but of the participants themselves.[192]

190 Michael Kirby, 'The New Theatre' *The Tulane Drama Review* (Winter 1965) 10.2. [Online]: http://www.jstor.org/stable/1125229 [accessed 23 April, 2011].
191 Personal conversation with Graham Caine, Montpelier, Bristol 29 November 2012.
192 Kirby, 'The New Theatre', 32.

In this sense there could be a sense of greater authenticity in the happening than in more traditional performance. Greater scope for improvisation could be both liberating and challenging. By the 1970s, happenings had somehow scaled the walls of the theatre, eluded the director and the spotlights and outpaced the ushers becoming a staple of the underground scene at such venues as the Roundhouse and the UFO Club. The late 1960s, early 1970s also saw a renewed enthusiasm for agit-prop (agitational propaganda), a strategy by groups such as the Cartoon Archetypal Slogan Theatre (CAST) to air and express political themes through drama, film and other performance media, that had been popular during the 1930s.

In some ways this seems like a digression, a world away from ideas about architecture. So what on earth were Street Farm playing at in their green boiler suits? What was innovative and unexpected about Street Farm and enabled their tractors to plough their own furrows was the transplantation of performance to the world of planning and environmentalism. As we have seen, their political and artistic concerns predated their architectural practice. Involvement with the Committee of 100, for instance, caused Crump to take part in direct action campaigns that were in in their own way performance interventions. Such actions sought to gain cultural leverage to challenge the ideas that bring about and sustain the war machine.

The experimental integration of multimedia also brought elements of the happening to the work of Street Farm. Recitals with a wholesome rock and roll background, collage and the introduction of super 8 film into their events enabled them to create an interest in ideas about the urban environment that reached beyond academia. This was a continuation of the unconventional approach that Crump and Haggart had taken while still students at the Architectural Association, as they deviated from the formal presentations expected upon such occasions. Improvisation and indeterminacy allowed the performers and, indeed the spectators, some relaxation of the formalities of the conventional predetermined lecture. This would in turn give spectators license to participate in developing events, giving rise to a creative freedom from constraints usually determined by the lecturer or creator. Greater liberty to improvise and to select alternate elements of a show rendered individual events unique occasions. Just as Street Farm railed against linearity of thought and produced magazines that could be read in the order of their readers' fancy, so they experimented with elements of non-matrixed performance. Simon Rycroft provides a fascinating account of the explosion of lightshows and multi-media environments in the counterculture from the late 1960s. He argues that the appearance of non-representational, experiential representations at this time belie the notion that hippy critiques of technocracy were technophobic but rather were a popular expression of new scientific thinking based upon an 'Einsteinian cosmology of matter and energy in flux to which humanity is intricately bound':

> Added to an evolutionary understanding of nature that suggested that humans were symbiotically entwined with natural processes then, was a revolution, suggested by Einstein and others, in the ways in which we understood the very matter of that nature. What was solid could easily become invisible as energy and vice-versa. This was something that, at the time, excited and influenced Op Artists, Pop Artists, cultural and media theorists, performers, filmmakers, architects, planners and the counterculture. Whilst infinitely varied, the project of each of these groups concerned making the invisible visible.[193]

Street Farm deployed multimedia technologies therefore which

193 Rycroft, *Swinging City*, 8.

were a means to gesture towards abstract, almost metaphysical, phenomena such as the transmogrification and alienation which constituted the basis of their critique of capitalism. In a similar way to the tactics of conviviality of earlier radicals such as the Clarionettes who cycled and picnicked for socialism, they were thus able to seamlessly merge propaganda and pleasure in a more creative and enticing way than the dour didacticism that could sometimes beset the earnest pronouncements of the old Left. Their arsenal in the war of image and sound was a core collection of slides (which sadly have not survived the intervening decades) and music. Crump recalls:

> We would give slide presentations from a collection of around 300 slides. These were projected while we read out some of our texts and rock music was played – such as Grace Slick with Jefferson Starship, the Rolling Stones and Neil Young. On one occasion the vocalist from the Pink Fairies sang an improvised 'Street Farming Man' adapted from the tune of the Stones' 'Street Fighting Man'.[194]

Later links between Street Farm and the Pink Fairies continued as Haggart and Caine cracked the semi-licensed squat in Flodden Road that developed into what Szczelkun calls 'a loose community formation' of buildings in south London in 1976 which included a church hall inhabited by Larry Wallis of the Pink Fairies and Motörhead.[195] The Pink Fairies were a band with anarchist ideas whose credentials were bolstered by playing for free outside paying festivals and taking an active role in supporting political underground papers such as the *International Times*. In the aftermath of Woodstock and the Isle of Wight, the free festival scene

194 Personal conversation with Peter Crump, Café Kino, Stokes Croft, Bristol 23 Feb 2011.
195 Szczelkun, 'EarthWorkshop', footnote.5.

was riding high as the epicentre for the countercultural resurgence. Reflected spangles from this colourful libertarian spirit grace the pages of *Street Farmer*, which in effect incites a future of permanent festivity. In *Street Farmer* 2, for example, Alan Mitchell imagined: 'articulated lorries are hijacked by folk-groups and used as mobile stages running along the motorways using the flyovers as festival platforms' (*SF* 2, 7).

Peter Crump enthused that one of the motivations for Street Farm was that the performance aspect of it could be developed into a kind of roadshow. He told Lydia Kallipoliti:

> While selling the magazine, more than anything else we were most interested in being on the road like a rock 'n' roll band. It was fun. We went to Holland and hitched to Italy.[196]

Why not rock 'n' roll architects as well as rock 'n' roll musicians? Once the Street Farm project had come together and they were equipped with their slide collection, they gave offbeat audiovisual presentations at various locations on the road. Street Farm's most adventurous road trip was a visit to Italy to participate in an event called the Mondial Festival, organised by two Florentine avant-garde architect groups, 9999 and Super Studio, in November 1971. This event, it seems, belonged more in the realm of an artistic happening than it owed to the concerns of conventional architecture and planning. The work of the participants and schedule was marketed in a square format prospectus covered in thick white fake fur.[197] God-like, 9999 created a universe to which bemused visitors were treated to the spectacle of indoor planets and an ecosystem complete with a mini-ocean, forest and vegetable patch accompanied by a live piano

196 Kallipoliti, interview with Peter Crump, Bristol, 11 July 2007, *Clip, Stamp, Fold*, 255.
197 In Peter Crump's personal archive.

recital. Other performers namely Renalto Renaldi, UFO, Zziggurat and Marc Balet, attempted to challenge, baffle and enthral with a sensory onslaught of dream sequences and nonsense. As we cannot step back into that crowded building in Florence in the lost autumn of 1971, we must content ourselves with Haggart's report written for *Architectural Design*, which provides a first-hand account of what a Street Farm performance entailed. Street Farm's first contribution to the happening was a presentation of:

> Street Scarecrow – a comic strip, 2 and 3 dimensional. (Defn. A Street Scarecrow is a street agent whose purpose is to scare from the streets menaces to the well being of the people (e.g. motor cars etc).[198]

Later they had the honour of concluding the Mondial Festival's schedule with some classic Street Farm fare. After introducing themselves, we are told, faces appeared in a slide projection on the walls from which speech bubbles appeared speaking Italian and engaged in the polemical exchange that is for the most part taken from the concluding dialogue in *Street Farmer* 1. Haggart reported:

> Then they saw a War movie starring motorways as linear forests/ trains as mobile parks/prisons as hotels/commuters rowing to work/tractors ploughing the wasted city/flats as the Ministry of the Environment and a Healthy Life Biscuit Works/ children harvested potatoes beside a sign reading NO BALL GAMES/buildings unbuilt/ buildings burnt. An applecart upset to see which way the apples roll.

Finally, Haggart continued, the event concluded under a sub-heading entitled 'a mass walkout at Street Farm performance':

198 Bruce Haggart, 'Italian Trip', *Architectural Design* 42.4 (April 1972), 202.

We finished distributing grass and sunflower seeds in paypackets. 'Plant in Pavements to push up slabs.' Smiles returned to faces.[199]

Crump recounted that they also took up the mayor of Eindhoven's invitation to give a presentation with the result, that, as 'scruffy hippies' they found themselves slightly out of their comfort zones, showing their slides in the recently constructed Eindhoven city hall as well as at the local school of architecture.[200] Caine mentioned further trips such as those to venues in Sweden, Paris, the Glasgow School of Art and driving to Wales in an old ambulance to give the previously mentioned presentation at Cardiff that Paul Downton recalled. Nearer to home they undertook an ambitious schedule of presentations at the Institute of Contemporary Arts, Goldsmiths, most English schools of Architecture, such as those in Bath and Leeds and a three-day trip to Blackpool where they talked about their ideas and work at local schools.[201]

Another important outreach event was Street Farm's participation, in 1974 and 1975, in Comtek (short for Community Technology), Bath Arts Workshop's festival for alternative futures, held in the city of Bath. This was an occasion to share their ideas with other alternative technology enthusiasts and showcase their work, such as a recently constructed windmill, as a practical demonstration of their experimental innovation (featured in their *Clearings in the Concrete Jungle* documentary). Haggart and Caine were based in the media tent from where they would 'present a multi-media exposition of the Street Farmhouse and the ideas which gave rise to it'.[202] They contributed a giant sailwing to the

199 Haggart, 'Italian Trip', 202.
200 Personal conversation with Peter Crump, Montpelier, Bristol, 24 August 2012.
201 Personal conversation with Graham Caine, The Farmhouse, St Werburghs, Bristol 21 May 2013.
202 Comtek, *Comtek '74* (Bath: Comtek, 1974), 15.

splendid array of alternative paraphernalia working on site. Writing of the groups in attendance at Comtek in 1975 Ian Hogan described the 'Situationist' Street Farmers as: 'enigmatic, given to produce precise, technological expositions which end abruptly in ribald joking and heavy rhetoric.'[203] This temporary microcosm of the alternative society included a sizable contingent from Kentish Town and Camden (video researcher Sue Hall of Graft On who showed a film about the Prince of Wales Crescent squat, members of Inter-Action, 'body awareness' guru Jym Macritchie and Herbert Girardet of Radical House) and several fellow tinkerers and potterers in radical technology (the Bath Arts Workshop, Undercurrents and the Rational Technology Unit). The vogue for community technology was underlined by the presence of a performance and music group called Harsh Mouse, billed as 'Britain's first technology/ street theatre company'. Their contribution included a workshop to create paper houses from newspapers (an idea that featured in one of Szczelkun's Survival Handbooks). Disappointingly however, it is recorded that 'Their pioneering attempt to sail down the River Avon on a 30ft inflatable sausage had to be abandoned when the craft sprang a leak.'[204]

Street Farm's travels and adventures illustrate their willingness to think globally and act locally. Their international orientation is also revealed in connections in Sweden (with the *Pow Wow* newsletter challenging the reformist premises of the UN Conference on the Human Environment at Stockholm), and the United States, where as we have seen *Mother Earth News* featured the Ecological House and comrades in the New Alchemy Institute undertook a similar fusion of alternative technology, ecology and political change. Such exchanges, as well as more the formal syndication of the underground

203 Ian Hogan, 'Comtek Windmills', *Architectural Design*, 55.10 (1975), 625.
204 *Comtek '74*, 11.

press, made for the rapid transmission of countercultural themes across borders and enhanced the cultural evolution of ideas and images.

Street Farm's greatest prominence in the national media was the broadcast of two BBC television documentaries. The first was a Street Farm contribution to 'Open Door', aired on 18th June 1973. This was an experimental series which, perhaps daringly, gave a platform to non-professional broadcasters – often controversial or contrarian grassroots voices – to tell untold stories about overlooked areas of life, offering them live airtime to express their viewpoints in their own words. Technical staff and state-of-the-art equipment were placed at their service. On the day of filming, the project didn't run as smoothly as Street Farm members might have hoped. The production team allocated to work with them, and with whom they had established a working rapport, went off shift shortly before the filming was scheduled, to be replaced by another team. Peter Crump recalled:

> The new production team didn't really know what was going on and I think that some of the intended frames may even have been out of sequence. We ended up more or less storming out of the studio when it was finished. In any case what we were trying to achieve in this space was possibly too complicated. I seem to remember a frame with Bruce digging his allotment in front of a dark blue sheet in the background – the idea was that it would have had a motorway projected onto it but in the event all that appeared was Bruce digging in front of a blue sheet. Another scene featured Graham and I trying to punch our way out of a very large box in a field. I think we were trying to get across an

idea about alienation or something like that.[205]

From the perspective of the viewer however, it was alright on the night. The film is an enjoyable pastiche of animation and cartoons, some revolutionary slogans and polemics, practical introductions to hydroponic gardening and methane digesters and one or two good visual jokes. The result is much like a transposition of *Street Farmer* into 3-D, resulting in a world where Monty Python meets Guy Debord, where complete self-sufficiency meets Jefferson Airplane and some Principal Edwards Magic Theatre for good measure. This is all appropriate in the search for a ludic, festive society where the divisions between the serious and the playful have been removed. Following images of Street Farm children enjoying themselves at Street Farmhouse, Bruce Haggart explains 'There are no boffins here but rather amateurs dabbling with tools and energy, like gardeners pottering in their garden, work and play have become work-play' (*Open Door*). Named after their amatory propensities, amateurs work for love not for bosses. Unalienated work is presented as creative tasks that are shared and enjoyed and where there is workers' control in place of wage slavery. Pinder notes that one of the chief features of the Situationist International's vision of utopian cities was that life would be a 'permanent game' in a 'civilization of leisure and play'. According to their concept of 'unitary urbanism' such binary divisions as work / leisure, home / workplace, public / private, reflected in the segmentation of present cities, would be abolished.[206]

A second documentary, *Clearings in the Concrete Jungle*, was screened as part of the BBC's 2nd House series, on 24th January

205 Personal conversation with Peter Crump, Montpelier, Bristol, 24 August 2012. Caine also pointed out that they were acting out an improvisation loosely based on an R. Crumb cartoon. Personal conversation with Graham Caine, The Farmhouse, St Werburghs, Bristol 21 May 2013.
206 Pinder, *Visions of the City*, 128-129.

1976. Featuring extensive footage of the practical example of the Ecological House, the programme provided Street Farm with an unprecedented opportunity to communicate their ideas to viewers. Electronic organ notes from Gong's 'The Octave Doctors and the Crystal Machine' adds to the mood music. Again pleasure and experimentation appeared to be essential to the process of creation through work-play. Graham Caine spoke of the amazing experience of exhilaration that the participants felt when constructing the Ecological House:

> There were only some sketches of the way it should roughly be so everybody involved with the house became the designer, the builder, the labourer and the joy that was experienced during the building process was something that couldn't be experienced I expect if you worked for Wimpeys (*Clearings in the Concrete Jungle*).

The kind of playful collaboration involved in assembling Street Farmhouse was also put to excellent effect in the process of film making, itself a kind of ludic labour that gave lots of opportunities to confront such serious issues as urban alienation and the future of the planet with weapons of wit and irony. Like their Situationist inspirers, Street Farm intuited that to learn the art of living by spending time as artistically as possible, they could challenge another powerful binary opposition – the collective separation of art and life – and thus achieve anti-capitalist Romanticism's most revolutionary potential; to abolish itself.[207]

Many years later, in a return to the medium of television, Graham Caine also guest presented *Travels with my Chainsaw*

207 See Blechman, *Revolutionary Romanticism*, 246-47.

(1998), a documentary in which he reflects on the architecture of Antoni Gaudì in Barcelona, as an inspiration for his own ideas and work (see Chapter 6). Graham first visited Barcelona during the 1960s when Gaudì's unconventional structures inspired his interest in architectural form and its potential to transform urban space.

Original pasteboard for Street Farmer 2, created by Peter Crump and Bruce Haggart, from the archive of Peter Crump.

Art in Revolution images reproduced with permission from architectural cartoonist Louis Hellman. Originally published in Architect's Journal (10 March 1971).

1979 cover from Undercurrents magazine which began in 1972. Cover design by Peter Bonnici. Often including the exploits of the Street Farmers, this inspiring magazine was a major forum for alternative view from green / libertarian socialist / anarchist perspectives during the mid-1970s and early 1980s.

ly 1970's agit-prop produced by London squatters

From Why Soft Technology?: Alternative Solutions to the Energy Crisis (1975), (p. 3). Reproduced with permission from Andrew McKillop

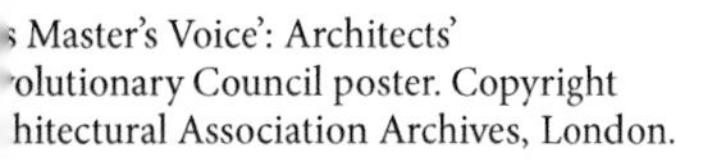

s Master's Voice': Architects' ·olutionary Council poster. Copyright hitectural Association Archives, London.

Front cover of Street Farmer 1 (1971). From the archive of Peter Crump.

ginal pasteboard for
et Farmer 1 (p. 6), with
tographs of Street Farm
re-cars' being worn at
fic protest in Oxford
et, London in 1971. From
archive of Peter Crump.

'This season's planting collage' from Street Farmer 2 (p. 22), created by Peter Crump and Bruce Haggart. From the archive of Peter Crump.

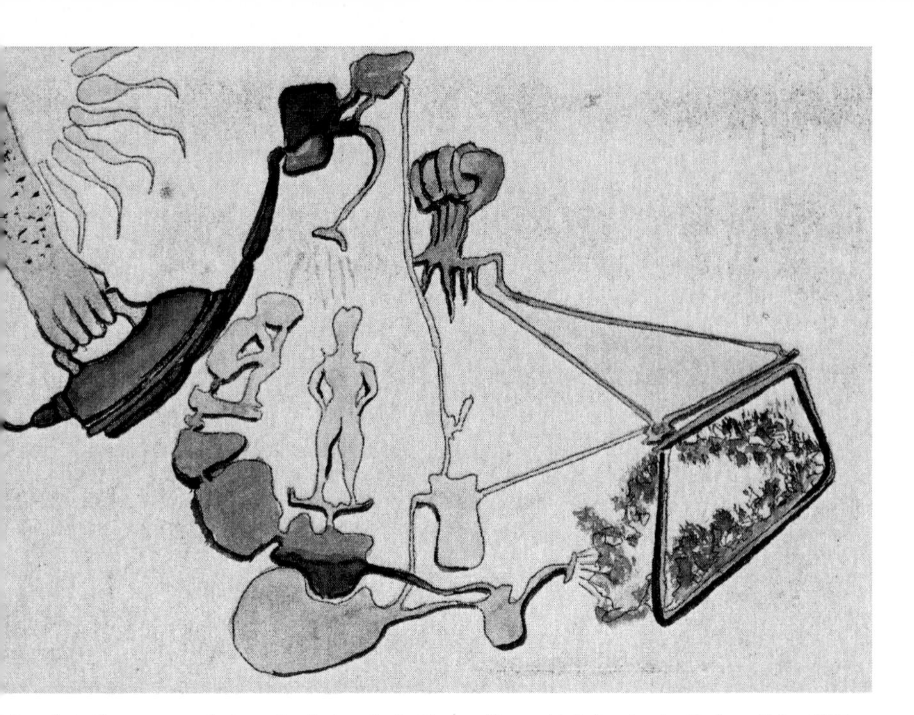

: iron fist of bureaucracy destroys the first ecological house. Pen and ink drawing by Graham Caine,1975. m the archive of Graham Caine.

'et Farmhouse c.1972. Photograph from the archive of Graham Caine

Street Farmhouse (1972) with call outs bearing the legends: 'Our rights are nobody's to give'; 'From here we grow'; 'Totality is hacking its way through'; 'Bite the hand that feeds you'. A flag with a green clenched fist fl from the dome. © Photograph from Graham Caine's personal archive

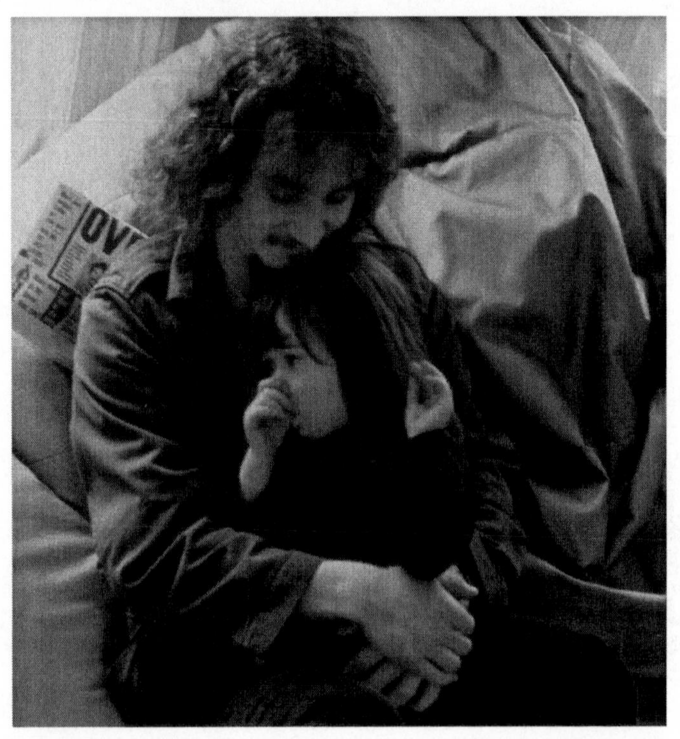

Pete Crump with his daughter, Bridget in Kentish Town 1971. Taken after delivering Street Farmer artwork and used as part of slide-show in Italy. From the archive of Peter Crump.

eet Farmhouse c.1972. Photograph from the archive of Graham Caine

n Stowell with Rosie at Street Farmhouse. Photograph from the archive of Graham Caine

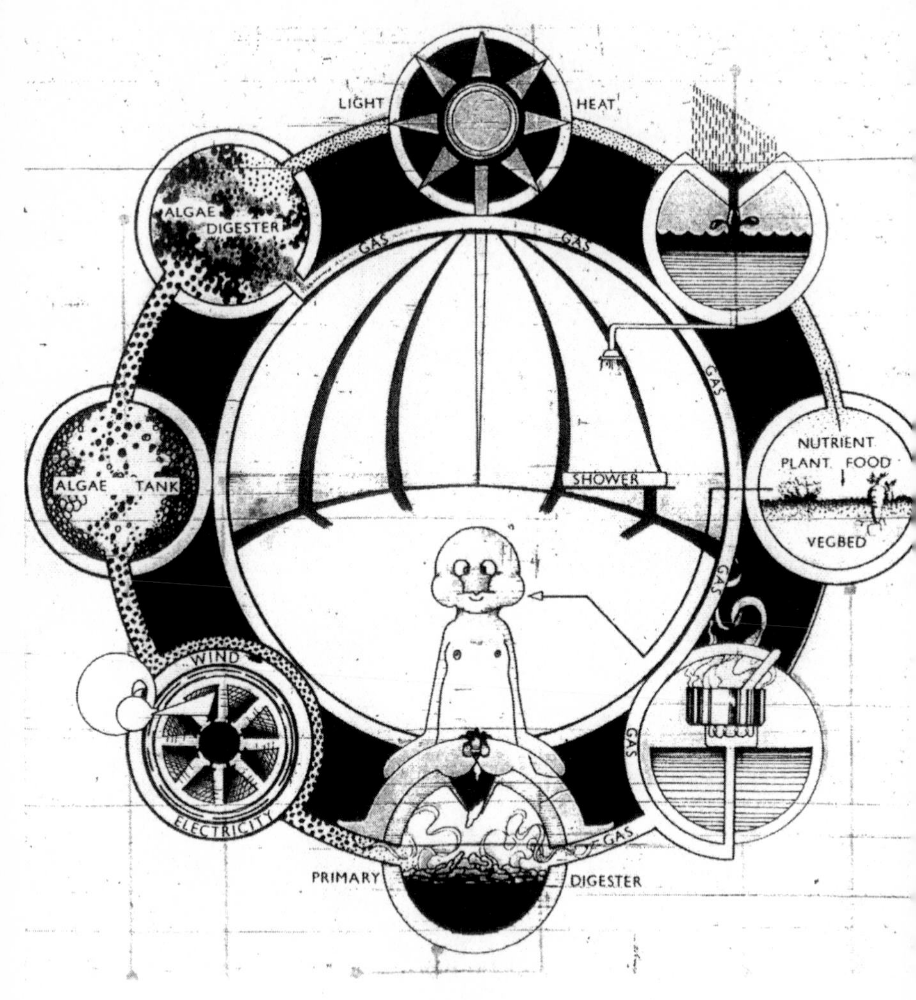

Graham Caine, Illustration from 'Revolutionary Structure', Oz magazine, November 1972 (p. 13).

Mother Earth News No 20 (March 1973), featuring the Eco-House. Reproduced with permission from Ogden Publications, publishers of Mother Earth News

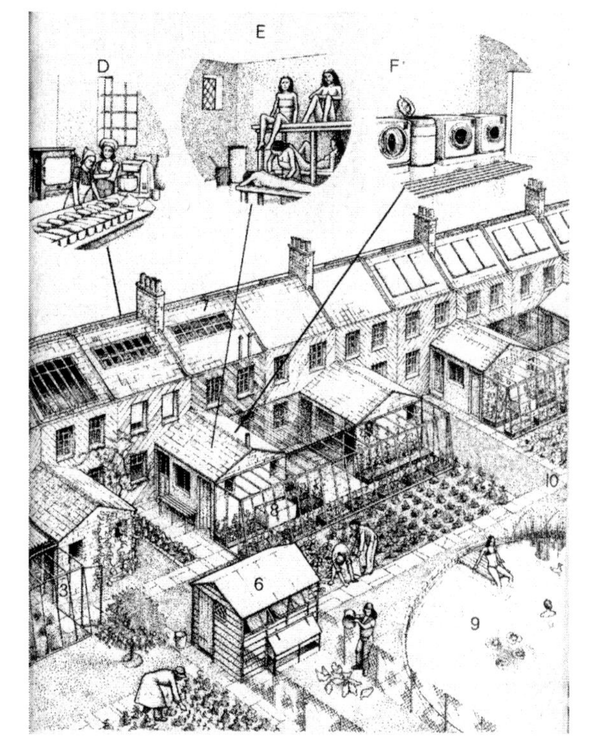

Autonomous Terrace' by Clifford Harper from © Radical Technology ed. by Godfrey Boyle and Peter Harper (1976), (p. 169). Reproduced with permission from Godfrey Boyle

Bristol 'Gnomework' at Little Tipple Off-Licence, Long Ashton. © Photograph by Stephen E. Hunt 2013

Graham Caine's 'Gnomework' at Barton Hill Settlement, Bristol, March 2011 (removed in 2013). © Photograph by Stephen E. Hunt, 2011

ham Caine by self-built house, St Werburgh's, Bristol. © Photograph by Stephen E. Hunt, 2013

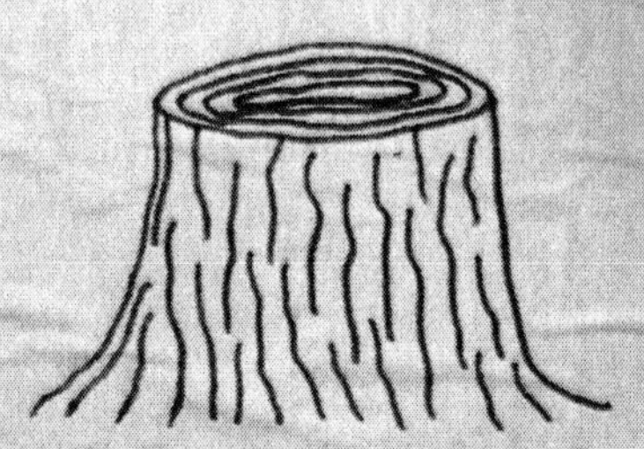

Protest poster in San Francisco on the occasion of the World Trade Organization talks at Cancun, Mexico 2003. © Photograph by Stephen E. Hunt 2003

The front cover of Issue 3 of ARse magazine lampoons Archigram. (© Reproduced with permission of Tom Woolley)

p.148 Eco-anarchy in the Naughties. Maypole dancing on Parliament Square. Reclaim the Streets guerrilla gardening action Mayday 2000. © Photograph by Stephen E. Hunt 2000

'Compost Capitalism'; Occupy London camp at St Paul's Cathedral, 2011. © Photograph by Stephen E. Hunt, 2011

Cover of programme for Comtek '74, organised by Bath Arts Workshop

Poster from early West Country ecological group, Abacus, circa. 1970. Reproduced with permission from Paul Downton

Street Farm Projects

You would hope that in an anarchistic society, one of the basics that would be shared as an ideal for everybody would be green policies. I mean why wouldn't you want to be green? Now wouldn't you want to share the planet with your grandchildren, rather than fucking it up? I can't see that you can be an anarchist without having green sympathies.[208]

The First Ecological House

Street Farm's first foray into the practical application of their theories about autonomous housing came in response to a competition, initiated by Bracknell Housing Corporation. The competition, run in early 1972, invited potential developers to present designs for a small housing estate of 90 dwellings in the vicinity of the town. Another entrant, Fortis Green Properties, proposed a moderately experimental venture that aimed to open up possibilities for dwellers' choice for affordable homes beyond standardised mass produced design.[209]

Graham Caine was aware that, inevitably, competition judges would expect entrants hoping to win this kind of project to present schemes within conventional parameters, consisting of housing dependent upon both a considerable initial input of materials and energy, and an ongoing, externally provided service infrastructure. In this way the Housing Corporation and developers could realise maximum profit from the sale of the units, while purchasers would be

208 Personal conversation with Graham Caine, The Farmhouse, St Werburghs, Bristol 21 May 2013.
209 Simon Conder, Jon Broome and Jennie Jones, 'Bracknell Housing', *Architectural Design* 42.9 (1972), 533.

locked into long-term mortgages. Graham's response was to submit a proposal in which residents would self-build structures made from giant bamboo and in which the development was organised so that private dwellings were integrated with generous allocations of communal space. As an article by Eve Williams in *Garden News* suggested, using rapidly growing bamboo meant that potentially such houses could grow themselves![210] In this way people could enjoy homes with the minimum of capital outlay and be liberated from the life-support system of state supplied utilities thereafter. Such an approach would have revolutionary social implications as it would reduce dependence upon wage slavery to fund the basic necessities of existence, promoting a form of development based upon meeting human needs rather than serving the interests of capital expansion. Reflecting his reading of Roszak at this time, Graham rejected the 'wasteland culture of our technocratic society' (*SF* 2, 20). To this end he confronted the capitalist model of enclosure. The assessors' panel at Bracknell recognised the radical implications of his proposal when they concluded: 'This unconventional solution would require a social revolution to enable its realisation' (*SF* 2, 20). Graham didn't win. In the event the award went to conventional housing units aimed at the 'executive market'.[211]

The practical 'real world' challenge at Bracknell, however, concentrated Graham's mind and provided an opportunity to sketch ideas that anticipate the construction of Street Farmhouse. This was Street Farm's most prominent practical achievement. Street Farmhouse was an ecological house that Graham constructed with his friends' help, after finally securing temporary planning permission, on playing fields at the Thames Polytechnic, Eltham. He recalled:

210 Eve Williams, 'The House that Grows', *Garden News* 722 (5 May 1972), 1.
211 Conder, Broome and Jones, 'Bracknell Housing', 533.

> At the age of 26 I started constructing the World's first 'Ecological House', which I had originated 18 months previous as a fourth year student. It was the first because I not only designed it, I christened it, and to the best of my knowledge, nobody had used that term before. By the time I came to build it, the term had already been abbreviated to 'Eco House'. In pursuing this project I gave up my architectural qualification in the greater belief I could and should be pursuing the betterment of the planet.[212]

Indigenous tribes have of course been building sustainable, self-build homes for countless millennia, and there were experiments in solar-heated housing before the Second World War. It is nevertheless correct to contend that the 'Ecological House', as it was known after Graham coined the name, can be considered as the earliest dwelling to be intentionally built in keeping with ecological principles. Peter Harper refers to the Street Farmers as having built 'the first (?) ecohouse'[213], a comment which, but for the question mark which allows some manoeuvre for doubt, tends to corroborate this from a contemporary perspective. A Wikipedia entry for Brenda Vale and Robert Vale cites their sustainable dwelling at Southwell in Nottinghamshire as 'the first autonomous building in the United Kingdom' but while this was groundbreaking, it was constructed more than two decades later than Street Farmhouse.[214] A more contemporary contender, the New Alchemists' Cape Cod Ark Bioshelter was built 1976.

The 'Ecological House' was ostensibly put together as Graham's

212 Graham Caine, e-mail message to the author, 2 October 2012.
213 Peter Harper, 'The New, Improved Undercurrents Alternative Technology Guide', *Undercurrents* 6 (March-April 1974), 24.
214 Wikipedia entry, 'Brenda and Robert Vale' http://en.wikipedia.org/wiki/Brenda_and_Robert_Vale [accessed 5 May 2013].

assessment submission at the Architectural Association.[215] However, his ambitions, and the practical utility of the construction, extended further. At the outset Alvin Boyarsky gave the project an auspicious boost by offering to refund the costs for the wood upon which Graham had spent his student grant.[216] This would have constituted a significant vote of confidence from Boyarsky, newly in place in his chairing role at the AA; as well as being no doubt indispensable in helping to secure the materials and time to get the job done. Kallipoliti argues that moral support from Boyarsky and Pawley 'allowed him to further his research within the academic framework of the AA.'[217] Yet more good news was permission from the planning department responsible for the Woolwich area to begin the project on the basis of a provisional two-year permit.[218] Graham recalled that a long meeting with the Chief Engineer at Public Buildings and Works that occurred almost by chance managed to secure official support for the experiment.[219]

While living in what Camden Council described as a 'slum' in the Archway, Graham, assisted by Bruce Haggart, Roger Stowell, Fran Stowell (Roger's sister and at this time Graham's partner) and others built the Ecological House in Kidbrooks Lane, Eltham between September and December 1972. An image of the framework under construction published in the November 1972 issue of *Oz* magazine shows a banner proclaiming 'This site is under workers' control'.[220] On completion it became the residence of Graham and Fran Stowell for more than two years. Graham designed Street Farmhouse with

215 Boyle and Harper, *Radical Technology*, 170.
216 Personal conversation with Graham Caine, Montpelier, Bristol 29 November 2012. Lydia Kallipoliti cites this as a £2, 000 donation in 'Review: Clearings in a Concrete Jungle', *Journal of the Society of Architectural Historians*, 70.2 (June 2011), 240.
217 Lydia Kallipoliti, 'From Shit to Food: Graham Caine's Eco-House in South London, 1972-1975', *Buildings and Landscapes*, 19.1 (Spring 2012), 89.
218 Kallipoliti, 'Review: Clearings…', 240.
219 Personal conversation with Graham Caine, The Farmhouse, St Werburghs, Bristol 21 May 2013.
220 Caine, 'Revolutionary Structure', 12.

the specific aim that it would be an 'autonomous' house, being as far as possible off the national grid and mains water supplies. To this extent the house was emancipated from dependence upon the state and private business for its basic utilities.

The ideal home that Graham and Fran moved into at the end of 1972 consisted of two integrated structures. The main living unit was an elongated two-storey timber cabin, measuring twenty-seven by forty feet.[221] Beneath this was a large greenhouse, a regular polyhedron made from glass clear acrylic. This resembled a low-elevation rotunda and was somewhat like a miniature version of the biomes now familiar at Tim Smit's Eden Project in Cornwall. The accompanying wooden panelled cabin anticipates the timber-fronted 'Scandinavian'-look buildings popular at the beginning of the Twenty-First Century. The irregular appearance and exploitation of an eclectic kludge of reused materials gave the dwelling a somewhat 'Heath Robinson' appearance, a fusion of the fantastical and eminently practical that was a hallmark of the Street Farm approach. At ground level was an extensive apparatus for biogas generation. In the 1971 prototype sketch, a bedroom and office space appears to be situated within the greenhouse dome, alongside hydroponic plant production and a fishpond (a feature that had appeared in the sketch for the housing competition at Bracknell, *SF* 2, 18). However, in the completed eco-house all domestic activities, with the exception of some washing and toilet facilities, were located in the main cabin. The bedroom, kitchen, bathroom and living space were upstairs, and enjoyed a view, while the workshop and growing areas were downstairs.

The first objective of the Ecological House was to be 'independent

221 Dickson, *Alternative Technology*, 132. Caine estimates the dimensions to have been: '2 storeys was about 10-12 feet wide, maybe 30 feet with an integral single-storey growing area probably 160° of a180° semi-circle, radius of about 20 feet, max'. Personal conversation with Graham Caine, The Farmhouse, St Werburghs, Bristol 21 May 2013.

of mains supply and waste services' (*SF* 1, [18]). To this end it featured an array of features for generating energy through ambient sources and maximising its efficiency. Solar energy was harvested by 'flat plate absorbers to provide domestic heating' (*SF* 1, [18]). Water was also solar heated by using black-painted domestic radiators and then 'thermosiphoned' to a large insulated cylinder. The wooden cabin was generously insulated using wood wool.[222] Ample windows, together with an acrylic panel to the rear of the living quarters, maximised the benefit from incoming daylight, although electric lighting was still required at night. The transparent 'double skin' of the greenhouse also exploited the potential for daylight lighting and heat retention (*SF* 1, [19]). Such measures for capturing daylight and heat appear, for the most part proved to be successful in achieving cosy domestic quarters. The energy from the greenhouse helped to keep the interior warm, backed up with a paraffin heater and cylinder gas for cooking.

However, Graham estimated that they had only needed to use three gallons of paraffin in the first year.[223] However, there were it seems limits to the comforts to be had. When Boyle asked in 1974, 'Does it get fucking cold in the winter?' Graham responded 'We're applying to the council to get a hot water system!' When Boyle prompted further about the shortage of hot water in the winter, for the necessities of washing up and showers, Caine further quipped that they owned 'plenty of dishes'.[224] David Dickson notes that 'supplementary electric heating' was also 'still necessary'.[225] Obligingly it seems that the Electricity Council offered good will by pledging to provide free electricity, although not waiving meter charges.[226] However, Graham soon added a wind generator to the

222 Sandy Halliday, *Sustainable Construction* (Amsterdam: Elsevier, 2008), 13.
223 Boyle and Harper, *Radical Technology*, 170.
224 Boyle and Harper, *Radical Technology*, 170.
225 Dickson, *Alternative Technology*, 132.
226 Gerald Leach, 'Living off the Sun in South London,' *The Observer* (27 August 1972), 1.

system which helped to further emancipate Street Farmhouse from the national grid.

Rainwater was harvested, filtered and stored in a 12 gallon drinking water tank. An extensive process of double filtration using a slow sand filter was used for water purification. Chronic air pollution was an unfortunate aspect of the industrial society that Street Farm were challenging. Caine was aware that London rainwater contained a dangerous level of 0.11 microgrammes of lead per litre and investigated filters to reduce the health risk.[227] He also conserved water by designing a toilet that used two pints rather than two gallons of water to flush.[228] Caine was to develop sewage biology as his professional specialism and it is therefore in respect of sewage treatment that he implemented some of the most innovative aspects of Street Farmhouse. Caine devised an anaerobic digester into which human sewage was channelled and collected for recycling. In keeping with the original sketches for Street Farmhouse, in which it was intended that 'organic waste will be recycled to provide a domestic gas supply', there was a gasometer outside of the main dome for this purpose (*SF* 1, [18]). In this way a virtuous closed circle is created to recycle the solids, liquids and gases from human waste. Nutrients were extracted from the effluent for a safe organic solution that was used as fertiliser for food production. The three-tank digester made use of algae to create gas in the gasometer, feeding it through to the cooker (*SF* 1, [19]). As Caine described it: 'To us, pollution is a greenhouse full of tomatoes and cucumbers and it's pretty healthy pollution'. Again Boyle queried: 'what about the E coli and all those other nasty things that public health inspectors don't like?' Caine characteristically defended his approach, claiming the 'the process takes so long that pathogenic bacteria die of old age', while making

227 Leach, 'Living off the Sun', 2.
228 Hughes, 'Ecologic House', 2.

the more serious point that the anaerobic system means that the human sewage is treated before it is used on crops, as distinct from systems for composting human waste which he believed carried more risks.[229]

The combination of hydroponic growing and adjacent allotment plots enabled Graham and Fran to produce a significant proportion of their vegetables for consumption. Collected rainwater, nutrients from the biogas digester and compost from kitchen waste were all fed back into the food production cycle. The variety of crops was an ambitious aspect of the drive towards self-sufficiency. Caine estimated that the family was able to grow nearly all of its own vegetables during the summer, and up to 70% in the winter, which, if accurate, is an impressive achievement given the limited space available.[230] A sketch that appeared in *Mother Earth News* featured a hothouse to produce 'bananas and other tropical food'.[231] Again the radically experimental nature of this Edenic project ensured that Caine was able to obtain support of a kind that would be unlikely to be provided were the construction of such dwellings to be scaled up to house a larger proportion of society. In this case the Royal Botanical Gardens at Kew were willing to donate some banana plants and it is recorded that sympathetic hydroponics expert James Sholto Douglas made some paw-paws available.[232] The project sketch for the Ecological House in *Street Farmer* 1 even featured a small 'paddy field' of brown rice, reflecting the 1970s enthusiasm for macrobiotic diet and this mighty grain's status as the single food item thought to be able to sustain all nutritional needs (*SF* 1, [18]). The spirit of experimentation extended to vegetarianism, again a means to increase self-reliance, creating an opportunity for Graham to

229 Boyle and Harper, *Radical Technology*, 170.
230 Boyle and Harper, *Radical Technology*, 170.
231 Graham Caine, 'Eco-House', *Mother Earth News* 20 [March 1973], 62.
232 Leach, 'Living off the Sun', 1.

investigate the health outcomes of strict vegetarian diet.[233] Graham's approach was always pragmatic as much as it was ascetic. He later joked 'we buy dairy produce and cat's meat – because we haven't got a vegetarian cat'.[234] Also essential was the incorporation of a beer brewing system in the dwelling.[235] Intriguingly, the prototype sketch indicates a 'growing grass carpet' (*SF* 1, [19]).

Tinkering and Bricolage

The swiftly constructed Ecological House was at once an end in itself and also an ongoing opportunity to provoke thought about the core processes of daily existence. As sustainability expert Adrian Smith points out, as well as the different functionality of the domestic technology, living in eco-housing connotes a different value system on the part of the occupiers that is distinct from those living in more conventional, volume-built housing. The users' relationship to their eco-home is likely to embrace both an 'active commitment to a green lifestyle' and more practically 'high user-involvement or self-build' as distinct from 'passive and conservative consumers'.[236]

The character of much formal employment is to add labour value to commodities to produce profit for others and to follow predefined procedures and transactions for standardised outcomes. By contrast the building and maintenance of the Ecological House was in the best tradition of salvaging and tinkering, in which constructive work is akin to a hobby. Caine consciously posits a mode of being in which social needs might be met outside of capitalist relations. As he described it:

233 Leach, 'Living off the Sun', 1.
234 Boyle and Harper, *Radical Technology*, 171.
235 Leach, 'Living off the Sun', 1.
236 Smith, 'Governance Lessons from Green Niches', 99, Table 5.1.

> It should project a different life style and thus expectations for the inhabitants... a more peaceful existence... a sort of pottering about to the sounds of Zappa and Lennon...[237]

Street Farm were fond of *The Ragged Trousered Philanthropists* from which an excerpt is reproduced in *Street Farmer* 2 (*SF* 2, 1). In the influential socialist novel of 1914, Robert Tressell characterises the precarious economic relationships in capitalist society as a 'battle for life' – a competitive struggle in which any act of altruism would be irrational and necessarily self-destructive. It is on a unique occasion on which the socialist hero, Frank Owen is able to channel his artistic potential into the design of an elaborate Japanese interior, that he is fleetingly able to transcend the utterly demoralising sense of alienation that besets his life as an exploited decorator in a provincial town. Significantly it is only when Owen takes this work out of the formal workplace, and away from the surveillance of the boss's foremen, to research in the Free Library and experiment with design at home in his own time, that he is able to focus his innate intellectual and creative propensities and accomplish a task to his own satisfaction. As we have seen the idea of alienation was fundamental to Street Farm's critique of affluence based on consumerism in the early 1970s. Caine speculates that the increasing enthusiasm for Do-It-Yourself at that time was an expression of an often unconscious experience of alienation due to the curtailment of creative expression:

> A lot of the Do-It-Yourself movement, I believe is the desire of people to witness their effectivity within their immediate surroundings; as a response to the alienation that is experienced in the majority of work situations of the specialised, industrialised

237 Caine, 'Revolutionary Structure, 13.

society in which we are immersed.[238]

There is a significant emphasis on direct participation so that occupants of eco-houses do not passively consume their houses as products, but undertake the kind of self-skilling and skills-sharing that enable them to engage with their homes on the most intimate practical level. In learning new processes and techniques first hand they increase understanding, de-mystify their relationship to their own domestic environment and obviate the need to rely upon outside experts. Communities are able to reclaim knowledge from specialists and benefit from the synergies that come from cooperation. Ideally, this increases confidence and autonomy in something of a virtuous circle. Such a tradition of people's technology continues today in the kind of initiatives that Californian radical Carl Carlsson updates and celebrates in *Nowtopia* (2008) with its splendid countercultural crew of DIYing biofuel alchemists, permaculturalists and open-source software gurus.

Positively then, this experimental autonomous space is an environment in which to find out what works best empirically, to learn from mistakes and modify accordingly. Yet experimentation brings with it spills as well as thrills, uncertainties, waste, insecurities, frustrations, at worst even dangers and calamities. In a real and more than metaphorical sense, the residents of the Ecological House enjoyed an intimate, symbiotic relationship with its interior habitat. They were even its vital internal organs and an essential part of its metabolism. First and foremost Street Farmhouse was a home. Caine stressed that 'it's a house not a laboratory, though we enjoy tinkering around with a few things.[239] Yet even after the eco-house's construction it seems that the family had to undertake many

238 Caine, 'Revolutionary Structure, 13.
239 Boyle and Harper, *Radical Technology*, 171.

domestic tasks such as maintaining the water and sewage system and keeping on top of the horticultural production that less dedicated folk might have considered onerous. Haggart put it bluntly: 'The reality is that twice a week you've got to get elbow-deep in shit'.[240]

In part due to the experimental nature of the project, Caine went to extraordinary lengths to monitor and regulate the Ecological House's working processes and seldom left home, a level of dedication that the rest of us may be reluctant to emulate. Kallipoliti suggests that the project 'denoted an intensive preoccupation with the physiology of inhabitation'.[241] Caine has since been keen to distance himself from Kallipoliti's characterisation of his role in the eco-home, stressing that while he was diligent about his work and aimed to 'research and inspire', he was never a scientist or 'a white-coated boffin'. While the originality of his approach attracted attention from the mainstream scientific community, with the result that Nobel-prize winning scientist Maurice Wilkins supported his research, Graham had no long term aspiration to develop his knowledge of sewage biology into a career as a professional scientist.[242] As such he remained an ambitious amateur, working for a love of trial and discovery but also to create a practical living space, a distinction Haggart identified between the ethos of the amateur and the boffin when the house was under construction (Chapter 5). It was therefore perhaps because, rather than in spite, of the fact, this was a full-time experimental home and not a workplace laboratory that Caine's relationship with his work was particularly intimate. As the system aspired to the perfect circle of a closed system of perpetual recycling of human bodily waste, a literal composting of self, it entailed a symbiotic, even co-dependent, relationship with its occupants. The demands of the perfect cycle must therefore be squared with some practical

240 Boyle and Harper, *Radical Technology*, 171.
241 Kallipoliti, 'Review: Clearings in a Concrete Jungle', 242.
242 Personal conversation with Graham Caine, Montpelier, Bristol 29 November 2012.

considerations of maintenance.

This raises a potential tension which Boyle and Harper explore with some probing and cogent questions about the friction between inclusion and self-skilling and the assumption that all members of society will have the necessary aptitude and application or even desire to live free of hierarchical constraints and to devote a proportion of their lives to their own subsistence. Robert M. Pirsig was to shortly explore the philosophical implications of a similar philosophical dilemma in his 1974 cult classic *Zen and the Art of Motorcycle Maintenance*, in which the mindfulness of the narrator willing to get his hands oily, understand and become one with his motorcycle contrasts with hands off approach of his fellow travellers, John and Sylvia Sutherland, who would prefer to leave such tinkering to expert mechanics. For all Caine's self-deprecating jokes about the doubtful quality of his own carpentry,[243] Street Farm unquestionably developed advanced technical abilities, time and support networks who were willing to take on projects that most people would give a wide berth. Caine's expertise in sewage biology, for example, kept the system in Street Farmhouse safe in a way that may have had dire consequences in the care of a less knowledgeable person. Nevertheless he later argued 'I was thrown out of woodwork at school – I became "skilled" when it wasn't alienated labour'.[244] They learned such skills in practice when cooperating on a project that was, as they had proclaimed, under worker' control, and consequently they were able to learn and reach a potential through participating in concrete labour rather than undertaking more conventional alienated labour which is often intentionally deskilled to retain economic power over so-called 'human resources'. The endeavour to democratise such knowledge by the means they are

243 Caine, 'Revolutionary Urbanism', 12

244 Personal conversation with Graham Caine, The Farmhouse, St Werburghs, Bristol 21 May 2013.

advocating is in my opinion the most progressive way forward. It is worth quoting Godfrey Boyle's comments on the issue at length:

> This theory that all of us seem to have at the back of our minds – that inherent to to every human being is the desire to be creative and be self-sufficient – I think it's like an act of faith. It's not corroborated with any particular evidence – it's like the belief that all men are equal: there's not much evidence for that. It's just something that we have to accept as a basic premise until proven otherwise. Of course it's just as hard to *disprove* the hypothesis that people are born *without* that innate ability. But don't you think that behind all this there's a notion somewhere of the 'whole man' or 'whole woman' – of a person who spends some of his time growing vegetables, some of his time playing guitars, building houses when the need arises or writing books or drawing cartoon strips? That, to me, is the ultimately seductive idea, and I don't think it's necessarily elitist to have that point of view.[245]

In a critical, though sympathetic analysis of the viability of autonomous living, Peter Harper also considers that any rigorous evaluation should factor in non-monetary 'hidden subsidies', in the form of such inputs as the builders' and designers' skills, the number of hours spent in constructing and maintaining such dwellings and the source of the 'spare' materials even if they are otherwise scrap parts.[246] Caine largely constructed Street Farmhouse from 'scrounged', donated and reused materials. It was thus freed from the usual requirement for substantial capital investment to purchase materials from suppliers and spared the full rigours of market

245 Boyle and Harper, *Radical Technology*, 171.
246 Boyle and Harper, *Radical Technology*, 156.

forces. Street Farmhouse was built extremely cheaply, even taking into account inflation since the early 1970s. Dickson records that materials to build the house cost just £650 (roughly equivalent to £7, 200 in 2013).[247] The practice of building quickly, cheaply and with limited technical expertise in order to avoid substantial capital input was integral to the Street Farm ethos for community architecture. Caine put forward the radical argument that a house could not be considered ecological only by virtue of the fact that its designers adhered to strict ecological principles in terms of incorporating an array of energy efficient features. Ironically, if large amounts of money were required to construct and purchase an eco-home, it followed that this capital would inevitably be generated by economic activity that was likely to be environmentally destructive. It was not possible to decouple economic growth from a detrimental environmental impact during the early 1970s. This remains true in the present day when, in a time of economic downturn, never-to-be-realised aspirations to a weightless economy are downplayed. This constitutes a valid critique of many present-day bespoke eco-homes designed to meet the needs of a niche market for wealthy clients with a sense of environmental responsibility.

Such difficulties illustrate the obstacles, indeed the impossibilities of achieving a environmentally sustainable economy within the capitalist free market. At the end of the 1970s economists Daniel Khazzoom and Len Brookes identified another apparent paradox that helps to account for capitalism's failure to deliver truly 'green' economics. In his environmental bestseller *Heat* (2006), George Monbiot argued that the Khazzoom-Brookes Postulate may explain the macroeconomic trend whereby improvements in increased energy efficiency have invariably been accompanied by increases in

247 Dickson, *Alternative* Technology, 132.

energy consumption.[248] The Khazzoom-Brookes Postulate suggests that, in a free market, reduced energy costs through energy-saving features mean that more economic activity can be undertaken for the same financial investment, thus generating a net increase, rather than reduction, in energy use. While this remains a postulate, and hence unproven, Monbiot points to some subsequent longitudinal evidence that suggests that this is the case. He draws attention, for example, to the fact that 'between 1980 and 2002, energy use in the thirty richest countries rose by 23 per cent, even while they exported their most energy-intensive industries to poorer nations'.[249]

Autonomous Houses, Liberated Homes

Alexander Pike's project team at the University of Cambridge's Department of Architecture took a more theoretical approach to the implementation of alternative technology. The contrasting motivations behind the 'Autonomous House Research Programme' explain a possible element of rivalry apparent between the projects. Pike's team was funded by the Science Research Council, the Department of the Environment and some manufacturing organisations. The immediate driver for the autonomous house was to relieve planning pressures on urban areas on the premise that the process to achieve more distributed development would be smoother if construction didn't need to be concentrated where there were pre-existing connections to centralised infrastructure for the supply of utilities. To this extent the team were designing a prototype that, it was envisaged, would be implemented within the

248 George Monbiot, *Heat: How we can Stop the Planet Burning* [2006], with research assistance from Dr Matthew Prescott (London: Penguin, 2007), 61-62.
249 Monbiot, *Heat*, 61-62. Monbiot's data is taken from Roger Levitt, 'Quality of Eco-Efficiency', *Energy and Environment*, 15 (2004), 1015-1026.

capitalist economy. Pike did, however, contextualise autonomous housing within holistic concerns for the predicaments starting to face humanity and planet Earth. Brenda Vale who, together with her husband Robert Vale, was a pioneering exponent of autonomous housing, recalls his impact on them:

> Alex Pike used to take his students for coffee in lieu of supervision and talk over world problems – Ehrlich and the population explosion, lack of resources, diminishing fossil fuel reserves etc. Obviously I believed every word since it has shaped our whole working life.[250]

Three predictions based on contemporary trends underpinned Pike's project: that during the following decade energy costs would rise substantially, there would be increasing constraints on urban land space and that the working week was expected to decrease incrementally to an average of three days.[251] The 'Autonomous House' was dedicated to the generation of reliable scientific data, and was an architectural laboratory rather than a residence. For this reason Pike's conclusions (after the project had run for three years) included a dismissal of the work of amateur members of the alternative technology movement:

> Some enthusiasts have worked on a purely experimental basis with insufficient theoretical knowledge, the motivation towards the goals being much more in evidence than the means of achieving them. Projects which have reached the stage of construction are, for the most part, insufficiently monitored, their usefulness limited by knowledge of actual performance.[252]

250 Brenda Vale, e-mail message to the author, 17 April 2013.
251 Alexander Pike, 'Autonomous House,' *Architectural Design*, 44.11 (1974), 686.
252 Pike, 'Autonomous House,' 689.

Caine recalled that he was invited to Cambridge to lecture to Pike's students and shared his research findings but felt that his work was condemned for being 'amateurish'.[253] This suggests that Pike included Street Farm among those he had in mind when he spoke of the perceived shortcomings of 'enthusiasts'. The intention behind the autonomous house was, in due course, to design a template and system that could be scaled up for mass production.[254] For their part Caine and Haggart rejected such an approach as an instance of the kind of consumerism that they were critiquing.[255] In order to afford the costs involved in the Cambridge House, Street Farm argued, a large capital outlay was necessary. Peter Harper referred to the 'really fancy Cambridge design that costs £20, 000'[256] (amount in 1972 roughly equivalent to £224, 000 by 2013). Even if the design incorporated state-of-the-art environmental features, to raise this capital might involve economic activity that would itself have a detrimental impact on the environment. By contrast, Caine and Haggart assembled Street Farmhouse with as little money as possible, not only for the practical reason that they were cash strapped, but also because they believed that borrowing financial capital from banks would inevitably compromise the ethos of autonomy. They therefore used materials such as reused acrylic sheeting, rather than glass for the greenhouse – even though they would have preferred the latter as 'greener' and more effective – because it was significantly more expensive to source. Caine stakes a claim to two significant distinctions; that the principles behind Street Farm's Ecological House were a combination of a pragmatic and holistic rather than instrumental approach, and that liberatory technology should be accessible to benefit all. He explains:

253 Personal conversation with Graham Caine, The Farmhouse, St Werburghs, Bristol 21 May 2013.
254 Pike, 'Autonomous House,' 686.
255 Boyle and Harper, *Radical Technology*, 171.
256 Boyle and Harper, *Radical Technology*, 171.

> To me an ecological house was about a biological system, so it had an ecology going on within it, it wasn't necessarily, but it should be you know, green materials, or environmentally friendly materials, it was about experiencing yourself as part of nature.

Caine further argued that 'The whole point about revolutionary technology was that it should be available to ordinary people, not just the rich'.[257]

Another autonomous house, 'De Kleine Aarde' built by Dutch architect Jaap t'Hooft near Eindhoven in 1975 attracted attention, this time in the *Sunday Times Magazine*. As well as investigating some of the technical features of autonomous housing, the feature's author, Tony Osman, comments on some of the incentives for investing time and money in such a project. He provides an important reminder that radical social change of a kind that Street Farm advocated was only one, and probably not the most widely shared, motivation:

> [...] if your imagination runs that way, you could, in your autonomous house, feel safe from interruptions of your supplies by trade unionists and strikers.
>
> The reasons for wanting autonomy are important. One group of the sybaritic rich wants to continue in the life style to which it has been accustomed, driving, if possible, its dishwashers and spin-driers and pop-up toasters from 'natural' (i.e. free) energy. At another pole, a radical drop-out, trying to solve the problems of a methane generator in a rural area will willingly live in a

257 Both quotations from personal conversation with Graham Caine, Montpelier, Bristol 29 November 2012.

> heavy jersey and thick socks. Somewhere in the middle come most of us, accepting that there will be some 'standard of living' traded against self-sufficiency.[258]

By 1976 the notion of an autonomous house had attracted enough mainstream interest for Granada TV to back the construction of a purpose-built self-sufficient home from the shell of an old coach-house in Cheshire. The Macclesfield house, designed by architect Donald Wilson, was to be the subject of a TV series based on the experiences of the Grant family in their new ideal autonomous home. Written in the years following the publication of the *Limits to Growth* report and *The Ecologist*'s 'Blueprint for Survival', the intention was to show how it was possible 'to live a normal life without draining away precious resources of energy, water, and other irreplaceable materials'.[259]

Street Farm were not alone in recognising the radical implications of autonomous housing, although they were at the forefront. In 1975 Brenda Vale and Robert Vale were prophetic in arguing that the adoption of autonomous housing and alternative technology had social ramifications as well as technical consequences:

> The autonomous house is not seen as a regressive step. It is not simply a romantic vision of 'back to the land', with life again assuming a rural pace and every man dependent upon himself and his immediate environment for his survival. Rather, it is a different direction for society to take. Instead of growth, stability is the aim; instead of working to earn money to pay other people to keep him alive, the individual is presented with the choice of

258 Tony Osman, 'Dome Sweet Dome', *Sunday Times Magazine* (30 November 1975), 68.
259 Terence McLaughlin, *A House for the Future*, 2nd rev. ed. with revisions by Don Wilson and Brian Trueman (London: Independent Television Books, 1977), 6.

self-autonomy or working to pay for survival.[260]

During the mid-1990s the Vales constructed pioneering autonomous houses at Southwell and Hockerton in Nottinghamshire. In their later book, *The New Autonomous House*, written a quarter of a century after the first title, they survey the presence of alternative technology in the utopian literary tradition. Brenda Vale's *Albion* (1982) is one of the rare novels whose futuristic action revolves around the implementation of radical technology. The Vales tentatively conclude that 'the alternative-technology approach to a house might be the more appropriate route to follow, as the one tending to encourage individual freedom.[261]

Similarly, rather than providing 'how-to' manuals for individual opt-outs, Street Farm were advocating assaults upon such fundamental articles of fiscal faith as the necessity of economic growth and wage labour. Inspired by Situationism, with its blend of Marxist and anarchist economic and cultural theory, as we have seen they particularly identified the problem of alienation as a problem. Such an approach is a radical departure from mainstream political rhetoric about economic growth, wealth creation and the creation of jobs. A strong ethos of autonomy and self-determination was built into the fabric of Street Farmhouse. The structure was therefore more than an experiment in sewage management, hydroponics and sun harvesting. It was an exercise in self-management and workers' control, of anarchy in action. It was, Caine proclaimed, a 'Revolutionary structure'. Writing for a countercultural readership, Caine was forthright about the sociopolitical and ecological impetus behind Street Farmhouse in an article entitled 'A Revolutionary Structure' published in the underground magazine *Oz* in November

260 Vale and Vale, *Autonomous House*, 8.
261 Brenda Vale and Robert Vale. *The New Autonomous House: Design and Planning for Sustainability* (London: Thames and Hudson, 2000), 35.

1972. In the early 1970s, as well as in the present-day, 'revolution' was a term that was much used and abused. It has a strong primary meaning in the sense of a conscious overturning and transformation of existing social relations. However, it is often, perhaps more frequently, used in diluted senses as a shorthand for any kind of change, novelty or technical innovation or even taken up by commercial enterprises attempting to accrue the zest of modish sophistication to their brand by claiming that their organisation, product or service has 'revolutionary qualities'.[262] Caine was clear that in a modest way, his construction of an eco-house was revolutionary in both of these senses. First, and most significantly, it was exemplary of an approach to life that rejected capitalist ideology and its socio-political expression in forms such as enclosure, consumerism, specialisation and centralisation. Second, it was revolutionary to the more limited, technical extent that it was innovative and synthesised several ideas from alternative technology, being experimental in the sense that the autonomous house constructed at Cambridge was to be. Caine felt that mainstream commentators more readily recognised, and accepted with greater comfort, the second, than they realised the implications for the first. He drew attention to the semantic slippage in the term 'revolutionary':

> The project has often been described as revolutionary, usually with reference to the concepts of its techniques, but I believe it to be revolutionary more in its implications within the existing

262 'Architecture Revolution', for example, felt the necessity to distance themselves from 1970's revolutionaries, clarifying on their online blog:

> 2009's ARCHITECTURE *REVOLUTION* is coincidently unrelated to 1975's Architects' Revolutionary Council (ARC). The motive for the ARC was a communist vendetta against the Royal Institute of British Architects (RIBA) while the REV is a positive social network for the creation of architecture for architects and their rights.

'1975's Architects' Revolutionary Council' [online entry] http://architecturerevolution.wordpress.com/category/architects%C2%B4-revolutionary-council-1975/ [accessed 1 February 2012].

> social situation… I mean, the world has been going round for millenias on the techniques involved, it's the political situation that is fucking them up that needs revolution.[263]

Caine wished readers of *Oz* to understand that this 'revolutionary structure' was the outcome of a hybrid relationship between his technical know-how and social ideas and that it would be a mistake to compartmentalise the two by stressing technical innovation without reference to social intentions regarding autonomy. The social and the technological components are mutually constitutive and should not be considered in isolation.

Haggart argued that the 'loveliest houses' were 'liberated houses' such as squats.[264] Despite their lip service (for example David Cameron's current enthusiasm for the 'Big Society'), mainstream politicians and local authorities are extremely wary of individual and community self-help, in any but the most superficial sense of referring to someone that is working for a wage rather than off welfare benefits. For the most part, autonomy and control over one's own life, is a privilege reserved for those above a certain wealth bracket – to extend them further would be to risk subversive consequences. The closing exchange in Boyle's interview with Street Farm is therefore somewhat prophetic as yet more of the environment has been enclosed and possibilities for self-determination have been considerably shut down during the intervening decades:

> **Godfrey Boyle:** An essential part of what you're saying seems also to be that the act of creating shelter for yourself should be, at the same time, an act of affirming your independence of the State and the System?

263 Caine, 'Revolutionary Structure', 12.
264 Boyle and Harper, *Radical Technology*, 171.

> **Bruce Haggart:** But there's more to it than that. There's got to be thought about what will survive in the future, realistically – not so much ecologically as politically. There's something that's happening that's making it harder for people to live with any kind of self-determination. And if there's going to be something that *can* survive – though it's not going to be one thing, it's going to be umpteen things – then one of them might well be a kind of Street Farm-type scenario.[265]

In Street Farm's microcosm of libertarian communism the material necessities of life – shelter, food and water, heat and energy – come free through the intelligent use of low-impact 'people's technology'. Street Farmhouse is therefore a showcase that puts into practice some of the ideas of the emergent 1970's ecology movement including alternative technology, low fossil fuel usage, organic gardening and vegetarianism. It is also exemplary of a different mode of production based upon self-reliance and mutual aid, radical decentralisation and that prioritises a form of wealth based upon use value rather than exchange value. This was not envisioned in terms of escapism on the part of individuals or couples, in the manner of their self-sufficient television counterparts Tom and Barbara Good, eponymous stars of the popular 1970's sitcom 'The Good Life'. Street Farm saw the proliferation of their ideas more through clusters of urban communes that would flow into a broad and inclusive community-based social movement. It is also significant that Caine was implicitly tuned in to the link between political power and power in the sense of energy resources, evident for example in the struggles between the government and the miners at this time. His work was not a response to the oil crisis of 1973, which as Kallipoliti

265 Boyle and Harper, *Radical Technology*, 171.

notes, it predated,[266] but a strategy for decentralising power in response to the state's command and control of energy resources as a means to control its population. Before the Ecological House was constructed, Caine wrote in *Architectural Design*:

> By treating shelter as an energy system to provide a basic life support system it is hoped to reduce the individual's dependence upon a centralised power structure, and thus increase the choice of an individual's area of contribution within the context of a life killing culture.[267]

The connection between autonomous architecture and the kind of closed-cycle technology that NASA (National Aeronautics and Space Administration) scientists were currently designing for spaceflight was another topical theme during the early 1970s. While the Ecological House may have resembled a spaceship, much to the bemusement of the neighbours, Street Farm reversed the functionality of such closed-cycle systems. Kallipoliti suggests that Street Farm attempted to repurpose NASA's technology of self-reliance so that it might operate to free ordinary people from dependence on the electricity grid and other components of state infrastructure. This would enable economic, and eventually political, emancipation from dependence on the institutions of state and capital, rather than use such technology to satisfy the technocratic hubris of the military-industrial complex. Kallipoliti concludes, however, that such an approach is inherently flawed, arguing that 'this view of the world is philosophically problematic, in its claims about a natural cosmic order, and also technically unviable'.[268] This perhaps misconstrues the intention of the kind of decentralised

266 Kallipoliti, 'From Shit to Food', 89.
267 Caine, 'Ecological House', 140.
268 Kallipoliti, 'Review: Clearings in a Concrete Jungle', 243.

'revolutionary urbanism' that Street Farm advocated. This was not, ultimately, to use closed-cycled systems to bring about entirely autonomous systems, entailing extreme social insularity. It was to bring about release from the controlling, self-serving and alienating influence of political and economic elites, in order to reconnect more widely with international networks based upon mutual aid to meet social needs.

Caine and the other Street Farmers consistently advocated a collective rather than individualistic conception of autonomy. Caine argued that while the intention behind the Ecological House was to construct an 'individual domestic unit', he recognised that this would require an onerous management commitment on the part of the occupants. His approach was flexible and pragmatic rather than rigidly upholding the principle of autonomy at this level. He argued:

> this limitation would be reduced with the expansion of this attitude applied to small low rise high density communities which also destroys the image of isolation of the autonomous house.[269]

The underlying principle, moreover, was to reclaim control at the grassroots level through connective empowerment and solidarity to address alienating isolation, not to fetishise a conception of domestic self-sufficiency that would be impossible, and in any case contrary to the underlying purpose that they were trying to achieve. After all greater reliance of ordinary people upon each other, met by an increased sharing of responsibilities, could hopefully cultivate stronger social bonds, thus meeting revolutionary urbanism's primary objectives to foster community empowerment and counter alienation. Autonomy is not to be conceived as a closed system.

269 Caine, 'Ecological House', 140.

Caine later explained:

> We have never actually tried to attain self-sufficiency at a nuclear family level which seems not only extremely difficult to do technically but also is socially undesirable. It's too much of the 'I'm alright, sod everybody else' (*Clearings in the Concrete Jungle*).

If achieved, community cooperation to administer basic provisions and services, underpinned by rigorous egalitarianism, would entail a far-reaching redistribution of wealth away from the current monopoly by the numerically tiny percentage of the population who currently control the means of production.

While Caine found points of interest within the high-profile developments at NASA, this approach to autonomy takes us a long way from the purpose and context of NASA's technological research programme. His work with alternative technology was always motivated by a desire to further the principles of revolutionary urbanism. In this sense it was linked to a political aim to achieve what is now sometimes referred to as 'modularity', a means to achieve connected autonomy in order to maximise the benefits of living for both individuals and communities.[270] A more accurate representation of the Street Farm vision than a nuclear family inhabiting an isolated domestic unit, therefore, is the kind of autonomous cooperative space that Peter Harper outlines and critically assesses in *Radical Technology*.[271] In Clifford Harper's accompanying depiction of an autonomous terrace, space is communalised to incorporate shared uses such as a bakery, library, sauna and collective garden as well as liberatory technology

270 Michael Lewis and Pat Conaty, *The Resilience Imperative: Comparative Transitions to a Steady-State Economy* (Gabriola Island, BC: New Society Publishers, 2012), 240.
271 Boyle and Harper, *Radical Technology*, 136-169.

including solar panels, hydroponics and an anaerobic digester. Furthermore, for Caine, the notion of connectedness was not only social but ecological in its wider concern for the planet. First coined by Kenneth Boulding, and further popularised by Barbara Ward, the term 'spaceship Earth' had more than metaphorical force.

Kallipoliti argued that just as big business has been willing to tap into the creativity of the counterculture to recuperate radical ideas to market its own expansion and profit, so savvy members of the underground were happy to hack into the ideas bank of the military-industrial complex to repurpose them for community-oriented applications. She cited Caine's preoccupation with the outputs of NASA research as a case in point. His dialectical encounter is an abrasive collision, part creative exchange, part culture war. It also counters any illusions regarding the neutrality of technology. In Kallipoliti's words:

> NASA's latest discoveries regarding the recycling systems of spaceships were appropriated by a countercultural generation of environmentally concerned architects who popularised 'autonomy' from the grid as a tool for social and political reform. These renegade architects and researchers promised to reinvent habitation anew as a synecdoche of Earth, exhibiting an unprecedented belief in the possibility of systematizing the household into an autonomous and regenerative circuit, capable of harnessing its waste and providing its own energy, ideas which have since moved from the fringe to become a part of the dominant paradigm.[272]

Caine later offered a corrective to Kallipoliti's representation of his work feeling that, although he had read through some of NASA's

272 Kallipoliti, *Clip, Stamp, Fold*, 11.

research literature with interest at the time, Street Farm were far more insistent upon taking an ecological rather than technocratic path. He rejected the overarching emphasis upon a connection between his autonomous ecological home and NASA:

> I was going no, no it's far more connected to another satellite organic system that is a closed system called the Planet Earth. You know it didn't take a fucking rocket ship to make people think that life exists in a cyclic, contained way. I mean you get the sunlight coming in and that's the only energy source that the Planet's got. That's all we've got to work with.[273]

Demolition of Street Farmhouse

Street Farmhouse was finally demolished due to lack of planning permission for a permanent structure in October 1975.[274] Despite initial blessings from both Greenwich Council and Woolwich Polytechnic, permission for a more long term experiment on the site was not forthcoming, leading to the destruction of the dwelling which, as we have seen, was known as 'Britain's first ecological house'. Opposition from several neighbours in Eltham, who regarded the structure as an 'eyesore',[275] did not help the longevity of the living experiment. They failed to be charmed by the makeshift wooden and plastic temple devoted to self-sufficiency, an ongoing difficulty facing experiments in alternative technology that do not conform to popular expectations in visual aesthetics. Indeed some neighbours even enthusiastically helped to pull down the home of Graham,

273 Personal conversation with Graham Caine, Montpelier, Bristol 29 November 2012.
274 Ward, 'Do-It-Yourself New Town', 33.
275 Kallipoliti, 'Review: Clearings in a Concrete Jungle', 240.

Fran and their new baby daughter, Rosie.[276] As it was submitted as part of Caine's educational assessment it was somewhat ironic that it also turned out to be a practical if disheartening learning experience in the sense that it corroborated something that Street Farm had always theoretically believed. The lesson that the nature of planning was as much about power, social control and economics as it was about shelter and design. Twenty years later the racist murder of black teenager Stephen Lawrence – a stone's throw away from Street Farmhouse's former site – means that today the location in Eltham is associated with tragedy rather than ecological experimentation.

During the intervening period capitalism's innate internal dynamism has continued to lead it to confront boundaries and to pull all materials, beings, transactions, services, communication and thought within the cash nexus and under corporate and state control in the name of growth, while undifferentiated expansion has accelerated to the detriment of human wellbeing and the natural environment.[277] In such a context more sophisticated technologies have often contributed to the reduction rather than enhancement of real wages and failed to address a sense of malaise in the face of permanent economic, military and environmental crises.

If we want to learn about the urban environment and the kind of problem the city is, I believe Jane Jacobs, the influential contrarian and author of *The Death and Life of Great American Cities* can still teach us much. Jacobs combined a celebration of the creative, socially progressive, liberating and regenerative potentialities of successful cities with some astute and prescient environmentalist arguments as early as 1961. Her insightful theoretical approach encouraged us to consider development and planning not as expert decisions

276 Kallipoliti, 'From Shit to Food', 87.

277 See Joel Kovel's sustained eco-socialist critique of capitalism's clash with the natural world, *The Enemy of Nature: The End of Capitalism or the End of the World?* [2002], updated and expanded ed. (London: Zed; Halifax: Fernwood), 2007).

about the judicious placing of bricks but more profoundly as condensed processes, dynamic expressions of complex physical and social relations; a built structure is at once an in-breath of historical forces and an exhalation influencing a locality's future change and direction. We all recognise that the qualitative phenomenon that is a home connotes a different concept to that quantitative entity that is a housing unit. A liberated home is distinct thing again.

After Street Farm

One of the other things we strongly believed in is that nothing should last very long; everything should be very temporary so that organizations could grow, mesh, and then come apart again.[278]

EarthWorkshop

After the publication of *Street Farmer* 2 Peter Crump and Glenys Crump effectively ended their direct involvement with Street Farm and became involved in EarthWorkshop, an environmentally oriented project set in the green valleys of mid-Wales. This was initiated with several comrades from their London network including Stefan Szczelkun, a lecturer at the Architecture Association for a brief spell during the early 1970s, and a friend and fellow traveller on the winding path to the alternative society. Szczelkun has written an online account of EarthWorkshop, set up as an 'eco-commune' in an Old Vicarage in 1973, some of the details of which Crump contests. The Crump family were members of the eco-commune alongside the seven residents that Szczelkun mentions, namely Szczelkun himself, Eric Raven and Chrissie Raven and their daughter Poppy and Bernard Seal, Roger [no family name given] and Brett [Bailey]. The vicarage was situated at Llandeussant, in the Brecon Beacons. The aims of the EarthWorkshop project were compatible with the ethos behind Street Farm:

> We intend to use our background experience from the broad based disciplines of art, architecture and literature to explore possibilities of life support systems that may be developed

278 Kallipoliti, interview with Peter Crump, Bristol, 11 July 2007, *Clip, Stamp, Fold*, 255.

> and controlled on a small scale and that will integrate most fully with the existing support systems of nature (Szczelkun, 'EarthWorkshop').

Despite such fine aspirations it nevertheless seems that it was a learning experience but was far from successful. Crump quickly found the economic arrangements underpinning the initiative impractical:

> The Old Vicarage was bought (not 'occupied') with a loan guaranteed by the value of Glenys and my London house (which we were paying a mortgage on) and all adult participants in Earth Workshop agreed to take up equal shares via individually arranged loans/capital input. In the end only Glenys and I put up the full amount, the others contributed various (small) percentages of their shares and it became obvious fairly quickly that there was either no way or no inclination to raise any more money than bare subsistence at the 'west end of the Brecon Beacons'.[279]

Peter Crump found himself in a situation where he was working a five-day week in London to service the loan, travelling through the night to make weekend visits to Llandeussant on Fridays and then returning to the English capital each Sunday. He quickly came to regard the arrangements as 'unsustainable' and 'inegalitarian'.[280] Crump became disillusioned with the scheme, due to both the absence of opportunities in the remote location and 'a personality clash' with Eric Raven.[281] In any case the EarthWorkshop proved to be a short-lived venture – the next site that it was offered was

279 Peter Crump, e-mail message to the author, 29 April 2013.
280 Personal conversation with Peter Crump, Montpelier, Bristol, 24 August 2012.
281 Szczelkun, 'EarthWorkshop'.

the abandoned site of a former slate quarry at Llwyngwern, near Machynlleth.[282] Following significant altercations, the Vicarage was sold and the Crumps returned to London while the other members of the EarthWorkshop also shortly moved on and dispersed. On reflection Crump dismissed the scheme as 'completely naïve' given the lack of income available in the area.[283]

Szczelkun's connection to Street Farm was to continue as he returned to London from Wales in 1976. He moved to Flodden Road in Camberwell where a collective that included the Haggart family had set up an alternative community in the buildings connected to an abandoned church (which Caine briefly inhabited). Szczelkun recalls:

> Larry [Wallis] of the rock group Pink Fairies lived in the hall and Lemmy (who would later form Motorhead was a regular visitor. The Street Farmer Bruce Haggart lived in the vicarage with his wife Kate and child Sholto. We had parties in the church in which the 101'ners played. They were led by Joe Strummer who later formed 'The Clash'.[284]

Peter Crump moved to Bristol in 1975. Consistent with his early activism in the Committee of 100, he became active in the resurgent peace and anti-nuclear movement in following years. He was an early member of the internationally renowned Greenham Common Peace Camp where he lived in a tipi before a women-only policy was adopted.

282 Later in 1973 this site was to realise its potential in the form of the Centre for Alternative Technology (CAT), founded by Gerard Morgan-Grenville. CAT was, and continues to be, the flagship for alternative technology.
283 Kallipoliti, interview with Peter Crump, Bristol, 11 July 2007, *Clip, Stamp, Fold*, 256.
284 Szczelkun, 'EarthWorkshop'. Szczelkun, a journalist, remains a prolific writer on countercultural matters.

Graham Caine: From Revolutionary Portugal to the Bristol Gnomes

As we have seen, Graham Caine's Ecological House survived for three years before its dismantlement on the orders of the local planning authorities. After ending his time as an Architectural Association student, Graham continued at Bedford Square, where he took up some work as an instructor. In 1974 he jumped in a van with community architect Bob Kindred and some other friends and journeyed to Portugal, a country still euphoric following the Salazar regime's overthrow in the coup and revolution of that year. An invitation from a Portuguese AA student to help out was a fresh opportunity to place practical alternative technology at the service of social change. Graham supported a self-build housing project by providing expertise to set up improvised solar heating systems, applying the skills he had developed in the construction of Street Farmhouse.[285] He recounted his exhilaration at being present in the throes of a real revolutionary situation and the novelty of being in a march of celebration with members of the police and army on the streets side by side with the people, and with banners flying against the fallen dictatorship.[286] In an uncanny echo of a Street Farm scenario, he found himself sleeping in a tent city in Lisbon on the first night, a repurposing of a camping exhibition that had been set up in the capital and had been about to open when the Carnation Revolution broke out.[287] Graham's group, described as 'six Street Farmers', worked at a village newly named the 'Bairro de Liberdad',

285 Graham Caine, e-mail message to the author, 2 October 2012. An analysis of the political dilemmas raised by the Street Farmers' implementation of alternative technology in a revolutionary situation is included in Marta Pinheiro, 'A.T. Days that Shook Portugal', *Undercurrents* 26 (February-March 1978), 9-12.
286 Personal conversations with Graham Caine, The White Hart, Bristol, 26 March 2013 and The Farmhouse, St Werburghs, Bristol 21 May 2013.
287 Personal conversation with Graham Caine, The Farmhouse, St Werburghs, Bristol 21 May 2013.

experimenting with liberatory technology to implement practical small-scale solutions to create heating systems using extremely limited resources.[288] Graham returned and shared his experiences at the Comtek festival in Bath later that summer.

After spending time living in a converted church in the squatted community with Bruce Haggart at Camberwell, Graham moved on to set up an urban farm in Thamesmead, where he was to live until eventual eviction in the early 1980s. Characterised by some of the forbidding brutalist tower blocks that were used as the dystopian setting for Stanley Kubrick's film *A Clockwork Orange* (1971), Thamesmead is a large modern development built in the 1960s to rehouse people following the slum clearances of the post-War era. At the time Graham lived in a large Nissen hut in which, he recounted, for six winter months they had no water and for more than a year they had no electricity. This made it an ill-advised choice for someone disabled, as it was, he quipped, so cold that 'it snowed inside when it wasn't snowing outside and their boots were frozen to the floor in the mornings'.[289] There were also many highpoints however. Parties took place at every solstice and equinox with Tony McPhee of blues rock band The Groundhogs stopping by to perform at the Nissen Hut.[290] Finally, he claimed, 'we got booted out of Thamesmead because we were anarchists basically'.[291]

After spending some time in France, in 1984 Graham moved to Bristol, where his friend Peter Crump was already living, and started to work as a craftsman on innovative projects in the West Country. Over the course of the next two decades he carried out unique, purposefully fashioned work, made from offcuts from a factory in

288 An account of their experiments appears in Street Farmers, 'Revolutionary Technology in Portugal', *Architectural Design*, 55.10 (1975), 619-623.
289 Personal conversation with Graham Caine, The Farmhouse, St Werburghs, Bristol 21 May 2013.
290 Personal conversation with Graham Caine, The White Hart, Bristol, 26 March 2013.
291 Personal conversation with Graham Caine, Montpelier, Bristol 29 November 2012.

Lydney, before terms like 'bespoke' and 'artisan' became clichés of middle-class interior design. Based in workshops in Mivart Studios, Easton and underneath his home in St Werburghs, Graham became part of a cooperative known as the Bristol Gnomes assisted by fellow Gnomes Martin, Chris and Danny. What was termed 'gnomework' livened up the heart of several inner-city locations with buildings that looked more suited to the glades of enchanted forests. The first project the Bristol Gnomes undertook was the entrance lobby of the Barton Hill Settlement. Caine lived on the premises while the courtyard entrance, library and meeting rooms were given gnome treatment during a refurbishment in 1984. However, the glossy wooden interiors were removed to make way for an extension and new lift in autumn 2012. Fortunately, and appropriately, Barton Hill Settlement administrators have stated that at least some of the 'gnomework' was retrieved, rehoused and recycled rather than destroyed. Other West Country gnomework projects include the interior of the Little Tipple off-licence in Long Ashton and premises in the courtyard of the Glastonbury Experience. The Gover family at Long Ashton featured in the documentary *Travels with my Chainsaw*. Norman and his parents David and Yvonne told me that a chance meeting with Graham was to change their lives as they were delighted with his work and it transformed their living and workspace.[292] They adored Slyply so much that they commissioned Graham and Martin Muller to design and create extensive features throughout the Little Tipple, house and adjacent annex building as well as their daughter's Cotswold Vintner off-licence in Chipping Sodbury. These include winding gnomework staircases, a large wooden hand to clasp a bottle of champagne, a matching foot to tread grapes, a large gaming table with pop-up roulette wheel and

292 Personal conversation with David, Yvonne and Norman Gover, The Little Tipple, Long Ashton, 4 June 2013.

fantastical gnomework table and chairs. The most recent addition to Bristol's gnomework by Danny O'Donoghue is to be seen at the Duke of York pub in St Werburghs.

The Bristol Gnomes also designed and built the Gaudìesque City Farm Café at Watercress Road, St Werburghs, a project completed in just over four months in 1985. It is made with 'sculpted' plywood which became something of a signature material and style for Caine, being stable enough to create structures with fantastical appearance. He is quoted as saying: "People cut down trees and slice them into plywood. We stick the ply together and carve them back into trees'.[293] The windows are irregularly shaped portals into the similarly woody, varnished interior. While the café is now showing some signs of deterioration, as the plaster on the wire mesh stretched over the wood framework has begun to flake, it has long been a popular and much loved local treasure.

The official opening of the café was an opportunity for the gnomes to indulge in some rockery and roll. In an online posting of February 2008, 'Harrymac' wrote that he was one of the team who commissioned the café, adding:

> The pinnacle of the gnome architecture movement was around 1987 when the City Farm organised a concert by Wild Willy Barrett at the City Farm Cafe – all WWB's instruments and the Cafe itself were Gnomemade.294

By way of rock trivia Barrett, who became an accomplished woodworker, lays claim to having produced the only record to boast a wooden cover sleeve for his 1986 album 'Organic Bondage'. The

293 St Werburghs, Bristol Community UK website, 'The Gnome House up for Sale' (3 December 2010), http://www.stwerburghs.org/index.php?section=news&story=the_Gnome_House_up_for_sale.txt [accessed 2 March 2012).
294 'Harrymac', St Werburgh's Forum Index, posting 26 February 2008.

'Gnomemade' instruments are used on the album, the title of which came from an in-joke Caine made in the course of a discussion between the two kinky carpenters after they created chained speaker structures at the time.[295]

In 1998 HTV West broadcast a documentary about Graham Caine's ideas and work with 'Slyply' called *Travels with my Chainsaw*, produced and directed by Steve Gear. Caine guest-presented the film as a part of the Art Trails series, grounding the narrative in his admiration and respect for Catalan architect Antoni Gaudì, whose buildings such as the Casa Battló and Sagrada Famìlia, he had found so stirring when first encountering them on a visit to Barcelona during the mid-1960s. It was partly a retrospect on some of Graham's own work from the days of Street Farm and the Ecological House through to projects undertaken over the course of two decades in Bristol. But it was also a chance for him to look at what he considered to be some of the shortcomings of the architectural profession throughout that period and continuing to the present-day. Interviewed in his own woody house in Bristol, Graham explained that:

> [the 1960s and 1970s] were also a time when architects were probably at their most ruthless. They were putting up some of the worst buildings that architecture has yet witnessed. They were chucking up these tower blocks and people were saying: 'We don't want to live like this, we don't want this!', and architects were saying: 'But it will be lovely, it'll be just the job, exactly what you want!' And they were so arrogant... it's put me off architecture for life. It's against that kind of background that we built this little house [Street Farmhouse].[296]

295 Personal conversation with Graham Caine, Montpelier, Bristol 29 November 2012.
296 Caine, *Travels with my Chainsaw*.

There is a continuity of themes, from a passionate advocacy of a people-centred approach to the human environment, to concern with issues of alienation, control, ecology and the place of individual artistic skills and craftwork. This was an opportunity for Graham to reflect back on the intervening years and comment from his position firmly situated outside of the architectural profession. An amicable exchange with Nigel Horner, architect at Bristol's Create Centre, set up by the local authority to raise environmental awareness in the city, implicitly illustrates the gap between the principles of radical urbanism underlying the Ecological House of the early 1970s and the energy efficient features of the uninhabited eco-house designed as demonstration model at the present-day environment centre. Horner's assessment is upbeat as he sees Graham's Ecological House as a technical 'starting point' for ongoing development, suggesting that 'where these types of houses are, where they're situated, more and more people can visit them'. Graham by contrast appears disillusioned with the lack of progress that has been made since Street Farmhouse, with its aspirations for social liberation and a more holistic approach rather than for generating 'green' economic growth. Graham responded:

> Well I felt a bit more radical than that when I built my house. I mean a major part of it was to try and influence. It is so important for an awareness of housing, of how to take care of one's environment.[297]

Unfortunately Graham's reservations about the influence of the Create Centre's eco-home during the 15 years since the documentary was broadcast have proven to be partly justified. The Create Centre is not only geographically marginalised from both the commercial

297 Caine, *Travels with my Chainsaw.*

and cultural centre of Bristol and immediately adjacent residential areas, but has also become less accessible through a reduction in opening times in recent years. Graham's critical reflection tells much of his continued recognition of the political constraints and limitations of such projects, despite their positive intentions:

> When I lived in my Ecological House, obviously I designed it, built it, but of course that was just to live in it. It became my home just because I needed a home. I was homeless. And we had lots of visitors, we had hundreds and hundreds. We didn't actually feel any pressure to be ecological people, you know we kind of wanted it to be an ordinary family home. And that's want we had. We were trying to achieve something with our lifestyle rather than just a piece of technology and the adoption of lifestyle was very important rather than technology. People who are now like I was then are probably people who live in trucks, and they are reducing their dependence on the state and moving around and they're getting jobs here and there, they're doing festivals and stuff like that. There are a lot of marginal lifestyles now. I think that is probably more interesting than the ecological housing at Bristol City Council.[298]

Some of the issues aired in *Travels with my Chainsaw* were soon to emerge in a direct manner in Graham Caine's own neighbourhood. In 2000 he became involved in a high profile, and ultimately controversial, project initiated at St Werburghs. At the outset, Ashley Vale was an uncommonly utopian scheme for an inner-city development, embracing a not-for-profit ethos. The following summarises some of the allegations made in an article written for *Bristle*, a local anarchist magazine, an exposé based on an

298 Caine, *Travels with my Chainsaw.*

anonymous interview with disaffected local residents and including comments from Graham, who felt free to speak his mind following his resignation from the scheme.[299] Graham's involvement tells much about his continued commitment to the ideas and ideals of sustainable and experimental planning design, coupled with community participation and social justice. It also illustrates the formidable obstacles to making positive progressive change within the broader context of a capitalist system which distorts such principles and divides communities. The story was later taken up with more attributed comments (but without acknowledgement of *Bristle*'s original article) by *The Guardian*.[300]

The site concerned, a former disused scaffolding yard outside Graham's own home, was an ideal location for development, on land adjacent to St Werburgh's City Farm. It is situated in one of the most desirable parts of Bristol with a thriving, close-knit alternative community, readily adjacent to the city centre, yet blessed with nearby allotments and green spaces for recreation. This community was characterised by a combination of residents living in mostly Victorian terrace houses and those living in an eclectic company of vans, caravans, trucks, buses and even a traditional horse-drawn roulotte or two. In order to prevent development by a high-volume corporate builder, Graham, together with a number of local residents, founded the Ashley Vale Action Group (AVAG). They collaborated to launch a self-build development with individually designed houses, in appearance somewhat similar to those erected at Christiania and other alternative havens. The development, as initially proposed, was presented as being innovative while still in keeping with the character and identity of the surrounding streets.

299 [Anon / some local residents of St Werburghs]. 'AVAG – Selfish Self-Builders?', *Bristle* 18 (Winter 2005), 26-28.

300 Steven Morris, 'Green Dream Site has become Bristol's Vale of Tears', *The Guardian* (21 February 2005), [online] http://www.guardian.co.uk/uk_news/story/0,,1419092,00.html [accessed 15 November 2012].

The scheme would be mixed-use in as much as there would be a small proportion of buildings which would accommodate workshops for artists and craftspeople. This was intended to generate some local employment and financial income which would be channelled into a maintenance fund to pay for the upkeep of Ashley Vale, without the need for additional local authority funding.

As such the self-build project to build around 30 homes was warmly welcomed by local residents. At first Graham was an enthusiastic initiator of, and participant in, the project, contributing his expertise to the outline design of the development. He had already created one of his finest examples of Bristol gnomework in the form of his own self-built home, a striking sylvan dwelling at the start of Boiling Wells Lane, the location of the AVAG scheme, built over a period of eighteen months between 1988 and 1990 (Haggart had briefly come to Bristol to work on the project too). In keeping with Hundertwasser's principles, the straight line has been banished in favour of a faery organic structure with a Gaudìesque tower, festooned with creepers. Complementary to the eldritch exterior there is a gorgeously quirky interior with gnomework banisters. Now there was an opportunity to take part in a genuinely community-driven experiment in green building within Graham's immediate environs. Or so it seemed.

However, according to its detractors, after the development was given planning permission, there quickly appeared several breaches of trust which began to divide local opinion. Critics claimed several aspects of the development directly contravened the spirit and letter of original agreements, including the failure to provide promised affordable housing, the construction of buildings with additional storeys that overlooked neighbouring houses, the slippage of schedules for the completion of work causing prolonged disruption to the wider neighbourhood, the creation of sub-lets for private profit which in turn raised occupancy numbers generating more traffic. Most serious were allegations of a kind of cultural cleansing as AVAG facilitated the systematic removal of live-in vehicles, resulting in the exclusion of travellers from the area. Critics held that such infringements were an almost inevitable consequence of handing over control to a private limited company, no longer answerable to the local community for its activities. The offices that it was hoped could be rented to generate to plough back into the community were sold for conversion to private dwellings. The legacy, therefore, was a development that, while its unconventional low-impact designs and location made it attractive to house buyers who could afford to live there, became a more conventional private housing estate in terms of its tenure. Graham had been opposed to the personal interests of the self-builders coming to dominate the make-up of AVAG which he'd originally conceived as not-for-profit and believed should have been constituted to represent the community as a whole. Saddened and disillusioned by the apparent triumph of private profiteering over community well-being, Graham resigned from AVAG and, disillusioned, moved to his present home in Ronda, Spain after living in Bristol for twenty years.

Conclusion: Eco-Anarchism - Refusing the Inevitable

The ideas behind [Street Farmer] magazine were modest; basically, we wanted to have a world revolution, get rid of the state and live in an anarchist utopia.[301]

As a case study, I believe my work with Street Farm demonstrates the unsurpassed value of oral-history interviews as a method for revealing the overlooked experiences of unofficialdom. The time when the post-War decades exist as living history in the memories of those who experienced them is of course limited. There is a continuous transition from living history – the recollection of the past in directly remembered experiences – to documentary history, available to us for interpretation only through records such as written accounts, photographs, archive film footage, physical artefacts and environmental evidence. This is a moving line; at the time of writing it could be placed at approximately 1923, a date when those born around 1913 were old enough to reasonably recall some details of their earliest years. By such a measure the 1970s are clearly well within living memory. Yet documents are lost, memories fail, personal networks are unknotted, generations pass on. History is notoriously fragile, so it is also true that only those born in the 1960s and earlier, already middle aged or older, can remember the early 1970s and many participants in the alternative scene during that era are no longer alive. The nature of the counterculture or the 'underground'

301 Peter Crump, 'Street Farm', talk at Bristol Anarchist Bookfair, 7 May 2011.

was especially marginalised and ephemeral. It is therefore all the more urgent to capture alternative and radical history so that it is allocated its rightful place in the collective memory and not erased. The task of such history is not only to record facts of the time but to offer a glimpse into what might have been; a counterfactual account of the past.

Beyond the prominent and now well documented underground of Pink Floyd and *Oz* there existed in London a perhaps larger, less documented network – the contributors to *Street Farmer* magazine were voices from that yet more subterranean underground, off-centre from the core grooviness of Archigram, Carnaby Street and the pop aristocracy, trying to reconfigure the new Jerusalem of the metropolis according to a different vision of the future.

Street Farm were a distillation of several features of the counterculture. They embraced political anarchism, drawing upon Situationism, a New-Left rejection of both capitalism and statist models of socialism and communism (widely discredited by the Soviet experience) and also an emerging ecological awareness. They took up many of the practices now often associated with the late 1960's, early 1970's period, including underground journalism, squatting, communal living, rock music, liberatory technology, self-sufficiency and multimedia performance. At the same time I hope that the preceding chapters keep sight of the fact that Street Farm were also a unique blossoming of that counterculture.

Street Farm took their first small, steady hoof steps towards the verdant pastures of London WC1 at the outset of the 1970s. In common with recent initiatives such as Transition Culture and the Occupy movement, they still provoke us to think about what an urban environment could be, as distinct from the physical reality of the traffic-choked interchanges, brutalist blocks and advertising hoardings that dominate city life. It is unlikely that anyone would rationally set out to design present-day metropolises, with their shoddy compromises between state planning and market forces. In this respect Barry Commoner's diagnosis of environmental problems remains as true today as when he wrote it in 1972:

> What is real in our lives and, in contrast to the reasonable logic of ecology, chaotic and intractable, is the apparently hopeless inertia of the economic and political system; its fantastic agility in sliding away from the basic issues which logic reveals; the selfish manoeuvring of those in power, and their willingness to use, often unwittingly, and sometimes cynically, even environmental deterioration as a step toward more political power; the frustration of the individual citizen confronted by this power and evasion; the confusion that we all feel in seeking a way out of the environmental morass. To bring environmental logic into contact with the real world we need to relate it to the over-all social, political, and economic forces that govern both our daily lives and the course of history.[302]

As we have seen, Street Farm proposed instead cities that were ecologically sustainable, organised for social needs not private profits or for the benefit of political elites, and run on principles of direct democracy. Street Farm were not anti-technology, but recognised the problems that beset urban living were not, finally, to be solved through technocratic solutions, requiring instead social and political transformation, indeed revolution. However, beyond toppling and replacing the current establishment to affect 'regime change', the kind of revolution required was nothing less than profound cultural renovation and a fundamental change in the human interaction with each other and our environment.

302 Barry Commoner, *The Closing Circle: Confronting the Environmental Crisis* (London: Jonathan Cape, 1972), 294.

'Revolutionary urbanism' therefore was a desire for liberation in the nature and quality of our daily lives; for a transformation of the visual appearance, sound and smell, the texture and ambience of the urban environment, for worker and community control of the means of production, for an upending and flattening of the hierarchic triangle of political structures and for a reconsideration of the human relationship with other species and their habitats. As such it was both a toolbox for practical change and a call for an upheaval of dominant cultural values and worldviews, somehow attempting to synthesise individual change and collective action (a contention that is still an endlessly repeated staple of political debate on the libertarian left).

The countercultural philosophy of the Woodstock generation represents the road not travelled. The politically orientated members of the hippy underground identified the problem of state power and its weapons of social control in the forms of repression, mystification, alienation, division and surveillance. They did not succeed, however, in building up a sufficiently numerous and inclusive constituency of contrarians who shared the solidarity, practical purpose and vision necessary to confront it. There may, to borrow the title of John Jordan and Isabelle Fremeaux's film, be many 'pathways to utopia', but, notwithstanding countless inspirational attempts, none of the alternatives at the end of these meandering green lanes has been scaled up and linked beyond the marginal or ephemeral. Tactical prefiguration is frozen in its nascent state, never actualised to a more expansive and durable configuration. How to explain this in broad terms? Needless to say there is, thankfully, no monolithic counterculture but multiple countercultures of which the revolutionary urbanism of eco-anarchism is but one tangled skein. In this sense a characteristic countercultural dilemma consists in the contradiction that great strength and vitality in diversity can at times be weakness in disunity and incoherence. By contrast the institutions of state and capital which revolutionary urbanism opposes have continued to engender and retain enough loyalty from a sufficient proportion of the population to systematically check, undermine and close down radical alternatives. Capitalism has, to date, also delivered adequate goods to enough people in terms of increasing economic growth, albeit at the cost of environmental degradation and extreme inequalities in wealth and power. Hitherto, therefore, strategies of repression, division and recuperation have enabled the mighty chest of the state to withstand pummellings from the clenched fists of dissidents.

Equally, collective political strategies of resistance have all too often collapsed of their own accord. It is beyond the purpose of the present discussion to add to the voluminous debates about why this may have been the case. The recent appearance of the Occupy movement, most promising in its international reach, showed that the counterculture can still blossom. However, the lack of a unifying cause, at once a sign of its strength in diversity and yet also a symptom of its failure to formulate and communicate a coherent and cohesive alternative, has become apparent in its meteoric rise and equally rapid tailing away. Occupy's people's assemblies were an attractive and impressive instance of the possibilities of an engaging face-to-face political process beyond the inane and disempowering exercise of the five-yearly ballot, a refreshing alternative transcending the limitations of hierarchical splinter groups. Yet, to up-scale horizontalism a system of mandated and instantly recallable delegates is required to connect with a wider federation if such decision making is to avoid the often repeated problem of the tyranny of structurelessness. Somewhat sceptical of horizontalism, David Harvey, presently one of the left's most prominent theorists in cultural geography, cites Murray Bookchin's libertarian municipalism as a possible solution to the impasse in the fortunes of grassroots countercultural groups.[303]

Whatever the political dilemmas that beset the New Left and its successors, Street Farm did not finally lay down their crooks and pitchforks because they found their wider politics wanting – certainly neither Crump nor Caine from the core collective has disavowed their 1970's radicalism. To acknowledge limits to the possibilities of individuals as agents for change is not to detract from that 1970's catchphrase 'the personal is political'. How many projects, communes, agit-prop papers, activist groups and alternative spaces must have foundered due to unresolved interpersonal conflicts and dysfunctional small-group dynamics? In this respect Robin Clarke shares a salutary tale of the difficulties that this perennial problem presents in his account of a short-lived self-sufficient rural commune in Wales.[304] At this time it was possible to buy a 43-acre farm with cottage and out-buildings for £10, 000. Clarke frankly acknowledged that it was interpersonal issues, rather than technical and economic difficulties, that defeated BRAD (Biotechnic Research and Development), a 16-strong community venture. This was despite the fact that all members approached the project as people of good will with a common purpose. Peter Crump's experience of the comparable EarthWorkshop scheme had been similar. Readers old enough to have watched the BBC's early reality television series *Living in the Past* (1978) may remember that interpersonal differences enlivened, though did not destroy, the experiment of the featured community who lived self-sufficiently for a year as Iron-Age villagers in rural Dorset. Like Street Farm, many have been unsuccessful in sustaining alternative collectives over a long period. Individual life paths almost inevitably diverge as members move on to pursue other projects, experience life changes that prove

303 David Harvey, *Rebel Cities: From the Right to the City to the Urban Revolution* (London: Verso, 2012), 84-85.
304 Robin Clarke, *Technological Self-Sufficiency* (London: Faber & Faber, 1976), chaps. 1 and 16.

incompatible or simply agree to part as personal differences emerge.

Street Farm also fit a model whereby radical groups form as a catalyst for radical change filling a niche when there is a particular need and opportunity and then disbanding before they ossify. Taoist like, the vitality and dynamism of such groups in some ways rests in their provisional, fluid nature and ephemerality, their propensity to fragment, disappear and coalescence anew with new formations, strategies and fresh impetus. Crump observed that such small countercultural groups either formed on an *ad hoc* basis for a particular reason and circumstances and then disappeared, or else turned into something rather less radical.[305]

Political Process Theory holds that groups and projects such as Street Farm emerge and thrive, or lose impetus, at particular historical moments as part of broader new social movements according to the prevailing political circumstances and opportunities of the time. Certainly members of Street Farm were able to exploit and expand a number of existing positives, and in doing so help to generate and keep open alternative spaces for others. By the early 1970s there were relatively high employment levels, real wages and educational opportunities in comparison with previous decades, a trend since reversing at a time of 'austerity'. This strengthened the working class's collective bargaining power and afforded improved life chances and flexibility of action. Idealistically motivated members of the counterculture were also willing to work long hours to take control over their lives and to pursue their hunger for revolutionary change. Caine recalled:

> I grew up in a corrugated asbestos prefab, [...] and I have done stuff in my life which I feel proud to have lived in so many ways with dignity, which I largely attribute to my mother's

305 Personal conversation with Peter Crump, Montpelier, Bristol, 24 August 2012.

> determination to provide my brother and I with the best chances as she struggled to provide by sewing bras together as our only source of income.[306]

Based in London, Street Farm members also had rich opportunities for what in present-day terminology would be termed social networking. They could access and connect into local, national and international networks of fellow activists with whom they recognised and shared a common cause. There was a proliferation of radical ideas and shared practice – facilitated by relatively cheap transport options, extensive telephone access, community bookshops and resource centres and alternative media such as the *Alternative London* directory. Concentrations of like-minded people, for example the diversity of people in Kentish Town's 'Squat City', made possible a cross-fertilisation of ideas and mutual aid. An alternative society of this kind – a phenomenon that US theorist Hakim Bey would later term a 'Temporary Autonomous Zone' – created opportunities by supporting a provisional infrastructure of ventures such as I.R.A.T. Printers and the wholefood, information and communication centre whose community supplies were consciousness raising as well as nutritional. Such developments required an availability of physical spaces, in the form of otherwise derelict buildings and unused land and people with enough disposable income to assure freedom from absolute material want. During the late 1960s and early 1970s there was were also cultural and political momentum towards to a more libertarian future, with the relaxation of statutes against 'homosexual acts' and abortion and the censorship of literature and the theatre and the abolition of the death penalty. The relatively liberal administrations of these years did not undertake the more extreme censorship and surveillance of

306 Graham Caine, e-mail message to the author 29 December 2012.

totalitarian regimes, while the extensive and sophisticated methods of social control and issue management by global corporations in the present day was yet to come.

All was far from well, however, in the early 1970s and the counterculture thrived because of the desperate need for alternatives, then as now. The ubiquitous psychological chill of the Cold War, accompanied by armed conflicts across the globe, most prominently in Vietnam and Ireland, set the context alongside social injustice, alienation and environmental destruction. These – and their root causes – were the ultimate target of all of Street Farm's output whether through physical projects, protests, roadshows or polemical communications. Disappointingly, less radical accommodations with unsustainable capitalism have since come to characterise the environmental movement, in the form of green consumerism and technocratic eco-pragmatism. As astute Situationists, Street Farm members are well aware that, ironically, some of the achievements of their generation's radical technology have been recuperated. Capitalism has dragged the vehicle for change into its chop shops, stripping off the practical components of alternative technology to sell while leaving the frame and bodywork of political autonomy behind.

What is left is to consider what a 'revolutionary urbanism' might be, both from the hints in Street Farm that we have seen, and, at a time of economic austerity and continuing, indeed accelerating, ecological crisis, today and in the future. At such a time the mist-shrouded shores of utopia seem a distant prospect indeed. Yet, in the context of mass disaffection with both state-socialist and neo-Liberal remedies for the deterioration of civic life, the need for a genuinely progressive, utopian approach is as great as ever. In Pinder's words:

> A utopian impulse remains necessary [...] for confronting the challenge of creating better futures through its emphasis on

> exploring possibilities and what could be. A utopianism for the present, furthermore cannot afford simply to ignore or discard past visions; it needs to come to terms with those histories, and may indeed find ways of using them as it forges its own poetry with different futures in mind.[307]

In keeping with the suggestion made in Chapter 4, the following components of what might constitute a 'revolutionary urbanism' can be visualised as a loose network of nodes comprising an overarching dome of associated ideas. By way of a conclusion, this amounts to a distillation of some of the key elements of eco-anarchism. Most of them appear one way or another in Street Farm's writings. In keeping with their libertarian ethos, Street Farm were keen to stress that they were not about dictating a prescriptive template for a future society. As Crump put it, in reference to one of David Shrigley's cartoons:

> "An unfinished plan for a better society" was really what we were about. We weren't really about designing a utopia, but we were about providing the means and the analysis to get you there.[308]

So I offer these elements, in the spirit that Street Farm offered their ideas, not as a rigid manifesto or blueprint but rather, to use the terminology of the 1970s, as an index of alternative possibilities.

1. Direct democracy and decentralisation: Libertarian polity aspires to authentic egalitarian empowerment and participation in a classless society, ensuring justice while making efficient decisions so that communities thrive. Dispersal and deconstruction of power vested in centralised hierarchies to make for radical decentralisation

307 Pinder, *Visions of the City*, vii.
308 Peter Crump, 'Street Farm', talk at Bristol Anarchist Bookfair, 7 May 2011.

of decision-making structures. Accountability no longer subordinate to the political interests of state, capital or religious elites. Principle of subsidiarity so that decisions are taken at the appropriate level for those affected by their consequences. Inclusive decision-making structures most appropriate to the functions for which they are responsible. Bookchin's notion of libertarian municipalism provides a model that constitutes a strong starting point for this approach. He envisaged local and regional governance through community participation best suited to decisions of locality, expressing the views and needs of those who know a particular area best. In the spirit of traditional anarchism, this would entail decision making in such entities as local assemblies and street communes. Provisional and recallable delegates on rotation rather than representatives undertake participation in a larger regional confederation, or 'a commune of communes' with powers limited to administrative roles.[309] Many eco-anarchists favour some version of bioregionalism.

Such structures work in tandem with workers' councils and cooperatives to deliberate upon issues concerning the production of goods and services. Delegates within an international federation might be best suited to coordinate particular services such as telecommunications, or productive enterprises such as ship building. Making use of knowledge sharing to inform and nourish decision-making process without thereby facilitating the re-emergence and domination of an expert class.

If chains of production, supply and consumption are shorter, then democratic participatory control over the whole process becomes more viable – there are 'well calibrated feedback loops'.[310] This empowers individuals and communities, hence reducing alienation and facilitating cooperation. An increase in regional or

309 Andy Price, *Recovering Bookchin: Social Ecology and the Crises of Our Time* (Porsgrunn, Norway: New Compass Press, 2012), 225-226.
310 Lewis and Conaty, *The Resilience Imperative*, 240.

local, rather than global, production of commodities would provide considerable ecological benefits, as current centralised supply operations are economically efficient only because of the artificial subsidy of non-renewable energy sources.

Issues: Hinges upon the fundamental intersubjective problem of what it means to be an individual in a society of others. Where does the community stop, and start? How to ensure that the interests of the current members of a neighbourhood take into account and respect the needs of its future members and wider local, regional and international society? How to overcome apathy and empower people for ongoing participation? How to ensure that the interests of young children and those with severe learning disabilities or severe mental illness are upheld? How to prevent privileging of certain personality types such as extroverts over introverts? While a successful decision-making process is an achievement in its own right as well as a means to an end, there is still a need for quick and efficient solutions without being burdened by endless disputative debate. Ensuring that horizontal structures do not entail a 'tyranny of structurelessness'. Ensuring the effective distribution of the productive commonwealth so that those with easiest access to natural resources such as fertile soil, valuable mineral deposits and abundant fresh water are integrated in a system of distributive mutual aid and do not exercise power and advantage through resource monopoly. The push and pull of potential tensions between the local needs of autonomous communities and the need to observe the wider needs of the bioregion or global confederation so that international priorities, for example, to observe human rights, distribute resources equitably and care for global ecologies, are not negated by, parochial self-interest and xenophobic perspectives. Would entail abolition of competing interests and conflicts of class society. Dependent upon the evolution of public-spirited citizens with internationalist sensibilities.

Street Farm: 'Workers of the world disperse' (*SF* 1); 'Within themselves all groups have the knowledge to make correct decisions about all matters which effect them. Only they do have the ability to make the correct decision. Any group which does not include all those people canNOT reach the correct decision!' (*SF* 2); 'The "problems will disappear as the whole force of the people's organism is brought to bear on them [...] The council is the only power it will itself tolerate. At its inception other organisations of state and party disappear because by its existence it makes them redundant and irrelevant.' (*SF* 2); 'The council is not finite, has no constitution, no legality, no quorum, no structure, it is not lasting, it is not the end of revolution, but where the revolution starts!' (*SF* 2).

2. Ecological awareness: Not only for human-centred purposes but that respects the integrity of the natural environment and autotelic worth of other species in their own right. Revolutionary urbanism must be ecologically sustainable.

Issues: Urgency to maintain biodiversity and stem the catastrophic extinction of species by converting from capitalist system of undifferentiated economic growth to steady-state economy. Need to accommodate human population, projected to continue to rise in the medium-term future, achieving and maintaining a decent standard of living for all. Requires a new ecopsychological understanding of human relationship to the natural environment. Spiritual growth required to cultivate relational, ecological selves for holistic consideration of the living world and future generations.

Street Farm: 'The alienation of people from their environment' (*SF* 1); 'Ecology appreciation... help restore your natural harmony by spending time up in a tree' (*SF* 1); 'Cows arise' ('Threatening Letter'); 'The land belongs to the communities of the biosphere, not individuals of the human race' ('Threatening Letter'); 'Modern urbanism, the physical manifestation of hierarchical systems, is but a further aspect of the ecological disorder that follows the very logic of capitalism' (*SF* 2).

3. Steady-state economy: Economic forces engaged to meet human needs not private profits. Eco-anarchists reject the imperative of perpetual economic growth as an inherent contradiction of capitalism. Physical constraints of life on a finite planet mean that unsustainable expansion cannot ensure the well-being of humanity or protect the survival of other species. As we are materially embodied beings this situation is unlikely to change in the short- to medium-term unless inhabitancy beyond the Earth becomes viable. While not available at the time of Street Farm, Michael Albert and Robin Hehnal's proposals for participatory economics provide promising groundwork for post-capitalist economics, combining social justice and environmental sustainability. Creative commons of ideas in cooperative society to unleash latent cultural renaissance.

Issues: Means of transition from capitalist system and state control!

Street Farm: 'Does capitalist free-for-all & communist five-year-plans mean the inevitable need to produce "ad nauseam" until we choke our planet to death… or can some people find a balance where living in harmony with the natural environment is enough to satisfy them?' (*SF* 2); 'All glory to the G.N.P' (*SF* 2).

4. Rational organisation of space: Changes of land use decided at an inclusive, participatory community level. Return of public buildings, thoroughfares and open spaces to common ownership. Infrastructure for the production of commodities and services likewise organised to meet social needs. Architects, designers and planners as enablers of community empowerment, rather than consolidating the inequities of a planning system based on private property. Efficient and rational use of land to prioritise the following: food production, accommodation, physical and mental health and social care, education, basic service utilities transport and telecommunications infrastructure, ready access to recreational land and (more) natural environment, resource centres as repositories for information and shared equipment and community venues. Production for commonweal rather than 'wealth creation' serving the interests of the economic elites who currently dictate through market domination. Reclaiming and imaginative repurposing or retrofitting of buildings and land currently unproductively used for car parks, office blocks, military purposes or the production of harmful and unnecessary commodities. Slow build if necessary to meet highest standards of design and construction.

Residential areas integrated with sustainable local production and green spaces. 'Greening' and dispersal of urban areas for local production of food and goods, enhancement of air quality and ecological diversity. Social impetus to redress vast imbalances between concentration of metropolis and sprawl of conurbations and dormitory towns lacking economic and cultural infrastructure. Implementation of restoration ecology and rewilding.

Issues: Conflicting opinions as to 'social needs'. Whether the character of space should best evolve organically according to social needs or whether those social needs are best met by factoring them in during a fresh start, along the pattern of Ebenezer Howard's garden cities. Tensions between competing needs, to accommodate increasing human population and to respect ecological imperatives.

Industrialism's legacy of contamination. What means to reverse current patterns of development? Exodus to the countryside could sometimes have progressive benefits, helping to change social conservatism of some rural areas.

Street Farm: 'The parks are urban campsites' (*SF* 1); 'Urbanism has been experienced as the capitalist definition of space' (*SF* 2); 'Provisional Farm Plan (subject to the whim of the people)' (*SF* 2); 'Provincialism is the manifestation of rurality, the illusionary salvation from urbanism' (*SF* 1); 'a change in the quality of both urbanity and rurality' (*SF* 1); 'the elimination of the duality of town and country' (*SF* 1); 'a process that means the end of the countryside just as much as the end of cities' ('Threatening Letter'); 'Fight back with nature, plant seeds in the pavement and push up the slabs' (*Open Door*).

5. Community ownership: Howard brought together several ideas for progressive planning reform to create the garden cities movement. A crucial feature was that the land was community leased; an aspect diluted in the garden cities and suburbs that were completed. This offered a third way to the binary options of private property or state control. Occupiers have provisional control of accessible housing rather than renting from private landlords, agencies or local government. To prevent speculation, however, such homes under community ownership cannot be sold for profit and have no automatic right of inheritance. It is hoped that occupiers would maintain and improve homes for the benefit of themselves and the community. Such a shift would help to end a legacy of enclosure and reclaim wider commons. It would also encourage longer tenure in so far as people would relocate when and if they desired to do so for personal reasons, rather than being coerced by demands to be 'flexible' in employment as at present. Other traditions of common ownership have incorporated traditional usufruct as a means to share and protect access to land, goods and amenities.

By the late 1960s several radical critics wished to enable, in Colin Ward's term, 'dweller control'.[311] The rise of political squatting drew attention to, and challenged, the widespread presence of empty buildings as a loss to the commonweal, scandalously existing alongside housing shortages and homelessness. Democratic planning for community benefit should aim to accommodate a variety of demographics and household structures, while discouraging the single occupation of large buildings. It should accept and enable self-build. It should encourage experimentation, while preserving historic buildings.

Issues: Who and how to assess and allocate fairly? What to do about anti-social neighbours! Recent criminalisation of residential squatting and constraints upon self-housing initiatives – such as canal boat dwelling and low-impact living – push ever greater numbers from independence into dependence upon over-stretched public housing or dysfunctional private sector.

Street Farm: 'People realise that the land belongs to everyone equally' (*SF* 1); 'If you want to own land, you can't have it 'cause it ain't only yours it's mine 'cause i can see it hear it smell it touch it speak to it and love it too' (*SF* 2).

6. Autonomous off-grid housing and more sustainable architecture: Aspiration to enhance self-reliance and reduce dependence on long supply chains for services and goods, while attaining decent, convenient and comfortable homes for all. Street Farm's practical

311 Colin Ward, *Housing: An Anarchist Approach*, new ed. with a postscript (London: Freedom, 1983), chap. 5.

experiments sought to develop appropriate technology that would liberate households and communities from dependence upon state agencies and private profit-making corporations for the basics of domestic life. A low-impact approach entails a preference for locally sourced or recycled materials with short supply chains. There is a need for a programme of retrofitting existing older housing stock to incorporate more recent innovations in energy efficiency and conservation. Such a programme would help to address the urgent necessity to curb climate change and create an infrastructure fit for a significantly more efficient, low-energy, low-carbon economy in the near future. In this respect the American environmentalist Richard Heinberg advocates an urgent process of 'cooperation, contraction, and conversion.'[312] Renewable technology and energy conservation has improved significantly since the early 1970s. State of the art developments such as Passivhaus technology promise to maximise heating of homes by combining airtightness with an air filtration and circulation system. Microgeneration could facilitate the greater decentralisation of society which would contribute towards the political imperative for an empowered, self-realised society.

Issues: Access to land. Intensive maintenance and availability of technical skills. Current planning issues. New houses still not being built to highest energy-efficient standard. Costs of latest developments prohibitive for most people (and implicitly requiring capital to be raised, usually by energy intensive means). Technical problems of storage and transmission of energy. Environmentalists lack consensus on the fundamental issues of whether high-density living in cities with advantages such as readily available public transport, outweigh those of great self-sufficiency in rural areas

312 Richard Heinberg, *Powerdown: Options and Actions for a Post-Carbon World* (West Hoathly, West Sussex: Clairview Books, 2004).

facilitating devolved production with shorter supply chains.

Street Farm: 'The award will be utilised to construct a domestic unit <u>independent of mains supply and waste services.</u>' (*SF* 1); 'Within the "Ecological House" which I believe is a REAL ALTERNATIVE to official architecture the individual is not only involved in its production, he is directly involved within the biological cycles that constitute so much of its life support systems' (Caine, *Revolutionary Structure*).

7. Commuting reduced to a minimum: Commuting is a colossal free subsidy that bosses get from their workers in a so-called free market. 'Forget the damned motor car and build the cities for lovers and friends.' So wrote Lewis Mumford in *My Work and Days* (1979). To end the hegemony of the private car would ease countless human problems. Extended networks of community-owned advanced passenger transit systems to liberate settlements from the gridlock of low-occupancy private cars. Homes situated near to creative, worthwhile, fulfilling work and necessary or desirable facilities and services – food, culture, hospitals and dentists, educational facilities for all. Improve health of population as a whole due to better air quality, fewer traffic accidents and increase in exercise. Reduce damaging emissions from private vehicles so addressing climate change and damage to fabric of historic buildings. Free up and reallocate land and buildings presently used for car infrastructure – road systems, car parking, fuel stations, refineries, prime agricultural land used for biofuel production. Locally; save time wasted and achieve transition to creative, pleasurable, sociable travel to replace commuter stress; more convivial, safer streets for adults and children. Internationally; reduce energy insecurity and political power of fossil-fuel producing nations.
Issues: Cultural addiction to cars has created personal dependency

that makes it difficult for many individuals to forgo this nineteenth-century mode of transport in the Twenty-First Century. Infrastructure has evolved to accommodate the car economy with facilities such as out of town superstores far from home, often unreliable and expensive public transport, constraints upon personal mobility and depopulated streets evoking fears for personal security. Dispersal of people requires' love miles' to maintain physical contact with friends and family. Difficulties in extending public transport infrastructure to thinly populated areas.

Street Farm: 'Every traffic jam makes us laugh' (*SF 1*); 'The plan to seed the pavements with grass makes it impossible to walk on the pavements resulting in the use of the streets for pedestrians, closing the streets to vehicular traffic (*SF* 2); 'The plan for rowing boat canal commuting makes what is already work in itself the total work and a pleasant task. On arrival the commuter would just have time to relax before having to set off home. No office work would be done. On wet days he could not travel to work. Of course he would soon realise that he did not have to go to work and could row anywhere or not at all' (*SF* 2); 'All car windscreens were painted black. All vehicular travel ceased. Motorway signposts felled and used to construct "cabins," using flyovers as basic roof and wall structures... good sites for these dwellings is on the path of motorways nearest to the industrial estate belt' (*SF* 2).

8. Transcendence of limited technocratic solutions to social problems: Pinder suggests that thinkers who have attempted to recommend an ideal city have foregrounded one of two aspects.[313] First, are those that aspire to perfection in the aesthetic and functional qualities of the city as a more or less bounded physical

313 Pinder, *Visions of the City*, 22.

space, which entails imagining the optimum, or most magnificent, architectural form, infrastructure and inventing and getting in place the 'right' technology. The second approach is taken by those thinkers who prioritise the political and psychological nature of urban space, concerning themselves with such issues as power relationships, communication and regulation within the city. For all their work in alternative technology, Street Farm propose that the crises of alienation, violence and injustice that beset conventionally constituted cities are for the most part the result of systemic political and economic failings rather than the outcomes of technological problems. As an expression of Situationism, itself within the tradition of Marxist cultural materialism, revolutionary urbanism demands that consciousness must be raised as to the dialectical relationship between physical conditions and the nature of a society's superstructure, such as prevailing psychological and political factors, if an ecologically sustainable, joyous utopia is to be realised.

Issues: How to take control of research, development and implementation of appropriate technology for the qualitative benefit of all, rather than being conditioned by present technological determinism.

Street Farm: 'The "environmental crisis" is a crisis of society not a crisis of technology and if one agrees with the theme that the technology of a civilisation is a reflection of its social structure it is not surprising that our civilisation has produced a life killing technology' (Caine, 'Revolutionary Structure').

9. Permaculture: Aspiration to sustainable production for social needs. Permaculture – intentional design for sustainability – takes a holistic approach to the art of living, working with local environments and ecosystems and using renewable resources to meet human needs. There is much common ground between the integrated approach of those like Street Farm who promoted autonomous housing, and the locally based solutions that Bill Mollison and David Holmgren favoured when they drew up the principles of permaculture during the late 1970s. Advocates of mixed production on micro-farms, smallholdings and in gardens hold that they can match agribusiness for the quality, and often the quantity, of their harvests.[314] Soil fertility prioritised as a matter of principle and aim to minimise input of fossil fuels.

Issues: While one of the twelve permaculture design principles is to 'use edges and value the marginal', advocates face the difficulty that, more than thirty years since the principles were set out, permaculture is itself still widely regarded as marginal when measured against agribusiness. As Street Farm discovered when they were forced to dismantle the Ecological House in 1976, constraints against access to land remain significant obstacles to building and growing alternatives. To paraphrase Pierre-Joseph Proudhon, current patterns of land allocation and planning laws all too often amount to insurmountable chains for low-impact permaculturalists, but easily evaded cobwebs for agribusiness and high-impact developers.

Street Farm: 'Our land has had FARMING confiscated from it… and an industry called AGRICULTURE imposed on it' ('Threatening Letter'); 'Chemical farming destroys the land. The expanding dependent populations of the rich nations continue to be fed by high intensity farming, but it is an illusion – the "soil-bank" is depleted year by year' (*SF* 2).

314 For example, see Fred Pearce, *The Landgrabbers: The New Fight over Who Owns the Planet* (London: Eden Project / Transworld, 2012), Chap. 27, or articles in the excellent magazine *The Land* (http://www.thelandmagazine.org.uk/).

10. Workers' control and cooperative production: In the post-capitalist utopian city we would expect to find maximum direct democratic control. Workers' cooperatives coordinate industrial production and farming. Decision-making process taking form of workplace democracy with consumer input. Communication and coordination with cooperatives representing all trades and services and across regions through federated model. Production for plentiful subsistence with balanced job complexes integral to participatory economics. Relationship between home, workplace and other human activities more integrated. Goods crafted-produced, with mass-production for standardised commodities to avoid tedious and hazardous toil where appropriate. Hardware goods designed for utility, aesthetics and long-life. Free sharing of skills and ideas in creative commons. Reconciliation of needs for abundance, social justice and sustainability through libraries of equipment, recycling and design for durability. For Goodman and Goodman, planned obsolescence is 'not only ugly and foolish but morally outrageous, and the perpetrators should be ostracized from decent society'.[315]

Issues: Transition from present-day dominance of unaccountable global corporations. Pathways from current control of individuals and populations through financial debt. Militant Syndicalist strategies represent the greatest potential for reclaiming power by non-military means but dependent upon a substantial growth in class consciousness, manifest through solidarity and mutual aid.

Street Farm: 'Business replaced by small scale super efficient cooperatives mass producing variety' (*SF* 1); 'We shall learn to live together satisfied with the shared rights of good food, clothing,

315 Paul Goodman, and Percival Goodman, *Communitas: Means of Livelihood and Ways of Life* [1947], new ed. (New York: Vintage, 1960), 174.

shelter and human companionship in nature' (*SF* 2); 'Uncataloguing is the antithesis of advertising' (*SF* 2); 'individual and collective production by the community (commune) will result in the production of what is needed' (*SF* 2).

11. Aesthetically pleasing: A revolutionary urbanism that aspires to the satisfaction of social needs and desires, must promote the establishment of conditions to create aesthetically pleasing buildings and encourage citizens' positive engagement with place and reinhabitation if it is to raise the quality of life for all and revitalise the totality of human experience. We might surely still learn much from earlier traditions, borrowing, for example, from the grace and beauty of indigenous handicrafts and artistic movements such as Arts and Crafts, Secession and Art Nouveau, Gothick, Surrealism and such thinkers as William Morris, Charles Voysey, Antoni Gaudì and Friedensreich Hundertwasser.

Planners of the garden cities movement, such as Raymond Unwin and Barry Parker, aspired to incorporate high standards of design to create housing that matched aesthetics to functional concerns such as making maximum use of natural light, achieving a sense of cosiness according to the best heat retention methods available at the time and, where possible, aligning dwellings to the south and providing focal points for pleasing views. Aesthetics would reflect and instil a social commitment to autonomy and vernacular distinctiveness by making use of local material. At the same time it would be wise to exploit standardisation where appropriate to share components and link services in order to cooperate within a wider confederation of communities across regional and even planetary networks of mutual aid. To stroll among the cooperative variety of a liberated neighbourhood would be an unending adventure through a living space.

Issues: Subjective nature of what is aesthetically pleasing; how to achieve consensus in this respect without being reduced to either a monotonous conformity or a free-for-all melange of styles detracting from and clashing with each other. How to prioritise cumulative, progressive development, given the legacy of existing environment.

Street Farm: 'OH GOD WHAT AN UGLY CITY EVERY CITY IS' (*SF* 1, quoting Vonnegut, *Cat's Cradle*); 'The most beautiful aspects of life are projected as the background to the stage of consumer society' ('Threatening Letter').

12. Thought to street furniture: Better design of common street furniture would help to transform urban life. The implementation of stand-alone, off-grid street lighting, angled to beam downwards to maximise lux at ground level would reduce light pollution and aid the appreciation of night skies. Light pollution affects the circadian rhythms of humans and other species and damages the ambience of life both in cities, and increasingly, rural areas. Two startling statistics illuminate the problem. The Campaign for the Protection for Rural England estimates that light pollution in England increased by 24 % between 1993 and 2000.[316] The British Astronomical Association's Campaign for Dark Skies estimates that lights that illuminate above the horizontal axis waste 30-50% of their energy output.[317] Street lighting designed on the principles of utopian technology would be aesthetically pleasing, like fine Victorian street lamps (the ammonite-shaped lights at Lyme Regis, for instance, are locally distinctive and elegant), while incorporating advanced features, such as microgeneration and possibly LEDs, to maximise efficiency

316 Campaign for the Protection of Rural England website, see http://www.cpre.org.uk/what-we-do/countryside/dark-skies/the-issues [accessed 4 October 2012].
317 Campaign for Dark Skies website, see http://www.britastro.org/dark-skies/inf003.htm [accessed 4 October 2012].

while minimising energy consumption. This would liberate communities from the need for excessive maintenance and energy generation and transmission, thereby facilitating greater autonomy by replacing dependence upon corporations and state infrastructure for the provision of centralised services. Alongside this could be the plentiful provision of equally elegant and durable (and vandal-proof) free public toilets, incorporating rainwater capture and urine harvesting and features such as beautiful bicycle racks that would function as public art when not in use.

Issues: Storage of adequate energy for stand-alone lights. Subjective differences about what is 'aesthetically pleasing'. Maintaining safe streets. Labour, time and energy required to retrofit existing system.

Street Farm: Instructions on how to prune and graft traffic signage and parking meters! (*SF* 1, [11]); 'lamp camp sites' in which street lights function as posts around which to anchor temporary shelters (*SF* 1, [17]); motorway flyovers re-used as stages for free festival performers (*SF* 2, 7).

13. Transformation of the conditions of alienation: The notion of alienation was a cornerstone of radical critique in the Twentieth Century. It was expanded in meaning to refer to the separation of workers from the control of productive processes in the workplace, the wider separation of people from the social and physical environment in which they live and the disconnection of humanity from the rest of the natural world. That the term is less frequently used in current social discourse may be not so much because the idea of alienation has been discredited or invalidated, but rather a sign that such disconnection has become so all pervading that the state of alienation is normalised and thus rendered invisible, an abstraction of social theory that is not seen as a sexy rallying cry for political agitation.

Issues: How can we turn this around when our current economic infrastructure and political systems are grounded in the separation that determines the conditions of our alienation? Could we organise society in such a way as to eliminate, or least ameliorate, conditions of alienation and anomie, reclaiming face-to-face relationships, while retaining the gains of inclusion fought for by new social movements and beneficial aspects of individual freedom over conformity?

Street Farm: 'Modern urbanism organises the reaction of all social life to a spectacle, but the only spectacle that it can stage is the that of our own alienation' ('Threatening Letter'); 'Any real alternative is an act of rebellion and is subversive. The quasi-alternative will make the alienation of our situation more tolerable: the real alternative changes the situation' (*SF* 2).

14. Communities in control not controlled communities: Safer streets for all.[318] Empowered communities with ethic of responsibility, trust and self-help. Transformation of property relations to reduce conflict and acquisitive crime. Just as police interrogators are said to employ 'a good cop / bad cop routine to, at turns, soften up and intimidate defendants at the individual level, then at the collective level the police force has a dual, contradictory role as community defenders to protect against anti-social behaviour and at once take on an ideological function in upholding the status quo which enables society's most powerful individuals, institutions and corporates to control and impose their wishes on disempowered populations. This ideological role has become clear recently as the police have

318 A succinct account of anarchist attitudes to crime, and further reading, appears within the Anarchist FAQ series: **http://anarchism.pageabode.com/afaq/secI5.html#seci58** [accessed 25 May 2013].

rapidly dropped their role as neutral community defenders, for example, in Greece where there has been widespread collaboration with the neo-Nazi Golden Dawn movement and in Egypt where police have taken part in attacks upon critics in Tahir Square, both before the Arab Spring and since. In a social revolutionary situation, authentic citizen community defence and people's tribunals for truly anti-social crime must emerge and be effective if the revolution is to survive. Reversal of increasing trend towards extending features of prison regime with gated communities, private security and intensive systems of surveillance. Raising next generation without instilling aggressive competition, alienation and prejudice.

Issues: Accountability of community defence initiatives to whole community. Incentives and dissuaders in a libertarian society.

Street Farm: 'The city is a replica of a power system based upon dividing and ruling, dependent upon the segregation of everything resulting in an anti-social society continually in competition and struggle' (*SF* 1); 'The city is the brain pattern of the bureaucratic mind that's aim is to simplify the control of people' (*SF* 1); 'City based communication exists for the manipulators not the manipulated – it is unidirectional it is simple it ensures surveillance and suppression' (*SF* 1); 'The same tactics that are employed by world police forces are used daily by the builders of our street corners. The same mentality that wages war, designs the cities we live in' (*Open Door*).

15. Convivial street life: A utopian city would be an urban commons greater than the sum of its parts. Even though no one has ever inhabited such a place in its existential totality, for cities are peopled by us humans with our imperfect behaviours, these parts may be familiar to us. Utopia is every place as well as no place; we experience it, glimpse it in fleeting moments and scent it among the stress, exploitation and pollution of existing cities. Its elements are known to us from art and literature but also to be found in the here and now, not only banished to the imaginaries of the prelapsarian past, the science-fiction future or the afterlife. It will be a healthy place with an abundance of the necessities of life and a positive relationship to the surrounding bioregion. Streets will be accommodating to all, the locally distinctive neighbourhoods cosmopolitan in outlook. Residents of convivial streets will be aware and in-touch with their history built up as a patina in well used buildings, artefacts and stories. We would expect to find convivial streets filled with the low-impact hedonism of game playing, discussion, music-making, creative work, feasting, exchanges of news and gifts, journeys into the respectfully experimental. This would be enhanced by the easy circulation of people travelling by sustainable public transport or by their own steam. Convivial streets would be sensuous, diverse, blossoming kinds of places, sprouting indoors and out with ruderals and cultivars and hydroponics, squawking and purring with life tame and feral. There would be endless opportunities for exhilaration and hilarity; reflection and inspiration; serendipity and happenstance. In place of countless office blocks, multi-storey car parks and traffic exchanges every acre would be a destination of sorts. Such places would not be transit zones to pass through, sacrificed and subordinated as means to infinitely deferred ends, but living spaces with intrinsic value. Even factories and industrial production could have aesthetic as well as utilitarian merit. A substantial shift to communal ownership would predominate, except private quarters expressive of the individuality of their residents, and respecting of personal space. A return to such public places as the square or plaza would reverse the trend towards gated communities and privatised shopping malls. Above all convivial street life entails an ethic of connected lookaftering and feeling of belonging in contrast to conditions of alienation.

Issues: Division between public and personal space. Increasing privatisation of public spaces in form of shopping malls, gated communities.

Street Farm: 'The real problems are to do with the isolation of individuals from the community and the disintegration of community' (*SF* 1).

16. Flexibility to adjust interior space and shift location according to need and desire: Archigram experimented with infrastructure to facilitate widespread nomadism, adapting the ideas of Buckminster Fuller. Likewise some of Street Farm's work suggested elements of a plug-in network, the idea being that people could tap into power sources wherever they roamed; in this respect, subsequent developments in ICT have increased possibilities. Another facet of a switch from a fixed to flexible infrastructure was consideration of means to design in adaptability so that it is integral to new building structures. An example would be future-proofing so that walls can be added, removed or redeployed to suit the requirements of shifting households. Standardisation of sizes and the design of interchangeable components would also aid such future-proofing and reduce the huge waste caused by competitive rivalry. Such standardisation does not preclude variety in style of fixtures and fittings. Enabling structures to evolve and adapt would avoid colossal wastage entailed in planned obsolescence which perpetuates the construction, demolition and regeneration of urban areas. In addition to enabling fixed structures to adapt and evolve, while retaining the propensity to acquire the patina of love and use and familiarity, there could be more fluid structures. More widely, greater tolerance and a supportive approach to alternative, low-impact lifestyles and accommodation of itinerant minorities such as travellers, Roma and boat dwellers.

Issues: Who would provide and control such plug-in networks? How to ease longstanding hostility of elements of settled community towards travellers.

Street Farm: 'Antibuilding shelter' (*SF* 1); 'The well-serviced field' (*SF* 1); 'lamp camp sites anywhere' (*SF* 1); tree house (*SF* 1).

17. Personal space and zoneing: The conflicting demands of personal space directly impacts upon the ambience and quality of day-to-day urban living. At present we are typically thrown together cheek by jowl with our fellow human beings, by accident of chance and market forces. Countless Eleanor Rigbys suffer the paradoxical loneliness of the city. Others bemoan the 'neighbours from hell' who perhaps, like weeds, are often just the equivalent of wild flowers whose energy is blossoming in an inappropriate way or in the 'wrong place'. People need moments to sleep, meditate, create and reflect without interruption from pneumatic drills, television and the ceaseless roar of traffic. They may also wish to try out primal scream therapy, to practice sousaphones or bagpipes, have shouty, grunty sex, party all night, to listen to bubblegum pop or prog rock or dubstep or opera or industrial noise. It is true that the negotiation of such tensions is a part of the business of living in society, but vast inequities in power still determine individual experience. The wealthy have opportunities to buy their way out of such difficulties by choosing a detached house in the leafy suburbs and to retreat to an idyllic second home in the country, their time management aided by nannies and cleaners. If there is to be a revolution in the conditions of human existence and the 'fabric' of daily life, such matters affecting well-being and mental health should be addressed for all. Neighbourhood assemblies could set up canteens to share work and create more convivial, less alienated public spaces. Areas could be more rationally zoned to reduce the kinds of conflicts mentioned above. Buildings could be effectively sound-proofed for greater energy conservation and reduction of personal conflict due to noise pollution.

Issues: How to reconcile the separation of activities such as industrial production with advantages of integration, abolishing the divisions between home and workplace? How to prevent the community from meddling in personal lives and imposing stifling conformity, while preventing anti-social behaviour and abuse?

Street Farm: 'Buildings seen to limit lifestyles are unbuilt' (*SF* 1).

18. International solidarity: The black flag of anarchism is a life-affirming anti-flag; it celebrates a thoroughgoing internationalism and cosmopolitanism in which our ultimate and unequivocal allegiance is to humanity at large and the Earth we inhabit. It upholds the principles of local distinctiveness and regional autonomy. In this respect Goodman and Goodman offer a corrective to parochial conceptions of autonomy: 'The fraction of necessary goods that can be produced in a planned region is very substantial, but it is still a fraction. And this fact is the salvation of regionalism! For otherwise regionalism succumbs to provincialism – whether we consider art or literature, or the characters of the people, or the fashions in technology. The regional industrialists in their meeting find that, just because their region is strong and productive, they are subject to strong circles of influence, they have to keep up.'[319] Desiring a world without borders, Anarchist-Communism seeks to confront and abolish imperialism, while transcending narrow, self-interested localism through wider coordinating federations. It aspires to an equitable and just global commonwealth of goods and services for

319 Goodman and Goodman, *Communitas*, 171.

human needs, abolishing the military conflict, extreme poverty and imbalances of wealth and population settlement that characterise the current capitalist era.

Issues: Residual racism, sexism and homophobia, religious conflict and political schism.

Street Farm: 'When we can live as we want to, at one with our brothers and sisters and with nature. When we can do the things we can enjoy and use our time for ourselves then we will have reached a state can be called living' (*SF* 1).

19. Much-loved dwellings to thrive in not just survive: Creation of comfortable, stimulating homes with charm, style and utility, rather than merely functional blocks. Interior spaces in keeping with the ideas of Gaston Bachelard's delightful *Poetics of Space*, providing optimum conditions for self-realisation. Homes with adequate space, incorporating shared good practice in ergonomic design, balancing conflicting human needs for privacy and autonomy, sociability and conviviality. Construction for, and often by, tenants. A sustainable infrastructure of buildings designed to endure and evolve with its users and residents rather than developments with short life expectancy due to in-built obsolescence. Currently, practices of repeated demolition and reconstruction generate profits for construction firms and landowners, rather than meeting demand for housing and other necessities for human well-being. At the same time there would remain a need for complementary structures that can be used flexibly and interchangeably for short term purposes and then removed with minimal environmental impact, for one-off events or seasonal tasks. An approach to building that exploits and expresses the vast and wondrous miscellany of human inventiveness to produce the entire natural history of habitations in all their variety. A celebration of bioclimatic architecture that reflects distinctive local conditions regarding available materials, geography and cultural embellishments. In short, structures fit for a society peopled by human beings not human resources.

Issues: Planning permission is currently easier for standardised housing estates with ever smaller rooms and single occupants than sustainable alternatives. City centres full of dead space of (often empty) office blocks alongside shortages of affordable housing and loss of more natural environment and land for farming. Quality assurance – self-builds might not be well designed and built. Means to achieve appropriate coordination of structures to suit purposes of wider community.

Street Farm: 'Older houses kind of transcend that alienation just because people will have lived there for so long and people will manifest themselves in the house' (*Clearings in the Concrete Jungle*); 'They were chucking up these tower blocks and people were saying: "We don't want to live like this, we don't want this!"... It's against that kind of background that we built this little house' (*Travels with my Chainsaw*).

The desirable elements or nodes in this framework have a direct bearing on the qualities of three of Hundertwasser's concept of five concentric skins – the home (3rd), society (4th) and ecological and planetary context (5th) as outlined in Chapter 2, thus providing the context for those more intimate skins, the epidermis and clothing. This unapologetically utopian outline seeks to suggest elements desirable in an ideal architecture and planning, predicated upon a revolutionary transformation to a post-capitalist society. After all, the notion of a progressive approach immediately begs the question: 'progress towards what?' The kinds of holistic aspirations set out above then, extend to an overarching aspiration towards human well-being and self-realisation at the individual and social level in a sustainable and more harmonious relationship with the natural world and the planet at large. In this sense the utopian wing of the 1960's and 1970's counterculture can be placed within a longer Romantic anti-capitalist tradition, sustained in a dialectical relationship with Industrialism for more than two centuries.[320] The exhortation to 'demand the impossible' was famously daubed on the walls around the Sorbonne.

The glosses to these ideas, however, are roughed up with the abrasion of countervailing issues. Herbert Marcuse, an influential figure for the emerging New Left, considered humanity's future in advanced technological society with trepidation. Would the forces of state and capital become all controlling and truly totalitarian in their reach, to an extent that earlier twentieth-century terror regimes could only aspire to? He envisaged such a society as one in which 'one-dimensional' individuals were preoccupied solely with the functional concerns of consumerism. Schooled in a language that inhibited the development of critical, dialectic thought, such 'one-dimensional' subjects would internalise habits of acquiescence. For critics such as Marcuse and Louis Althusser, dominant ideology would be instilled not only by blunt repressive measures but also by extending more insidious persuaders through Orwellian manipulation and control, first of information and communication but beyond them to our linguistic modes of cognition and so to our desires and impulses, indeed to our very psyche. Despite his cultural pessimism, Marcuse was not without hope for revolutionary change, noting that the 'spectre' of Marx's *Communist Manifesto*:

> is there again, inside and outside the frontiers of the advanced

320 See Löwy and Sayre, *Romanticism Against the Tide of Modernity.*

> societies' [...] But the chance is that, in this period, the historical extremes may meet again: the most advanced consciousness of humanity, and its most exploited force.[321]

At the time of writing in 1964, Marcuse concluded in *One-Dimensional Man*, that it was an open question whether such forces might prevail; it is still too early to tell.

Half a century later many of the expectations of 'techno-optimists' have not come to pass. At a time when the productive capacity of the economy is vastly greater, there are almost universal calls for increased economic growth, even though consistent and untrammelled economic growth has been trailed by austerity across Europe. Terraforming other planets has not come to be – Eugene Cernan's parting steps in 1972 turned out to be the last Moon walk, (a year when Street Farm were eyeing up the likes of Piccadilly for their horticultural potential). Nuclear power has not delivered its promise to produce electricity too cheap to meter; post-scarcity society is not with us; as the pension age recedes we are far from universally working a three-day week due to increased automation; the undoubted gains in universal access to health and education are threatening to stall and reverse. In real terms household income has kept in line with those of the 1970s, but this is maintained following a substantial shift of women into the workplace so more often made up of the combined income of two earners rather than a single wage packet. Robots do not pamper us by fulfilling our every need, nor do we dine on capsules of space-age wonder food or for the most part wear shiny metallic suits. The energies of the 1950s – coal, gas and nuclear power – continue to make up the bulk of today's energy portfolio, while in the transport sector, gasoline and other fossil fuels still propel the vast majority of ships, cars and planes, as they

321 Marcuse, *One-Dimensional Man*, 257.

did a century before. Policies that sought to make new build housing carbon neutral are being diluted on the grounds of cost and far from becoming autonomous; indeed homes are becoming more greedily dependent and addicted to high energy and service inputs than ever before.

The soothsaying capabilities of catastrophists, however, like those of techno-optimists, have also had their shortcomings. The popular television series 'The Survivors' captured the eschatological mood with its dramatisation of a world in which civilisation had collapsed. Yet 1970's predictions of apocalyptic Doomsday scenarios have not, at least hitherto, come about. The Cold War did not end in a nuclear Armageddon followed by nuclear winter (notwithstanding that proliferation remains a live threat).The human race has not been universally irradiated and annihilated. Garrett Hardin's predictions of famine due to overpopulation within twenty years proved wide of the mark in that, with notable exceptions such as sub-Saharan regions, the human race has not been starved. The anticipated increase of the human population to around 10 billion by 2050, particularly alongside a concomitant increase in domesticated animals, remains a significant challenge in terms of land use, though Paul R. Ehrlich and Anne Ehrlich's *Population Bomb* (1968) has not been detonated. Alvin Toffler's *Future Shock* (1970) warned of the 'disease' of inexorable change upon well-being, yet material living standards have undoubtedly mitigated the convulsions of rapid change for much of humanity.

We are now denizens of the future that early 1970's ecofreaks feared. Despite efforts to implement 'sustainable development', summits to tackle environmental degradation over the past forty years, such as those at Stockholm, Rio, Kyoto, Cancun, Johannesburg, Copenhagen and Doha have produced unfulfilled commitments and failed to reverse the trajectory of climate change. Risky older technologies such as nuclear energy are being expanded and joined by further invasive innovations such as genetic modification, nanotechnology and Unmanned Aerial Vehicles ('drones'), while the use of fossils fuels continues apace with fracking for oil shale gas and exploitation of the furthest reaches of the planet such as the Arctic and the south Atlantic. In the roll call of countless human tragedies, those that have registered most prominently include Bhopal, Chernobyl, Cambodia, Rwanda, September 11th, Katrina, Iraq, Afghanistan and currently Syria. As well as war and famine, the effects of climate change increasingly displace populations. Species extinctions due to habitat destruction and other anthropogenic causes are continuing unabated. Less dramatically there are concerns in the West about more subtle social trends – the effects of 'nature deficit disorder', the demographics of an aging population profile, single-occupant households and the inclination towards 'cocooning' in the home.

As I mentioned previously, the *Limits to Growth* and 'The Blueprint for Survival' reports received particular attention among warnings against the consequences of business as usual for the planet's future. This was not least because both reports were voices from within enclaves of wealth and industry and received a cautious endorsement by several prominent scientists and intellectuals of the day. Published in 1972, *Limits to Growth* was put together by the Club of Rome at the instigation of group of prominent figures from politics, science, education and business. *The Ecologist*'s 'Blueprint for Survival' was also published in 1972. It was co-written and part financed by James Goldsmith, an author who, in keeping with his ecologically minded nephew the Conservative MP Zac Goldsmith, was authentically green but also more right-wing than many radical greens could readily accommodate. As such, New-Left critics received such reports with scepticism regarding any change of heart on the part of big business. Graham Caine found that, as ecological ideas began to gain wider currency, a publication such as *Street Farmer*, which made appeals to 'grow your own house' and featured intergalactic tractors and such likes, 'suddenly didn't seem so silly' during the mid-1970s. However, as already quoted, Caine commented '"Limits to growth" only seemed to apply to the working class'.[322]

The debates continue. In respect of key predictions such as global population, environmental degradation and economic inequalities the *Limits to Growth* report seems to have been accurate in its estimates.[323] It forecasted, for example, that the world's population would be 6 billion by the year 2000, a total that humanity did indeed reach in 1999.[324] Certainly, despite the outrageous scandal of continuing malnutrition in a world of plenty, human populations as a whole have not suffered the cataclysmic bouts of widespread global starvation forecast by the gloomiest of 1970's jeremiads. Today world poverty is a notoriously slippery statistical challenge, based on shifting figures and subject to politicised interpretations. At the time of writing it seems that while the proportion of the world population living in poverty may be decreasing, the absolute numbers could well be increasing (particularly when the impact of rapid, but likely unsustainable, industrialisation in China is bracketed out). Without contradiction it can be statistically possible that there are at once more people living above the poverty line, and also more people living in poverty than at any point of history. Longitudinal studies of poverty must take account of shifts in relative definitions of poverty making benchmarking and comparison problematic. Definitions of poverty are further complicated by the confusion between use value and exchange value. It can be misleading to consider people as living in poverty if they earn less than $50 per week, if they live in a

322 Personal conversation with Graham Caine, The Stillage, Redfield, Bristol 25 October 2010.
323 Felix Dodds and Michael Strauss with Maurice Strong, *Only One Earth: The Long Road via Rio to Sustainable Development* (London: Routledge, 2012), 6 and 247.
324 Donella H. Meadows *et al*, *The Limits to Growth: A Report for the Club of Rome on the Predicament of Mankind* (London: Earth Island, 1972), 33.

subsistence economy in which most of their transactions take place outside of the monetary economy, as this is a measure of exchange value within market transactions, not use value.

Within bounds, the interest of business leaders and industrialists in the environment signified by *Limits to Growth* indicated recognition of serious underlying problems, due to the impact of economic externalities such as habitat destruction and pollution. To this extent, such attention was an encouraging sign of efforts to respond positively. At the same time, New-Left critics feared that the role of capitalism in enforcing the dominant growth paradigm remained unchallenged, arguing also that social justice and the equitable distribution of wealth were essential to viable programmes for change. For example, an anonymous commentator on 'The Blueprint for Survival', writing as 'a leftist suffering from grumbling ecology', noted that the report combined laudable concerns for the plight of the planet, with ill-conceived anti-migration sentiments. Calling for a critical and balanced appraisal, and a coherent response, the anonymous commentator recorded the Left's mostly antagonistic approach to the publication. However, the 'leftist' also noted the *Socialist Worker*'s initial recognition that the 'Blueprint's authors were at least acknowledging that the ecological crisis is primarily a 'political problem'. He or she concluded that 'The ecology movement must be radicalised. The Left must be ecologised'.[325] For radicals of the 1970s and subsequently, too often efforts to present a greener image of business, seemed to be motivated by attempts to outflank, neutralise and recuperate support for the increasingly popular ecology movement. As we have seen, as self-styled revolutionary urbanists, Street Farm regarded capitalism as incompatible with human well-being and environmental sustainability. In my opinion

325 [Anon], 'The Left's Reaction to "The Blueprint for Survival"', *Architectural Association Quarterly* 4.3 (Summer 1971), 35.

subsequent events have not discredited this analysis, despite efforts to achieve sustainable development in the interim.

Calls to recognise common ground between the red and green soon proved to be well founded. Towards the end of the 1970s the exploitation of the vast Brent Oilfield led to the North Sea oil and gas boom which helped to shore up the environmentally profligate Thatcher administration. The availability of such an alternative energy supply contributed to the defeat of the miners in the 1984-85 strike and subsequent pit closures, leading in no small measure to the political dominance of neo-Liberal policies over organised labour. Many eco-anarchists rightly had the foresight to support the miners, realising that the defeat of this most militant section of the working class would undermine the struggle to achieve an economy for social needs, while the dismantlement of a 'dirty industry' at home would merely be offshored and imported using energy intensive transportation (currently Russia, South Africa and Columbia are significant suppliers). The use of fossil fuels has not decreased so there have been no ecological benefits, while coal has been mined by low-paid workers, enduring poorer employment rights and lower health and safety standards than conditions at home won through decades of hard political struggle.

In 1975 Patrick Rivers attributed to the then prime minister Edward Heath the counterintuitive notion that 'the struggle against pollution requires massive resources which can only come from economic expansion'.[326] Heath's view largely remains political orthodoxy, despite evidence during intervening years that such an approach to environmental degradation has not worked; carbon dioxide emissions, for example, have continued to rise inexorably since the 1997 Kyoto Protocol. In the present day advocacy for the benefits of undifferentiated economic growth is being deployed

326 Rivers, *The Survivalists*, 48.

(with some success) as a means to off-set and neutralise underlying social tensions and conflicts of interests. Thus David Cameron's coalition government argues that is it imperative for ordinary people to work harder in order to compete effectively with rivals on the global market and defeat austerity, variously blamed on spendthrift political opponents, the lazy and feckless and 'immigrants'. Trends in economic expansion with particular consequences for the living world currently include, for instance, ecologically invasive extractive industries such as oil and gas exploration in the Arctic, deep sea mining and hydraulic fracturing ('fracking') to release shale gas and other previously locked-in fossil fuels. Wealth created from such sources will, their proponents assert, ensure jobs and prosperity, national energy security and stop the lights from going out. The wealth created from the production of surplus value (in which long-term externalities are not fully costed) will trickle down to the benefit of all. Rejecting this logic, radical environmentalists and anti-capitalists on the libertarian left such as Joel Kovel, Noam Chomsky, Vandana Shiva and Michael Albert continue to point out that it has remained impossible to decouple economic growth from ecological degradation. They counter that real sustainable wealth is not to be derived from a degraded environment.

Such debates concerning the future direction of Industrialism in an era of advanced capitalism and globalisation have long formed the discursive battleground between broadly sketched positions characterised as catastrophism and cornucopianism.[327] While, as I have discussed, the worse-case scenarios of the catastrophists have not come to pass, the trajectory of unfolding events since the 1970s has often confounded the optimism of the cornucopians too. Consequently, in the West, younger generations

327 Stephen Cotgrove, *Catastrophe or Cornucopia: The Environment, Politics and the Future* (Chichester: Wiley, 1982).

can no longer assume a bequest of ever more plentiful goods and opportunities than their parents. Present-day pundits speak of the phenomenon of austerity, not of coming abundance. Cornucopian economists such as Julian Simon challenged the assumptions of the catastrophists. *The Ultimate Resource* published in 1978 made a not unwarranted corrective to elements of anti-humanism in the writings of the Ehrlichs and Hardin. However, Simon's Promethean spirit, adding lighter fuel for 'Reaganomics' and the triumphalism of neo-Liberalism, was based on premises that have not been actualised. Confidence in human ingenuity working under the motivation of market forces has led neo-Liberal cornucopians to believe that economic growth can continue exponentially and indefinitely. For all their self-proclaimed rationalism, pragmatism and belief in scientific methodology, such faiths are based upon assumptions that derive from the realms of the occult and science fiction. Simon's assertion that the price of metals would inevitably decrease, for example, was in part based on the prediction that it would soon be possible to engineer atomic structures in such a way that they could be reconfigured into any element, thus rendering material shortages a thing of the past. This sounds like an updated extension of alchemical belief. Another favourite cornucopian idea has been that it will soon be possible to mine other planets for raw materials or that terraforming will facilitate the colonisation of space. Dematerialisation likewise takes its cue from science fiction, assuming that a rapid transformation into a weightless, virtual economy would ensure that the material limits of economic growth would no longer apply. This triumph of spirit over matter has yet to come. However, that such ideas have held sway in American Republican circles is consistent with, and intimately connected to, Christian fundamentalists' supernatural beliefs in the Rapture. This is not to say that such technical achievements are inconceivable in the distant future, but that they are nowhere on the horizon in the present, or I would speculate, within the timeframe of change necessary to address the consequences of the ecological crisis that is already with us. In practice economic policies and attempts to address the issue of climate change through a carbon market have not reduced emissions, even in the West where there has been a substantial transition from industrial production to predominantly service and information economies.

Eco-anarchism as exemplified by Street Farm was free of the anti-immigration sentiments that appear in 'The Blueprint for Survival' and neo-Malthusian concentration on the population bomb. Furthermore, 'The Blueprint for Survival' notoriously led to a desire for a neo-primitivist anti-urbanism, the logical corollary of which was Edward Goldsmith's apparent sympathy for the objectives of the Khymer Rouge. Subsequently social ecologists and libertarian socialists have been hostile to the kind of anarcho-primitivism expressed in an anti-humanist bent apparent among Unabomber sympathisers, some (but by no means all) members of Earth First! in the United States and the direction taken by *Green Anarchist* magazine during the 1980s (a trend that the present-day group Deep Green Resistance would do well to avoid). By contrast, for libertarian socialists the best hope for a levelling population was, and remains, support for women's empowerment and control over fertility, educational opportunities, social security in old age and an end to precarity. Planetary consciousness and an internationalist commitment to the welfare of humanity as a whole was a point of principle, exemplified by often repeated maxim that one should act local, think global. Against the predictions of groups such as Optimum Population and Migration Watch, as the West's population levels and decreases, migration will help to ensure that the demographic trajectory does not lead to imbalanced societies in which older generations substantially outnumber the young. At the same time it is obviously preferable that large scale relocations take place as positive life choices rather than purely due to imbalances in concentrations of capital, or on the part of severely traumatised people fleeing conflicts, extreme poverty, abuse and oppression or disasters. The reduction of refugees rather than migration for choice can only be achieved by international solidarity and cooperation working on principles of social justice, not by nationalistic and racist polemics and ever more draconian measures such as surveillance at borders, detention centres and forcible repatriation.

Such global considerations and imperatives clearly formed the context for the propagation of ideas in the 1970's radical ecology movement, including Street Farm. Eco-anarchism, libertarian socialism, green politics and other approaches within the radical counterculture sought viable alternatives to previous political options that had prevailed in Europe such as capitalism, state socialism, fascism or theocracy, without reverting to primitivism. Street Farm, my particular 'case study' if the foregoing can be called such, were a group of friends involved mostly with practical projects and who produced a limited published output. This in no way either constituted or aspired to be any kind of coherent manifesto for an alternative society. The more modest aims were to explore and promote passionately held ideas, to put some of these ideas into practice... and hopefully to have a good time in the process. Nevertheless present-day initiatives such as the Occupy movement and Transition Culture would do well to learn from earlier countercultural movements, revisiting the kind of revolutionary urbanism that Street Farm exemplify.

A Street Farm approach suggests that to tackle the environmental crisis it is necessary to raise consciousness of the underlying problem of capitalist expansionism. This seemingly impregnable and nebulous force cannot be confronted in the abstract or by isolated acts of insurrection. In order for the Occupy movement's self-identified 99% of society to take back wealth and power from the remaining1% using a Street Farm strategy, it would be necessary to immediately begin to take control over the production of the absolute material basics of food, energy and shelter, working collectively and democratically through our nearest and dearest, our communities and our networks. In this way it is hoped that a significant boost to social solidarity would enable a critical shift beyond individual acts of refusal to creative, confidence-boosting community organisation that would start to wrench back power back by producing sustainable alternatives. The strategic intention is not only to recruit members by attracting only like-minded members of the alternative society but to generate and be constitutive in the process of awakening wider political consciousness. This would occur by making explicit the struggle to keep open – and reverse – the process by which capitalism seeks to shut down spaces (psychological, economic and geographical) for personal autonomy and independence, through its perpetual operations to enclose and secure monopolies. Were this struggle to be successful, communities would be progressively liberated from dependence on the wages, loans, mortgages, benefits, corporate control of commodities, supply chains and services, that currently keep them in place and in thrall. To reclaim resources, time and the benefits of one's own labour would expand resilience at the individual and community level. As critical friends Paul Chatterton and Alice Cutler articulated in the 'Rocky Road to a Real Transition'[328], the Transition Towns network has undertaken well-meaning attempts to downplay political aspects of social change in order to attract mass involvement. While this is pragmatic in seeking to prevent factionalism, therefore understandable, it may, they argue, ultimately be counterproductive in obscuring the social relations that are intrinsic to the twinned problems of social injustice

328 Paul Chatterton and Alice Cutler, *The Rocky Road to a Real Transition: The Transition Towns Movement and What it Means for Social Change* (Trapese Collective, 2008) [online]: http://trapese.clearerchannel.org/resources/rocky-road-a5-web.pdf [accessed 12 January 2013].

and environmental destruction. By contrast the struggle for political autonomy along eco-anarchist lines entails recognition of authentic self-interest in cooperation and rejects the competition of all against all that the capitalist free market exalts. While eco-anarchism shares with Transition Towns a common theme of environmental resilience, an underlying promotion of intrinsic values of personal fulfilment through connectedness and empathy and aspirations to towards self-realisation through being over having, it is critical of its reluctance to confront the political and economic control of the land and urban space.

At a time when the West is facing serial crises, policies that have led to economic austerity, environmental destruction and cultural pessimism are being implemented all the more forcefully and stubbornly. Despite different emphases between right and left on spending cuts, privatisation and economic growth there are no alternatives to the current capitalist system on offer among the political mainstream. In truth, in an era of rapid and accelerating change there is no such thing as the status quo. It is only the paradigm in which such transformation takes place that appears frozen. However, there are always a range of options available to us and it is important to reject totalitarian suggestions that the system of capitalist globalisation is the only model that is possible because of its current dominance. In their updated book *Communitas*, published at the outset of the 1960s, Paul Goodman and Percival Goodman argued that modern Americans were, really for the first time in history, starting to experience a scenario in which the 'iron necessity is relaxed'. They stressed the range of directions that society could take:

> We could centralize or decentralize, concentrate population or scatter it. If we want to continue the trend away from the country, we can do that; but if we want to combine town and

> country values in an agrindustrial way of life, we can do that. In large areas of our operation, we could go back to old-fashioned domestic industry with perhaps even a gain in efficiency, for small power is everywhere available, small machines are cheap and ingenious, and there are easy means to collect machined parts and centrally assemble them. If we want to lay our emphasis on producing still more mass-produced goods, and raising the standard of living still higher, we can do that; or if we want to increase leisure and the artistic culture of the individual, we can do that. We have the solar machines for hermits in the desert like Aldous Huxley or central heating provided for millions by New York Steam. All this is commonplace; everybody knows it. It is *just* this relaxing of necessity, this extraordinary flexibility and freedom of choice of our techniques, that is baffling and frightening to people.[329]

Among such possibilities the eco-anarchist wing of the 1970's counterculture Street Farm represent is a path not taken. It advocated production for social needs in self-sufficient, autonomous communities under direct democratic control, federating regionally and internationally on a cooperative basis. In such a way the socialist ideal of a commonwealth would be established, dedicated to the material security of all, and made resilient and sustainable by a responsible concern for the natural environment. Through a variety of practical projects, avant-garde happenings and performances and multimedia output Street Farm presented an approach that was experimental, fun and inclusive by contrast to conventional politics. In this sense they adopted a strategy that I have termed 'tactical prefiguration'. Such attempts to be the change they wanted to see sought to reverse the alienation of hierarchical politics in favour

329 Goodman and Goodman, *Communitas*, 12-13.

of participative and horizontal structures, anticipating the radical environmental networks of the following decades.

Eco-anarchist critics have held that capitalism as presently constituted cannot solve the problems that beset humanity and the planet. Against its undoubted productive efficiency, advanced capitalism imposes an enormous systemic burden of social costs in terms of alienation and the poor distribution of wealth, leading to deprivation and countless expressions of individual and social dysfunction. The inevitable concentration of political power that such inequalities of wealth entails makes truly participative democracy impossible. Oligarchic business leaders, largely unaccountable to their workforce, consumers and the communities in which they operate, make the microeconomic and macroeconomic decisions that define each individual's waking hours and the context in which politics operates. It has not been possible to decouple economic growth from environmental degradation, incrementally turning the biosphere into dead matter in the process. This has led to a failure to protect the natural world upon which humanity and other species rely. Eco-anarchism is sceptical of the proposition that we can grow the economy to produce the wealth and knowledge to solve our most fundamental problems, insisting rather that the ecological crisis is a political problem, inextricably embedded within the existing paradigm of state and capital. It advocated, and still advocates, collective action for change and resistance outside of leverage attained through ethical consumerism or attempts to get the 'right people' into party politics, preferring practical grassroots projects, industrial and direct action and the communication and exchange of ideas to lobbying.

In the present day there are still different paths available to us, even if there is less confidence than the Goodmans were to express at the outset of the 1960s that humanity is advancing beyond the iron law of necessity. The anticipated plateauing of population during the coming century presents humanity with an unparalleled opportunity to realise a higher quality of life than ever before. If this is to be achieved, a shift is required so that economic production is for social needs, not undifferentiated expansion according to the crude measure of Gross National Product. Too often during recent decades the introduction of new technologies has been accompanied by job losses in heavy industries, retail and services, and in the worst case scenarios of the Thatcher years, physical conflict with sectors such as mining and printing to the detriment of working-class communities. If we need to phase out coal burning for the sake of combating climate change the decimation of the UK coal industry was an example of how *not* to do it. Three decades on, the post-industrial wastelands of former mining communities remain some of Britain's most depressed areas. Choosing an appropriate policy pathway means the difference between vastly increasing suffering and economic insecurity or making life experiences significantly more fulfilling and pleasurable than the Twentieth Century – there will be no status quo.

In this respect, Michael Albert's observation in *Parecon* is startling:

> Considering the US from the period after WWII – the golden age of capitalism – to the end of the twentieth century, [Juliet] Schor notes that per-capita output approximately doubled. She points out that an important decision should have been made in conjunction with that increase in productive capability. That is, should we maintain or even expand the work week to enjoy the much bigger social product that increased productivity made possible? Or should we retain the productive output of the 1950s, using the increase in productivity per hour to reduce the work week [...] with no reduction in overall output per person. You do not have to decide which option you prefer to note that

> in fact no such democratic decision ever took place because the issue never arose. The market ensured that work pace and workload climbed as high as they could without causing the system to reach a breaking point.[330]

As the Occupy movement has conspicuously reminded us, if the 99% of society were to positively recognise its social power and interests, there could be an infinite improvement in the human situation. Major obstacles to this include the firm grip on the means of production by a tiny economic elite and the inability to federate and cooperate locally, regionally and internationally due to a legacy of sectarian hostility on patriotic, racist and / or religious grounds. After all, the real parameters of life on earth are ecological rather than the arbitrary parameters of state borders. The role of national rivalry as an obstacle to agreements on environmental protection and social justice was apparent at the United Nations Conference on the Human Environment – held in Stockholm in 1973. Prominent voices on environmental issues behind the Stockholm Conference, Barbara Ward, Malcolm Strong and René Dubos (who coined the phrase 'Think Globally, Act Locally'), recognised that supposed conflicts of national interests consistently thwart the kind of global cooperation and coordination that is necessary to tackle such problems. They became advocates of supranational organisations able to address environment and development issues at the global level.[331] At the same time there was a move towards advocacy of decentralisation, particularly following the publication of *Small is Beautiful* by Barbara Ward's friend, E. F. Schumacher. By contrast, the inattention to increasing ecological austerity following the economic downturn is particularly concerning.

330 Michael Albert, *Parecon: Life After Capitalism* (London: Verso, 2004), 239.
331 Meredith Veldman, *Fantasy, the Bomb, and the Greening of Britain: Romantic Protest, 1945-1980* (Cambridge: Cambridge University Press, 1994), 214-215.

Forty years later David Cameron – a prime minister who once boasted that he would lead 'the greenest government ever' – failed to attend the Rio+20 environmental summit, even though the date had been adjusted to accommodate his schedule, illustrating the capacity of the continued demands of undifferentiated economic growth and national interest to distort political priorities.[332]

We have seen that the pages of the underground magazine *Street Farmer* provide us with some hastily sketched signposts to a countercultural pathway not taken. Voices from the forgotten summers of the early 1970s, their pasted-together imaginings offer an analysis that retains relevance for the present day as well as a wealth of historical interest. These hints encourage us to negotiate some stepping stones between the quotidian and the utopian. In doing so the eco-anarchist collective directly attempted to engage with the local, without losing sight of the planetary, even cosmic. Bruce Haggart remarked that Street Farmhouse looked like 'something that landed on the earth rather than growing out of it',[333] which is apposite given that it had ideas about the microcosm of the local and practical, and the macrocosm of the planetary, built into its fabric. As we have seen, fast moving current affairs motivated Street Farm to affect change by participating in several international happenings as well as building the Ecological House in Eltham, disseminating subversive ideas from Kentish Town and traffic blockading in Oxford Street. They were able to make radical and very literal interpretations of the consequences of living. If we were to extrapolate some terms from the pages of *Street Farmer* to create a word cloud some keywords and ideas that might be writ large could be: revolutionary urbanism, grow, a creative society not a consumer

332 John Vidal, 'David Cameron Criticised for Skipping Rio+20 Earth Summit', *The Guardian* [online]: http://www.theguardian.com/environment/2012/jun/11/david-cameron-rio-earth-summit [accessed 22 June 2012].
333 Kallipoliti, 'Review: Clearings in a Concrete Jungle', 240.

society, transmogrification, collective, renaturalise, cooperation, demystify, community, methane, digester, planting and, perhaps in the largest, boldest font of all, vision. With a blend of humour, rage and practical know-how, they refreshingly articulated a broad vision of change rather than defensive objections to the latest round of cuts, social injustice and ecological folly, as necessary as such campaigns are. In the here and now and near at hand this vision peers down to the potential of manure to produce energy and of sunflower seeds to crack concrete, but also scans out to a bigger picture beyond the capitalist present, deemed inherently unstable, unjust, dysfunctional and unsustainable, to a worldwide struggle for change. At its rare best the 1970's counterculture, beyond the violence and consumerism it shared with mainstream culture, advocated an expanded consciousness rather than the oppressively expansionist mentality of the 'square' world of the leaders they feared, fought and ridiculed. Their challenge was to achieve qualitative social and ecological change that permanently transcends alienation and resists recuperation. This would amount to a true urban revolution. Even if they did not succeed, surely that endeavour was worthwhile in itself. Their challenge remains our challenge. If we can demand the impossible, we can also refuse the inevitable.

BIBLIOGRAPHY

Primary materials: Street Farm in their own words

Boyle, Geoffrey and Peter Harper. 'Interview: Street Farmers', 170-171 in *Radical Technology*, ed. by Godfrey Boyle, Peter Harper and the editors of *Undercurrents* (London: Wildwood House, 1976).

Caine, Graham. 'The Ecological House', *Architectural Design* 42.3 (1972), 140-141.

Caine, Graham. 'A Revolutionary Structure', *Oz*, 45 (November 1972), 12-13.

Caine, Graham, Bruce Haggart and Peter Crump. 'Some Proposals on the Reservicing of an Urban Terraced House', *Domeletter*, 4, ed. John Prenis, 1–6 (Philadelphia, Penn: Self-Published, 1972).

Camden Street Farmers. [Dear Maya letter], *The International Times* 3.2 (July 1975), 6.

Crump, Peter. 'Street Farm', talk at Bristol Anarchist Bookfair, 7 May 2011. [online] Bristol Radical History Group website: http://www.brh.org.uk/site/events/street-farming/ [accessed 15 December 2012].

Haggart, Bruce. 'Italian Trip', *Architectural Design* 42.4 (April 1972), 201-202.

Haggart, Bruce and 'Dr John' [Pollard]. *Community Gardening* ([London]: Farmage Press, November c. 1972-1973) [A4 paper for Kentish Town squatters].

Haggart, Bruce. *The Street Farmers' Windworkers Manual* (London: Peace News, [1973]).

Haggart, Bruce and Graham Caine. 'Ramifications and Propagations of Street Farm' [A3 information sheet on the Ecological House] [1972].

Haggart, Bruce and Graham Caine, ['From Here we Grow'] [A3 information sheet on the Ecological House, featuring images and text relating to Street Farmhouse, and references to sources of information on liberatory technology on one side and 'Revolutionary Structure' article from *Oz* on the other] [c.1972].

Haggart, Bruce. Street Farm website: http://www.streetfarm.org.uk/streetfarmer_one.html [accessed 30 August 2012].

Kallipoliti, Lydia. Interview with Peter Crump, *Street Farmer*, Editor, 1971-72 , Bristol 11 July 2007, 252-56 in Beatriz Colomina and Craig Buckley (eds.), *Clip, Stamp, Fold: The Radical Architecture of Little Magazines 196X to 197X* (Barcelona and New York: Actar and Media and Modernity Programme Princeton University, 2010).

A London Farmer [probably connected to Street Farm]. 'Urban Farming', *The International Times* 3.4 (November 1975), 3.

Street Farm. *Street Farmer* 1 (Sept 1971). [NB. *Street Farmer* abbreviated in text as *SF* 1 and *SF* 2]. Can be accessed online from here: http://www.streetfarm.org.uk/Streetfarmer_One.html#0

Street Farm, *Street Farmer* 2 [1972].

Street Farm. 'A Threatening Letter to ALL Architects', *Architectural Association Quarterly* 4.4. (Autumn 1972), 17-20.

Street Farmers. 'Revolutionary Technology in Portugal', *Architectural Design*, 55.10 (1975), 619-23.

Films

Open Door. Television documentary by Street Farm (Peter Crump, Bruce Haggart and Graham Caine), broadcast BBC2 18th June 1973.

Clearings in the Concrete Jungle. Television documentary featuring Graham Caine and Bruce Haggart, broadcast as part of BBC's 2nd

House series, 24th January 1976.

Travels with my Chainsaw. Television documentary produced and directed by Steve Gear and guest presented by Graham Caine for Art Trails series. Broadcast HTV West, 20th September 1998.

Secondary Materials

Agria, Andi Stasis. 'An Image from the Future of Revolutionary Ecology:
Greek Insurrection and the Eco-War to Come', excerpts from *We Are an Image from the Future* (AK Press, 2010) *Earth First! Journal* (2010) [online] http://www.earthfirstjournal.org/article.php?id=525 [accessed 17 September 2012].

Albert, Michael. *Parecon: Life After Capitalism (London: Verso, 2004).*

Allaby, Michael. *The Eco-Activists: Youth Fights for a Human Environment* (London, Charles Knight, 1971).

[Anon]. 'The Left's Reaction to "The Blueprint for Survival"', *Architectural Association Quarterly* 4.3 (Summer 1971), 32-35.

[Anon]. 'Save the AA'. *Architectural Design* 42.9 (September 1972), 588.

[Anon]. 'Frontiers. Energy: a Choice for Reading' [review including Bruce Haggart's *Windworkers Manual*], in *Manas: The Journal of Intelligent Idealism*, XXVII. 11 (13 March 1974), 12-13. [Online]: http://www.manasjournal.org/pdf_library/VolumeXXVII_1974/XXVII-11.pdf [accessed 14 November 2012].

[Anon]. 'Comtek', *Undercurrents* 8 (October-November 1974), 26-28.

[Anon / some local residents of St Werburghs]. '*AVAG* – Selfish Self-Builders?', *Bristle* 18 (Winter 2005), 26-28.

[Anon]. 'Meet the first resident of Dubai's palm-shaped man-made island', *Daily Mail Online*, 22 June 2007: http://www.dailymail.co.uk/news/article-463694/Meet-resident-Dubais-palm-shaped-man-island.html [accessed 25 August 2011].

[Anon]. 'Can Permaculture Save Detroit?', *Punk Rock Permaculture E-Zine* [online blog] http://punkrockpermaculture.wordpress.com/2010/01/11/can-permaculture-save-detroit/ [accessed 16 August 2012].

An Anarchist FAQ Webpage: http://anarchism.pageabode.com/afaq/index.html [accessed 25 May 2013].

Appleyard, Donald, with M. Sue Gerson and Mark Lintell. *Livable Streets* (Berkeley. CA.: University of California Press, 1981).

Architectural Association. *Architectural Association: 125th Anniversary* (London: Architectural Association, [c.1973]).

Ariadne. [commentary in the] *New Scientist* 55.807 (3 August 1972), 264.

Awan, Nishat, Tatjana Schneider and Jeremy Till. *Spatial Agency: Other Ways of Doing Architecture* (London: Routledge, 2011).

Bachelard, Gaston. *The Poetics of Space* [1958], trans. by Maria Jolas (Boston, MA.: Beacon Press, 1994).

Biehl, Janet. *Mumford Gutkind Bookchin: The Emergence of Eco-Decentralism* (Porsgrunn, Norway: New Compass Press, 2011).

Blechman, Max (ed). *Revolutionary Romanticism* (San Francisco, CA.: City Lights Books, 1999).

Bolger, Julian. 'Anarchists and Blackshirts take up their Spraycans in War of Words', *The Guardian* (12 May 2012), 22-23.

Bookchin, Murray [writing under pseud. Lewis Herber]. *Our Synthetic Environment* (New York: Knopf, 1962).

Bookchin, Murray. *Post-Scarcity Anarchism* (London: Wildwood House, 1974).

Bookchin, Murray. *Ecology and Freedom: The Emergence and Dissolution of Hierarchy* (Palo Alto. CA.: Cheshire Books, 1982).

Bookchin, Murray. *Remaking Society* (Boston, MA.: South End Press, 1990).

Bookchin, Murray. *From Urbanization to Cities: Towards a New Politics of Citizenship* [1992], rev. edn (London: Cassell, 1995).

Bottoms, Edward. 'If Crime Doesn't Pay: The Architects' Revolutionary Council', *AArchitecture, 5* (Winter 2007-08) [online] http://www.aaschool.ac.uk/aalife/library/arc.pdf [accessed 24 November 2012], 14-16.

Bottoms, Edward. Architectural Association website, 'AA History' http://www.aaschool.ac.uk/AALIFE/LIBRARY/aahistory.php [accessed 30 December 2011].

Bristol Anarchist Bookfair Collective. [programme for Bristol Anarchist Bookfair], 7 May 2011.

Buick, Adam and John Crump. *The Alternative to Capitalism* ([s.l.]: Theory and Practice, 2013).

Callenbach, Ernest. *Ecotopia: A Novel about Ecology, People and Politics in 1999* [1975] (London: Pluto, 1978).

Campaign for Dark Skies website, see http://www.britastro.org/dark-skies/inf003.htm [accessed 4 October 2012].

Campaign for the Protection of Rural England website, see http://www.cpre.org.uk/what-we-do/countryside/dark-skies/the-issues [accessed 4 October 2012].

Carlsson, Carl. *Nowtopia: How Pirate Programmers, Outlaw Bicyclists, and Vacant-Lot Gardeners are Inventing the Future Today!* (Oakland, CA.: AK Press, 2008).

Carson, Rachel. *Silent Spring* [1962], (London: Penguin, 1999).

Chalk, Warren. 'Touch not…', *Architectural Design* 4 (April 1971), 238.

Chatterton, Paul and Alice Cutler. *The Rocky Road to a Real Transition: The Transition Towns Movement and what it Means for Social Change* (Trapese Collective, 2008), [online] www.paulchatterton.com/2009/08/17/the-rocky-road-to-a-real-transition-reprinted-with-new-preface/ [accessed 12 January 2013].

City Farm Group. *Where to Find City Farms in Britain*, produced and ed. by the City Farm Advisory Service (London: Inter Action Group / City Farm Advisory Service, [1980?]).

Clarke, Robin. *Technological Self-Sufficiency* (London: Faber & Faber, 1976).

Colomina, Beatriz and Craig Buckley (eds.). *Clip, Stamp, Fold: The Radical Architecture of Little Magazines 196X to 197X* (Barcelona and New York: Actar and Media and Modernity Programme Princeton University, 2010).

Commoner, Barry. *The Closing Circle: Confronting the Environmental Crisis* (London: Jonathan Cape, 1972).

Comtek. *Comtek '74* (Bath: Comtek, 1974).

Conder, Simon, Jon Broome and Jennie Jones, 'Bracknell Housing', *Architectural Design* 42.9 (1972), 533-34.

Cook, Peter *et al* (eds.). *Archigram, Rev. ed.* (New York: Princeton Architectural Press, 1999).

Cotgrove, Stephen. *Catastrophe or Cornucopia: The Environment, Politics and the Future* (Chichester: Wiley, 1982).

Crompton, Dennis (ed.). *Concerning Archigram* (London: Archigram Archives, 1998).

Daly, Herman E. *Steady-State Economics*, 2nd ed. (London: Earthscan, 1992).

DaSilva, E. J. 'Biogas Generation: Developments, Problems, and Tasks – An Overview', *Food and Nutrition Bulletin* (1979) Suppl. 2, 84-98.

Dearling, Alan. 'Not Only But Also: Some

Historical Ramblings about the English Festivals Scene', [online] http://www.enablerpublications.co.uk/pdfs/notonly1.pdf [accessed 25 September 2012].

Debord, Guy. *The Society of the Spectacle* [1967] ([s.l.]: Rebel Press, 1987).

Debord, Guy. *Comments on the Society of the Spectacle* [1988], trans. by Malcolm Imrie (London: Verso, 1990).

Dickson, David. *Alternative Technology and the Politics of Technical Change* ([London]: Fontana/Collins, 1974).

Dodds, Felix and Michael Strauss with Maurice Strong. *Only One Earth: The Long Road via Rio to Sustainable Development* (London: Routledge, 2012).

Downton, Paul F. *Ecopolis: Architecture and Cities for a Changing Climate* (Dordrecht: Springer, 2009).

Elliott, Dave. 'Glimpses of Socialism', *Undercurrents* 12 (September-October 1975), 27.

Engwicht, David. *Street Reclaiming: Creating Livable Streets and Vibrant Communities* (Annandale, NSW: Pluto Press Australia, 1999).

Fairlie, Simon. *Low Impact Development: Planning and People in a Sustainable Countryside*, 2nd enlarged edition (Charlbury: Jon Carpenter, 2009).

Featherstone, David. *Solidarity: Hidden Histories and Geographies of Internationalism* (London: Zed Books, 2012).

Federation of City Farms and Community Gardens Oral History Project webpage: http://www.farmgarden.org.uk/farms-gardens/oral-history-project [accessed 22 May 2011].

Goodman, Paul and Percival Goodman. *Communitas: Means of Livelihood and Ways of Life* [1947], new ed. (New York: Vintage, 1960).

Gowan, James (ed.). *A Continuing Experiment: Learning and Teaching at the Architectural Association* (London: Architectural Press, 1975).

Gutkind, E. A. [Erwin Anton]. *Community and Environment: A Discourse on Social Ecology* (London: Watts and Co., 1953).

Gutkind, E. A. [Erwin Anton]. *The Expanding Environment: The End of Cities – The Rise of Communities* (London: Freedom Press, 1953).

Halliday, Sandy. *Sustainable Construction* (Amsterdam: Elsevier, 2008).

Hanley, Lesley. *Estates: An Intimate History* (London: Granta, 2007).

Harper, Clifford. *New Times Class War Comix Number 1* (Brighton: Epic Productions, 1974).

Harper, Peter. 'The New, Improved Undercurrents Alternative Technology Guide', *Undercurrents* 6 (March-April 1974), 23-24.

Harper, Peter. 'Directory of Alternative Technology', *Architectural Design* 44.11 (1974), 690-698.

Hart, Robert A. de J. *Forest Gardening: Rediscovering Nature and Community in a Post-Industrial Age* [1991] rev. ed. (Totnes: Green Earth Books, 2001).

Harvey, David. *Rebel Cities: From the Right to the City to the Urban Revolution* (London: Verso, 2012).

Hay, Nikki (ed.). *Architectural Association* (London: Architectural Association, 1975).

Heinberg, Richard. *Powerdown: Options and Actions for a Post-Carbon World* (West Hoathly, West Sussex: Clairview Books, 2004).

Hellman, Louis. 'NAM Working to Redistribute Power in Architecture', *The Architects' Journal* 163 (2 June 1976), 1067.

Hern, Matt. *Common Ground in a Liquid City: Essays in Defense of an Urban Future* (Oakland. CA.: AK Press, 2010).

Higgott, Andrew. *Mediating Modernism: Architectural Cultures in Britain* (London: Routledge, 2007).

Hogan, Ian. 'Comtek Windmills', *Architectural Design*, 55.10 (1975), 624-26.

Holmgren, David. *Permaculture: Principles and Pathways Beyond Sustainability* (Hepburn, Vic.: Holmgren Design Services, 2002).

Holt, Jonathan. 'That Plywood Obsession', *Follies* 10.3 (Winter 1998), 14-15.

Hopkins, Rob. *The Transition Handbook: From Oil Dependency to Local Resilience* (Totnes: Green Books, 2008).

House of Commons Parliamentary Papers [online database], *Report of the Commissioner of Police of the Metropolis for the Year 1971* (Cmnd. 4986, 1971-72), 45 [accessed 22 November 2012].

Howard, Ebenezer. *Garden Cities of To-morrow*, 2nd ed, (London: S. Sonnenschein, [1902]).

Hughes, F. P. 'Ecologic House', *Mother Earth News* [20] (March/April 1973). Online: http://www.motherearthnews.com/nature-community/ecologic-house-zmaz73mazraw.aspx [accessed 22 April 2012].

Jacobs, Jane. *The Death and Life of Great American Cities: The Failure of Town Planning* [1961] (London: Penguin, 1965).

Jencks, Charles, with a contribution by William Chaitkin. *Current Architecture* (London: Academy Editions, 1982).

Kallipoliti, Lydia. 'No More Schisms', *Architectural Design* 80.6 (3 November 2010), 14-23.

Kallipoliti, Lydia. 'Review: Clearings in a Concrete Jungle', *Journal of the Society of Architectural Historians, 70.2 (June 2011), 240-244.*

Kallipoliti, Lydia. 'From Shit to Food: Graham Caine's Eco-House in South London, 1972-1975', *Buildings and Landscapes,* 19.1 (Spring 2012), 87-106.

Karpf, Anne. 'The Pressure Groups', *Architects' Journal*, 166 (1977), 728-734.

Kentish Town City Farm webpage: http://www.ktcityfarm.org.uk/history.htm [accessed 22 May 2011] and Kentish Town Memories: 40 Years of Kentish Town City Farm webpage: http://40years.ktcityfarm.org.uk/ [accessed 28 September 2013].

Kimber, Richard and J.J. Richardson (eds). *Campaigning for the Environment* (London: Routledge and Kegan Paul, 1974).

Kirby, Michael. 'The New Theatre' *The Tulane Drama Review* (Winter 1965) 10.2. Online: http://www.jstor.org/stable/1125229 [accessed 23 April 2011].

Kirby, Michael. 'Happenings: An Introduction', in *Happenings and Other Acts*, ed by Mariellen R. Sandford (London: Routledge, 1995).

Kovel, Joel. *The Enemy of Nature: The End of Capitalism or the End of the World?* [2002], updated and expanded ed. (London: Zed; Halifax: Fernwood), 2007).

Kultermann, Udo. *Art-Events and Happenings*, trans. by John William Gabriel (London: Mathews Miller Dunbar, 1971).

Kyes, Zak and Wayne Daly. 'Street Farmer', *AArchitecture*, 4 (Summer 2007), 19-22: http://www.aaschool.ac.uk/Downloads/AArchitecture/AArchitecture04.pdf [accessed online 24 January 2012].

Leach, Gerald. 'Living off the Sun in South London,' *The Observer* (27 August 1972), 1-2.

Lewis, Michael and Pat Conaty. *The Resilience Imperative: Comparative Transitions to a Steady-State Economy* (Gabriola Island, BC: New Society Publishers, 2012).

Liddell, Howard. *Ecominimalism: The Antidote to Eco-Bling* 2nd ed. (London: RIBA, 2013).

Lovelock, J.E. *Gaia: A New Look at Life on Earth* [1979], (Oxford: Oxford University Press, 1989).

Lowe, Philip and Jane Goyder. *Environmental Groups in Politics*, Resource Management series no. 6 (London: George Allen and Unwin, 1983).

Löwy, Michael and Robert Sayre. *Romanticism Against the Tide of Modernity*, trans. by Catherine Porter (Durham, NC.: Duke University Press, 2001).

McKay, George. *Radical Gardening: Politics, Idealism and Rebellion in the Garden* (London: Frances Lincoln, 2012).

Mackillop, Andrew. *Why Soft Technology? Alternative Solutions to the Energy Crisis* (London: Methuen, 1975).

McLaughlin, Terence. *A House for the Future*, 2nd rev. ed. with revisions by Don Wilson and Brian Trueman (London: Independent Television Books, 1977).

Marcuse, Herbert. *One-Dimensional Man: Studies in the Ideology of Advanced Industrial Society* [1964], 2nd ed. (London: Routledge, 1991).

Marcuse, Herbert. *The Dialectics of Liberation*, ed. by David Cooper (Harmondsworth: Penguin, 1968).

Marcuse, Herbert. 'An Essay on Liberation', [online] http://www.lifeaftercapitalism.info/downloads/read/Philosophy/Herbert%20Marcuse/Herbert%20Marcuse%20-%20An%20Essay%20on%20Liberation%20(Beacon,%201969).pdf [accessed 9 September 2012].

Marx, Karl. *Grundrisse: Foundations of the Critique of Political Economy (Rough Draft)* [first pub.1939], trans. by Martin Nicholaus (Harmondsworth: Pelican / Penguin, 1973).

Meadows, Donella H. *et al. The Limits to Growth: A Report for the Club of Rome on the Predicament of Mankind* (London: Earth Island, 1972).

Merchant, Carolyn. *Radical Ecology: The Search for a Livable World* (New York: Routledge, 1992).

Mills, George and Peter Moloney. 'Architects Revolutionary Council – Its History and Its Present Aims', *Building Design*, (297) (7 May 1976), 9.

Morris, Steven. 'Green Dream Site has become Bristol's Vale of Tears', *The Guardian* (21 February 2005), [online]: http://www.guardian.co.uk/uk_news/story/0,,1419092,00.html [accessed 15 November 2012].

Nicholson, Max. *The Environmental Revolution: A Guide for the New Masters of the Earth* (London: Hodder and Stoughton, 1970).

Nicholson-Lord, David. *The Greening of the Cities* (London: Routledge and Kegan Paul, 1987.

O'Riordan, T. *Environmentalism*, 2nd rev. ed. (London: Pion, 1981).

Osman, Tony. 'Dome Sweet Dome', *Sunday Times Magazine* (30 November 1975), 68-75.

Pawley, Martin. 'The Need for a Revolutionary Myth', *Architectural Design*, 42.2 (1972), 73-80.

Peace News. 'Blocking Oxford Street', *Peace News* (17 December 1971), 5.

Pearce, Fred. *The Landgrabbers: The New Fight over Who Owns the Planet* (London: Eden Project / Transworld, 2012).

Pike, Alexander. 'Autonomous house,' *Architectural Design*, 44.11 (1974), 681-89.

Pinder, David. *Visions of the City: Utopianism, Power and Politics in Twentieth-Century Urbanism* (New York: Routledge, 2005).

Pinheiro, Marta. 'A.T. Days that Shook Portugal', *Undercurrents* 26 (February-March 1978), 9-12.

Pirsig, Robert M. *Zen and the Art of Motorcycle Maintenance: An Inquiry into*

Values [1974] (London: Black Swan, 1989).

Plumwood, Val. *Environmental Culture: The Ecological Crisis of Reason* (London: Routledge, 2002).

Pollard, John. *Squat: A Report Written in Conjunction with the Squatters in West Kentish Town, September 1972* (London: [self-published?] 1972).

Pollard, John. 'Squatting in the City', *Architectural Design* 43.8 (1973), 504-506.

Poyner, Daniel (ed.). *Autonomy: The Cover Designs of Anarchy 1961-1970* (London: Hyphen Press, 2012).

Price, Andy. *Recovering Bookchin: Social Ecology and the Crises of Our Time* (Porsgrunn, Norway: New Compass Press, 2012).

Richardson, Dick. 'The Green Challenge: Philosophical, Programmatic and Electoral Considerations', 4-21 in *The Green Challenge: The Development of Green Parties in Europe*, ed. by Dick Richardson and Chris Rootes (London: Routledge, 1995).

Rivers, Patrick. *The Survivalists* (London: Eyre Methuen, 1975).

Rosen, Nick. *How to Live Off-Grid: Journey Outside the System* (London: Doubleday, 2007).

Roszak, Theodore. *The Making of a Counter Culture: Reflections on the Technocratic Society and Its Youthful Opposition* [1968] (Berkeley. CA.: University of California Press, 1995).

Roszak, Theodore, Mary E. Gomes and Allen D. Kanner (eds.). *Ecopsychology: Restoring the Earth Healing the Mind* (San Francisco. CA.: Sierra Books, 1995).

Rycroft, Simon. *Swinging City: A Cultural Geography of London 1950-1974* (Farnham: Ashgate, 2011).

Sadler, Simon. *Archigram: Architecture Without Architecture* (Cambridge, MA.: MIT Press, 2005).

Sadler, Simon. 'An Architecture of the Whole', *Journal of Architectural Education*, 61.4 (May 2008), 108-29. [online] http://onlinelibrary.wiley.com/doi/10.1111/j.1531-314X.2008.00194.x/pdf [accessed 24 January 2012].

Sandbrook, Dominic. *State of Emergency; The Way We Were: Britain, 1970-1974* (London: Allen Lane, 2010).

Saunders, Nicholas. *Alternative England and Wales* (London: Nicholas Saunders, 1975).

Sayre, Robert and Michael Löwy. 'Figures of Romantic Anti-Capitalism', *New German Critique*, 32 (1984), 42-92.

Schmied, Wieland. *Hundertwasser 1928-2000. Personality, Life, Work* (Köln: Taschen, 2005).

Schumacher, E. F. *Small is Beautiful: A Study of Economics as if People Mattered* (London: Blond & Briggs, 1973).

Schumacher, E. F. *Good Work* (London: Jonathan Cape, 1979).

Shane, Grahame. 'Obituary: Alvin Boyarsky (1928-1990)', *Journal of Architectural Education*, 45.3 (May 1992) [online] http://www.jstor.org/stable/1425256 [accessed 22 March 2011].

Shaw, Alison. 'Howard Liddell (1945-2013): Architect, ecology activist and charity worker', *The Herald* (Glasgow), [Features], 20.

Smith, Adrian. 'Governance Lessons from Green Niches: The Case of Eco-Housing', 89-109 in *Governing Technology for Sustainability*, ed. by Joseph Murphy (London: Earthscan, 2007).

Spatial Agency. 'Alternative Publishing / Zines', http://www.spatialagency.net/database/where/organisational%20structures/alternative.publishing.zines, [accessed 17 May 2011].

Spatial Agency. 'Architects' Revolutionary Council', http://www.spatialagency.net/database/architects.revolutionary.council.arc [accessed 2 January 2012].

Steedman, Neil. 'Student Magazines in British Architectural Schools', *Architectural Association Quarterly* (Summer1971), 36-40.

Sunwoo, Irene. 'From the "Well-Laid Table to the "Market Place": The Architectural Association Unit System', [online] *Journal of Architectural Education*, 65.2 (April 2012), 24-41.

Szczelkun, Stefan. *Survival Scrapbook* 5: *Energy* (Brighton: Unicorn, 1973).

Szczelkun, Stefan. 'EarthWorkshop' [n.d.] Online: http://www.stefan-szczelkun.org.uk/phd103.htm#_ftnref2 [accessed 23 April 2011].

Towers, Graham. *Building Democracy: Community Architecture in the Inner Cities* (London: UCL Press, 1995).

Tressell, Robert. *The Ragged Trousered Philanthropists* [1914] (London: Panther, 1965).

Vale, Brenda and Robert Vale. *The Autonomous House: Design and Planning for Self-Sufficiency* (London: Thames and Hudson, 1975).

Vale, Brenda. *Albion* (Barnstaple: Spindlewood, 1982).

Vale, Brenda and Robert Vale. *The New Autonomous House: Design and Planning for Sustainability* (London: Thames and Hudson, 2000).

Vale, Brenda and Robert Vale. 'Is the High-Density City the Only Option?', 19-26 in *Designing High-Density Cities: For Social and Environmental Sustainability*, ed. by Edward Ng (London: Earthscan, 2010).

Vaneigem, Raoul. *The Revolution of Everyday Life* [1967] ([s.l.]: Left Bank Books / Rebel Press, 1983).

Veldman, Meredith. *Fantasy, the Bomb, and the Greening of Britain: Romantic Protest, 1945-1980* (Cambridge: Cambridge University Press, 1994).

Vidal, John. 'David Cameron Criticised for Skipping Rio+20 Earth Summit', *The Guardian* [online]: http://www.theguardian.com/environment/2012/jun/11/david-cameron-rio-earth-summit [accessed 22 June 2012].

Walker, John A. *Glossary of Art Architecture and Design Since 1945*, 3rd ed. (London: Library Association Publishing, 1992).

Wall, Derek. *Earth First! and the Anti-Roads Movement: Radical Environmentalism and Comparative Social Movements* (London: Routledge, 1999).

Walters, Nicholas. 'Obituary of Alan Albon: Radical and Lovable', [online] *The Guardian* (25 May 1989).

Ward, Colin. *Anarchy in Action* [1973], new ed. (London: Freedom Press, 1982).

Ward, Colin. 'Do-It-Yourself New Town', *Undercurrents* 16 (June-July 1976), 30-33.

Ward, Colin. *Housing: An Anarchist Approach*, new ed. with a postscript (London: Freedom, 1983).

Ward, Colin. *Talking Houses: Ten Lectures* (London: Freedom Press, 1990).

Wates, Nick and Charles Knevitt. *Community Architecture: How People are Creating their own Environment* (London: Penguin, 1987).

Wells, Graham. 'London Squatters', 100-101 in Lloyd Kahn (ed.) *et al. Shelter* [1973] (2nd ed. Bolinas. CA.: Shelter Pub. [nd]).

Whitford, David. 'Can Farming Save Detroit?', *Fortune*, [online] CNN Money website,http://money.cnn.com/2009/12/29/news/economy/farming_detroit.fortune/index.htm?cnn=yes [accessed 16 August 2012].

Williams, Eve. 'The House that Grows', *Garden News* 722 (5 May 1972), 1 and 13-16.

Williams, Heathcote. *Autogeddon* (London: Jonathan Cape, 1991).

Williams, Raymond. *Keywords: A Vocabulary of Culture and Society* (London: Croom Helm, 1976).

Wines, James. *Green Architecture* (Köln: Taschen, 2000).

Wolch, Jennifer. 'Zoöpolis', 119-138 in *Animal Geographies: Place, Politics, and Identity in Nature-Culture Borderlands*, ed. by Jennifer Wolch and Jody Emel (London: Verso, 1998).

Woolley, Tom. 'Alternative Practice', *Architects' Journal* 42.166 (19 October 1977), 735-37.

Wright, Frank Lloyd. *The Living City* [1958] (New York: New American Library, 1963).

INDEX